Doing Conversation Analysis

INTRODUCING QUALITATIVE METHODS provides a series of volumes which introduce qualitative research to the student and beginning researcher. The approach is interdisciplinary and international. A distinctive feature of these volumes is the helpful student exercises.

One stream of the series provides texts on the key methodologies used in qualitative research. The other stream contains books on qualitative research for different disciplines or occupations. Both streams cover the basic literature in a clear and accessible style, but also cover the 'cutting edge' issues in the area.

TITLES IN SERIES

Using Foucault's Methods
Gavin Kendall and Gary Wickham

The Quality of Qualitative Research
Clive Seale

Qualitative Evaluation
Ian Shaw

Researching Life Stories and Family Histories
Robert L. Miller

Researching the Visual
Michael Emmison and Philip Smith

Categories in Text and Talk
Georgia Lepper

Focus Groups in Social Research
Michael Bloor, Jane Frankland, Michelle Thomas and Kate Robson

Qualitative Research Through Case Studies
Max Travers

Qualitative Research in Social Work
Ian Shaw and Nick Gould

Methods of Critical Discourse Analysis
Ruth Wodak and Michael Meyer

Qualitative Research in Information Systems
Michael D. Myers and David Avison

Qualitative Research in Education
Peter Freebody

Using Documents in Social Research
Lindsay Prior

Doing Research in Cultural Studies
Paula Saukko

Gender and Qualitative Methods
Helmi Jarviluoma, Pirkko Moisala and Anni Vilkko

Qualitative Research in Sociology: An Introduction
Amir B. Marvasti

Narratives in Social Science
Barbara Czarniawska

Criminological Research: Understanding Qualitative Methods
Lesley Noaks and Emma Wincup

Doing Qualitative Health Research
Judith Green and Nicki Thorogood

Using Diaries in Social Research
Andy Alaszewski

Constructing Grounded Theory: A Practical Guide Through Qualitative Analysis
Kathy Charmaz

Qualitative Marketing Research: A Cultural Approach
Johanna Moisander and Anu Valtonen

Doing Conversation Analysis

Second Edition

Paul ten Have

SAGE Publications

Los Angeles · London · New Delhi · Singapore

First edition published 1999
Reprinted 2000, 2002, 2004, 2005, 2006
Second edition published 2007

SAGE Publications Ltd
1 Oliver's Yard
55 City Road
London EC1Y 1SP

SAGE Publications Inc.
2455 Teller Road
Thousand Oaks, California 91320

SAGE Publications India Pvt Ltd
B 1/I 1 Mohan Cooperative Industrial Area
Mathura Road
New Delhi 110 044

SAGE Publications Asia-Pacific Pte Ltd
33 Pekin Street #02-01
Far East Square
Singapore 048763

Library of Congress Control Number 2007922041

British Library Cataloguing in Publication data

A catalogue record for this book is available from the British Library

ISBN 978-1-4129-2174-9
ISBN 978-1-4129-2175-6 (pbk)

Typeset by C&M Digitals (P) Ltd., Chennai, India
Printed and bound in Great Britain by TJ International Ltd, Padstow, Cornwall
Printed on paper from sustainable resources

In memory of Hanneke Houtkoop.

Contents

Preface to the Second Edition

The main purpose of the first edition of this book was to support the learning process of people who aspired to become proficient in actually doing conversation analysis (CA). As I wrote in the preface: 'The book does not just invite you to practise CA, but it also tries to support your process of learning the trade by trying to practise it. Therefore, it contains not only reflections on doing CA, but also instructions, warnings, and encouragements. See it as a collection of instruments, then, among others, in your becoming a conversation analyst.' In actual teaching situations, however, the book was also used to introduce novices to CA, often students with various disciplinary backgrounds. In preparing this second edition, I have tried both to preserve the original 'practical' orientation and to adapt the text to a broader introductory usage. This was most explicitly done by adding a section on motives and requirements for doing CA in the first chapter, and a completely new chapter, Chapter 4, on CA as it can be related to various disciplinary and critical agendas, including ethnomethodology, membership categorization analysis, discursive psychology, and feminist studies. Furthermore, I have, as far as it seemed sensible, updated the text of most chapters by adding some new examples and quite a lot of more recent references. I have also made an effort to incorporate aspects of the technologies that are currently being used in doing CA, but in order to avoid these being too dated later, I have not given detailed descriptions and instructions. A glossary of technical terms should also make the text more accessible to novices.

I am very grateful to the staff at Sage, in the person of Patrick Brindle, for inviting me to prepare a second edition of *Doing CA* and encouraging me along the way, especially when I encountered an unexpected setback.

In the preface to the first edition I had a long list of people to whom I felt indebted. Adding new friends to this list would make it too long, so I have decided not to include it this time. But, as time goes on, one has also to face the loss of dear friends and colleagues. I regret the early deaths of Carolyn Baker, Deirdre Boden, Hanneke Houtkoop, and Clare Tarplee. Obituaries for them are available at my website, www.paultenhave.nl. Hanneke Houtkoop was a special friend and close colleague. She supported me in the writing of the original text and wrote an appreciative review of the first edition. As I do miss her, I dedicate the present edition to her memory.

Paul ten Have,
Heiloo

Part 1

Considering CA

1

Introducing the CA Paradigm

Contents

Conversation analysis[1] (or CA) is a rather specific analytic endeavour. This chapter provides a basic characterization of CA as an explication of the ways in which conversationalists maintain an interactional social order. I describe its emergence as a discipline of its own, confronting recordings of telephone calls with notions derived from Harold Garfinkel's ethnomethodology and Erving Goffman's conceptual studies of an interaction order. Later developments in CA are covered in broad terms. Finally, the general outline and purpose of the book is explained.

What is 'conversation analysis'?

People talking together, 'conversation', is one of the most mundane of all topics. It has been available for study for ages, but only quite recently, in the early 1960s, has it gained the serious and sustained attention of scientific investigation. Before then, what was written on the subject was mainly normative: how one should speak, rather than how people actually speak. The general impression was that ordinary conversation is chaotic and disorderly. It was only with the advent of recording devices, and the willingness and ability to study such a mundane phenomenon in depth, that 'the order of conversation' – or rather, as we shall see, a multiplicity of 'orders' – was discovered.

'Conversation' can mean that people are talking with each other, just for the purpose of talking, as a form of 'sociability', or it can be used to indicate any activity of interactive talk, independent of its purpose. Here, for instance, are some fragments of transcribed 'conversation' in the sense that there are people talking together.[2]

EXCERPT 1.1, FROM HERITAGE, 1984A: 236 [NB:VII:2]

```
E:    Oh honey that was a lovely luncheon I shoulda ca:lled you
      s:soo[:ner but l:]l:[lo:ved it.
M:          [((f)) Oh:::][(   )
E:    It w's just deli:ghtfu[:l. ]
M:                          [Well]=
M:    I w's gla[d         you] (came).]
E:             ['nd yer f:] friends] 're so da:rli:ng,=
M:    =Oh:::  [: it w'z ]
E:            [e-that Pla:t isn'she a do:[ :ll?,]
M:            [iYe]h isn't she pretty,
             (.)
E:    Oh: she's a beautiful girl.=
M:    =Yeh I think she's a pretty gir[l.=
E:                                   [En' that Reinam'n::
             (.)
E:    She SCA:RES me.
```

EXCERPT 1.2, FROM FRANKEL, 1984: 153 [G.L:2]
[GLOSSES OMITTED]

```
Pt:   This- chemotherapy (0.2) it won't have any lasting effects on havin' kids
      will it?
             (2.2)
Pt:   It will?
Dr:   I'm afraid so
```

The first excerpt (1.1), from a series of telephone conversations among friends, would generally be considered part of 'a conversation', while the second (1.2), from a medical consultation, would not. The social import of the two occasions is rather different, but the excerpts could be both items for serious conversation-analytic study since they are both examples of what Emanuel Schegloff (1987c: 207) has called *talk-in-interaction*. Conversation analysis, therefore, is involved in the study of the orders of talk-in-interaction, whatever its character or setting.

To give a bit of a flavour of what CA is all about, I will offer a few observations on the two quoted fragments. In excerpt 1.1, E apparently has called M after having visited her. She provides a series of 'assessments' of the occasion, and of M's friends who were present. E's assessments are relatively intense and produced in a sort of staccato manner. The first two, on the occasion and the friends in general, are accepted with Oh-prefaced short utterances, cut off when E continues. 'Oh' has been analysed by John Heritage (1984b) as a 'news receipt'. The assessments of Pat are endorsed by M with 'yeh', followed by a somewhat lower level assessment: 'a do::ll?,' with 'Yeh isn't she pretty,', and '<u>Oh</u>: she's a beautiful girl.', with 'Yeh I think she's a pretty girl.'. These observations are in line with the tenor of findings by Anita Pomerantz (1978; 1984) on 'compliment responses' and 'down-graded second assessments'. The 'Oh-receipted' assessments can be seen to refer to aspects of the situation for which M as a host was 'responsible', while it might be easier for her to 'share' in the assessments of the looks of her guests, although she does so in a rather muted fashion. The 'work' that is done with these assessments and receipts can be glossed as 'showing and receiving gratitude and appreciation, gracefully'.

In the second fragment, excerpt 1.2, the context and the contents of the assessments are markedly different. The patient proposes an optimistic assessment as to the effect of her forthcoming chemotherapy, after which the physician is silent, leading to a remarkably long, 2.2-second pause. In so doing, he can be seen as demonstrating that he is not able to endorse this positive assessment. Thereupon, the patient 'reverses' her statement in a questioning manner, 'It will?', which the doctor then does confirm with: 'I'm afraid so'. We can say that the conversational regularity which Harvey Sacks (1987) has called 'the preference for agreement' has been used here by the physician to communicate that the situation is contrary to the patient's hopes, while she uses it to infer the meaning of his 'silence' (cf. Frankel's 1984 analysis of this case). In both cases, aspects of the 'pacing' of the utterances, as well as the choice of 'grades' or 'directions', contribute to the actions achieved. It is such aspects of 'the technology of conversation' (Sacks, 1984b: 413; 1992b: 339) that are of interest here.

The emergence of conversation analysis

The expression 'conversation analysis' can be used in wider and more restricted senses. As a broad term, it can denote any study of people talking together, 'oral communication', or 'language use'. But in a restricted sense, it points to one particular tradition of analytic work that was started by the late Harvey Sacks and his collaborators, including Emanuel Schegloff and Gail Jefferson. It is only in this restricted sense that 'conversation analysis' or 'CA' is used in this book.

In this restricted sense, CA was developed in the early 1960s in California.[3] Harvey Sacks and Emanuel Schegloff were graduate students in the Sociology Department of the University of California at Berkeley, where Erving Goffman was teaching. Goffman had developed a rather distinctive personal style of socio-logical analysis, based on observations of people in interaction, but ultimately oriented to the construction of a system of conceptual distinctions. Simplifying complex historical influences, one could say that Goffman's example opened up an interesting area of research for his students, the area of direct, face-to-face interaction, what he later has called 'The interaction order' (1983). Sacks and Schegloff, however, were never mere followers of Goffman.[4] They were open to a lot of other influences and read widely in many directions of social science, including linguistics, anthropology, and psychiatry.

It was Harold Garfinkel, however, who was to be the major force in CA's emergence as a specific style of social analysis. He was developing a 'research policy' which he called 'ethnomethodology' and which was focused on the study of common-sense reasoning and practical theorizing in everyday activities. His was a sociology in which the problem of social order was reconceived as a practical problem of social action, as a members' activity, as methodic and therefore analysable. Rather than structures, functions, or distributions, reduced to conceptual schemes or numerical tables, Garfinkel was interested in the procedural study of common-sense activities.

This apparently resonated well with Sacks' various interests, including his early interest in the practical reasoning in case law, and later in other kinds of practical professional reasoning such as police work and psychiatry. These things came together when Sacks became a Fellow at the Center for the Scientific Study of Suicide in Los Angeles in 1963–4. There he came across a collection of tape recordings of telephone calls to the Suicide Prevention Center. It was in a direct confrontation with these materials that he developed the approach that was later to become known as conversation analysis.

Two themes emerged quite early: categorization and sequential organization. The first followed from Sacks' previous interests in practical reasoning and was not essentially bound up with these materials as interactional. The second, however, was in essence 'new' and specific to talk-in-interaction as such. It can be summarized briefly as the idea that what a doing, such as an utterance, means practically, the action it actually performs, depends on its sequential position. This was the 'discovery' that led to conversation analysis per se.[5]

From its beginnings, then, the ethos of CA consisted of an unconventional but intense, and at the same time respectful, intellectual interest in the details of the actual practices of people in interaction. The then still recent availability of the technology of audio recording, which Sacks started to use, made it possible to go beyond the existing practices of 'gathering data', such as coding and field observation, which were all much more manipulative and researcher dominated than the simple, mechanical recording of 'natural', that is non-experimental, action.

Audio recordings, while faithfully recording what the machine's technology allows to be recorded, are not immediately available, in a sense. The details that the machine records have to be remarked by the listening analyst and later made available to the analyst's audience. It is the activity of transcribing the tapes that provides for this, that captures the data, so to speak. In the beginning, transcripts were quite simple renderings of the words spoken. But later, efforts were made to capture more and more details of the ways in which these words were produced as formatted utterances in relation to the utterances of other speakers. It was the unique contribution of Gail Jefferson, at first in her capacity as Sacks' 'data recovery technician' (Jefferson, 1972: 294), and later as one of the most important contributors to CA in her own right, to develop a system of transcription that fitted CA's general purpose of sequential analysis. It has been used by CA researchers ever since, although rarely with the subtlety that she is able to provide.[6]

It was the fitting together of a specific intellectual matrix of interests with an available technology of data rendering that made CA possible. And once it became established as a possibility, which took another decade, it could be taken up by researchers beyond its original circle of originators and their collaborators. There are many aspects of its characteristics and circumstances that have contributed to CA's diffusion around the world (of which the present book is one manifestation), but the originality of its basic interests, the clarity of its fundamental findings, and the generality of its technology have certainly contributed immensely.

The development of conversation analysis

For a characterization of CA's development, one can very well use the ideas that Thomas Kuhn developed in his *The structure of scientific revolutions* (1962). As Schegloff makes clear in the 'Introduction' to Sacks' edited *Lectures on conversation* (1992a; 1992b), Sacks and he were on the look-out for new possibilities for doing sociology which might provide alternatives to the established forms of sociological discourse, or 'paradigms' in Kuhn's parlance. And what they did in effect was to establish a new 'paradigm' of their own, a distinctive way of doing sociology with its particular interests and ways of collecting and treating evidence. As a 'paradigm', CA was already established when Harvey Sacks died tragically in 1975. The work that remained to be done was a work of extension, application, and filling in gaps, what Kuhn has called 'normal science'. What was already accomplished was the establishment of a framework for studying talk-in-interaction, basic concepts, and exemplary studies. What still could be done was to solve puzzles within the established framework. I will now discuss some of these later developments.

From its early beginnings in Sacks' considerations of tapes of suicide calls, CA has developed into a full-blown style of research of its own, which can handle all kinds of talk-in-interaction. When you scan Sacks' *Lectures on conversation* (1992a; 1992b), you will see that most of the materials he discusses stem from two collections, the already mentioned suicide calls and a series of tape-recorded group therapy sessions. Quite often, the fact that these recordings were made in very specific 'institutional' settings is ignored, or at least it is not in focus. Similarly, Schegloff's dissertation (partly published in Schegloff, 1968, and 2004), although based on calls to a disaster centre, mostly deals with general issues of conversational interaction as such, rather than with institutional specifics.

Gradually, however, Sacks, Schegloff, and their collaborators turned to the analysis of conversations that were not institutionally based.[7] The general idea seems to have been that such non-institutional data provided better examples of the purely local functioning of conversational devices and interactional formats such as 'turn-taking' or 'opening up closings'. From the late 1970s onwards, however, later followers of the CA research style turned their attention 'again' to institution-based materials such as meetings, courtroom proceedings, and various kinds of interviews. Their general purpose was to 'apply' the acquired knowledge of conversational organization specifically to these institutional interactions in order to show how these institutions were 'talked into being', to use a much quoted phrase coined by John Heritage (1984a: 290). In an introduction to this problematic, he has written:

There are, therefore, at least two kinds of conversation analytic research going on today, and, though they overlap in various ways, they are distinct in focus. The first examines the institution *of* interaction as an entity in its own right; the second studies the management of social institutions *in* interaction. (Heritage, 1997: 162; 2004: 223)

For simplicity, I will often refer to the first type as 'pure CA', while calling the latter 'applied CA', no specific evaluation of these kinds being intended. Within the latter kind, one could distinguish two different interests, which can be balanced in various ways. On the one hand, there can be an interest in the institutional arrangements as these pertain to the organization of interaction, such as turn-taking, the distribution of speaking rights, etc., in relation to various aspects of the institution's functioning. On the other hand, the interest may be in studying the specific institutional activities, the specific interactional situation, its local, interactional requirements, and especially the ways in which the interactants show their orientations to these situations and requirements. These issues will be discussed at greater length in Chapter 9 (cf. also: Boden & Zimmerman, 1991, and Drew & Heritage, 1992a, for examples and discussions of these issues; and Drew & Sorjonen, 1997, and Heritage, 1997, or 2004, for introductions and overviews).

I have suggested that a basic enabling condition for CA's emergence was the availability of the technology of *audio* recording. Therefore, one could expect that the later availability of *video* technology would have had a similar impact, but this does not seem to have happened, at least not to the same extent. Again simplifying a more complicated history, one can say that video analysis has been mostly used in a complementary fashion to audio-based CA.

Some CA researchers – most prominently Charles Goodwin, Marjorie Harness Goodwin, and Christian Heath – have used video recording with ingenuity and subtlety to study visual aspects of interaction (cf. C. Goodwin, 1981; 1987; 1996; 2000a; 2000b; Goodwin & Goodwin, 1996; Heath, 1986; 1989; Heath & Luff, 1996; 2000, for some particularly inspiring examples). When one looks at these analyses in detail, however, one can see that in most cases the verbal production by the participants is taken as a baseline for the understanding of the interaction, with selected visual details being added to this understanding to make the analysis more completely an analysis of *face-to-face* interaction. Prominent among these details is the direction of the gaze of the participants, with marked gestures as a good second. Furthermore, many ways of handling material objects and features of the environment can be included in the analysis. The general and recommended practice seems to be to start with an audio transcription, following the proceedings discussed earlier, and later to add the visual details one wants to consider (cf. Heath & Luff, 1993). This practice seems to be reflected in the fact that, while there is one basic system for the transcription of language, there is no equivalent system for the description of non-vocal action.

As I indicated, CA has been developed as 'a kind of sociology', but the sociological community was for a long time not very hospitable to this new offspring. Sacks and Schegloff made it clear from the beginning that their problematic was a sociological one, and that they did not start from a deep interest in language per se (cf. some of the quotes from classic CA studies in Chapter 2). The first CA papers, however, were published in anthropological, linguistics, and semiotic journals, and from the early days many people have seen CA as contributing to the study of 'language use' or 'oral communication'. Today, CA is still practised by sociologists, but also by anthropologists, linguists, and communications scientists. Linguists and researchers in communications may have a slightly different conception of CA's subject matter, and a different technical expertise and vocabulary, than sociologists and anthropologists, but this does not seem to hinder the exchange of ideas within the CA community. What does make a difference, however, is that people have to defend themselves, and CA, in different ways in relation to their different disciplinary backgrounds (see Chapter 4). One can also discern some differences in conceptions of CA's general background and purpose, sociologists generally having a stronger ethnomethodological orientation than linguists. In this book, I will mainly deal with aspects of CA that are generally shared, but from time to time my sociological roots will inevitably show.

Why do conversation analysis?

Conversation analysis is a rather specific endeavour, different from the established approaches in the social and human sciences. It would seem, therefore, that to 'do CA' one would need to have special motivations and arguments. These can be positive – what one likes and appreciates in CA – and negative – what is less inspiring or acceptable in the established ways of investigating and conceptualizing human activities. I will discuss some of these arguments and differences in a summary fashion, though they will return in various places elsewhere in the book.

Contrastive properties

Major differences of CA in contrast to other approaches are:

- CA operates *closer to the phenomena* than most other approaches, because it works on detailed renderings of interactional activities, recordings, and detailed transcripts, rather than on coded, counted, or otherwise summarized representations; because of this it can take into consideration details and subtleties of human interaction that are lost in other practices and that have proven to be important for participants.
- CA favours *naturally occurring data* rather than 'experimental' or 'researcher-provoked' ones, because it considers talk-in-interaction as a 'situated' achievement rather than as a product of personal intentions, to be studied in interviews, or external forces, that can be manipulated in a laboratory; it is therefore less 'artificial'.
- CA's perspective on human interaction is *organizational* and *procedural*: when people talk with each other this is not seen as a series of individual acts, but rather as an emergent collectively organized event; the analytic purpose is not to explain *why* people act as they do, but rather to explicate *how* they do it.

- CA can be seen as a study of language-as-used, but this is not done in terms of a linguistic system as such, although there is a rising interest in the different interactive resources that various languages provide; and while more traditional forms of linguistics are mainly based on written language, strictly following normative rules of correct usage, CA studies oral language as actually used interactionally in 'natural' situations.

CA is then based on a range of choices, and in order to be motivated to 'do CA', you have to be convinced that these are reasonable ones, or at least curious to explore these further.

A basic assumption of CA is that talk-in-interaction is important in social life, both at the level of everyday concerns and at the level of society at large. It does not take much effort of observation and reflection to conclude that talking together is *basic to the social life of humans*. When we grow up we 'become human' in and through talk and much of our social life is in fact enacted as and in talk. Think of education, medical care, politics, commerce, and, indeed, science; none of these crucial social activities could do without talk in some way. But even in situations which are not generally seen as 'important', like chatting during a break, we manifest ourselves and perceive others largely through our talking together.

Requirements

So in order to 'do CA' you have to have some affinity with arguments like the ones above. But you also need some more personal qualities and sensibilities. You should have a deep *interest* in the details of human behaviour and the urge to *understand* what people are doing. And you also have to be able and willing to *switch* between that level of concrete understanding and one of abstract reasoning. CA is based on an 'analytic mentality' that seeks to explore the connections between the particularities in the details of human action and the generalities of shared organizational problems and resources.

Furthermore, in order actually to 'do CA', you need to have the *patience* to work laboriously for hours on end at the production of detailed transcriptions like the ones quoted above. And for most projects one would need quite a large collection of recorded and transcribed events. In cases in which you collect your own recordings, you need to have or acquire the ability to work with cameras, microphones, and recording equipment. And, as for any scientific work in our era, you need to be able to work with computers and specialized software.

Rewards

A sensible question before deciding to 'do CA' would be 'what's in it for me?' Firstly, it can be, depending on your circumstances, a sensible choice in an academic career. But it may also be a difficult one when CA is not an accepted and appreciated option in a specific academic environment. In such a case you may have to struggle to get it accepted, or at least tolerated. It helps if you are not completely on your own, and to connect to like-minded people in your environment or elsewhere.

In my personal experience, CA is a *community*, although with various degrees of intensity. As it has become established as a quite solidly and specifically defined approach in the human sciences, you can, by working in the CA tradition, become 'a member' of that community. The problems you may encounter when you try to become a member, ranging from practical and methodological ones to issues of theory and philosophy, will not be new or unique. So it can be helpful to share such problems and seek advice from more experienced members. As a community of researchers, CA is essentially international and interdisciplinary. Although it was first developed in one particular discipline and local setting, it now operates in a wide range of disciplinary fields and in many countries, scattered over the world. Websites and email lists are good ways to connect to the CA community, but personal relations are also important. Going to conferences, workshops, and informal get-togethers is helpful to get to know both 'the ways of the tribe' and some of its members.

While the CA paradigm is quite firmly established, CA is not 'finished', so each member can, in principle if not always in practice, produce *discoveries*. The core phenomena have been identified, but they can be explored further and there exists an enormous variety of settings, conditions, and languages for which the local organization of talk-in-interactions can be fruitfully studied.

The possibilities for *applied CA* are quite varied, as will become clear in later chapters, especially 9 and 10. This means that for any activity that involves the details of talk, CA can be 'applied' to elucidate both the routine practices as well as some of the 'problems' that may arise in that particular field of activity. Just to give you a flavour of that variety, I can mention: the socialization of children from a very early age, educational and instructional practices in specialized settings or at work, social talk among friends, colleagues, and in families, working with clients in an enormous range of institutional settings such as primary health care, social work or psychotherapy, meetings of all kinds, judicial settings like law courts, police investigations, and 'plea bargaining', politics at all levels and in various formats, work-related talk especially in technologically complex settings, interaction with and among people with impaired communication abilities like deaf people, aphasics, etc.!

Conversation analysis, then, offers a unique opportunity actually to make discoveries in a field that is essential for human life, within a methodological and theoretical framework that has proven its value in numerous studies.

Purpose and plan of the book

The book has a dual purpose: to introduce the reader to conversation analysis (CA) as a specific research approach in the human sciences, and to provide students and novice researchers with methodological and practical suggestions for actually doing CA research. The first part is primarily oriented to the first purpose. After an introductory chapter (1), there is one (2) elaborating basic ideas by discussing three classical studies. Then CA's approach is further clarified in terms of some core concepts in qualitative social research (3) and by a confrontation with some neighbouring disciplines and critical concerns (4). The second, practical purpose comes to the fore in the later parts of the book. The second and third parts detail the specifics of CA in its production of data, recordings (5), and transcripts (6), and its analytic strategies (7 and 8). The final part discusses ways in which CA can be 'applied' in the study of specific institutional settings (9) and for certain practical or critical interests.

The focus in this book will be mostly on working with *audio* recordings of talk-in-interaction, since *video* analysis, as noted, has been mostly used in addition to an analysis of the 'vocal track' (cf. Heath, 1997; 2004), but see some notes on video and visual analysis in later chapters. (Some of my discussions will apply to what I will call 'pure CA', others to 'applied CA', and most to both. As noted above, 'pure' CA is meant to gloss analyses that focus on procedures of talk-in-interaction abstracted from any specific institutional context, while 'applied' CA focuses on practices typical of setting- and institution-specific (inter)actions (Chapter 9) and/or is framed in wider concerns than *just* studying talk-in-interaction (Chapter 10).)

Each chapter will end with a short list of suggested basic *reading*, sometimes with a few words of introduction. These include general introductions, discussions of special topics, and especially exemplary studies.

After the text of each chapter, I will suggest one or more practical *exercises*, diversified for different options. These options have to do with whether you are working alone or in a group, and whether you prefer to select your own theme or choose to focus on a particular theme that will also be used in the text quite often: 'questioning activities'. When you are working in a *group*, I recommend that the major focus of the group discussions should be on the individually accomplished practical exercises. For the first three, introductory, chapters, the exercises suggest ways in which the group could discuss the recommended texts; for the practical chapters that follow, the experiences and results of the exercises could be reported to the group and discussed in detail. The educational cycle I have in mind is: (1) background reading and instruction, (2) practical exercise, (3) reporting experiences and results, and (4) exchange and discussion. If you are using the book as an *individual*, I would still strongly recommend doing the exercises seriously after you have studied each individual chapter, and before you start the next one.

The instructions are thus diversified for the four options:

A. individual/open;
B. individual/focused;
C. collective/open;
D. collective/focused.

As a support for the main text, there are three appendices: A, detailing the transcript conventions used in CA; B, a glossary of technical terms; and C, suggestions for designing presentations and publications.

EXERCISE

Read one of the short introductions to CA, included in the 'Recommended reading' section below. Make a list of the questions and points for debate which this introduction raises for you. Keep this list at hand and write down 'answers' to the questions, or 'arguments' for the debate, when you encounter relevant points in your reading of the next three chapters.

For option A, individual/open, there are no special instructions. For option B, individual/focused, you should make an effort to note especially those issues that might be relevant for 'questioning activities', like the status of 'questions' and 'answers', their relations, any reaction to or take-up following the answers, etc. For option C, collective/open, take care to read different items; you might first discuss the questions and points for discussion in the group and compose a collective 'list' of answers and arguments before you proceed with reading the next two chapters. For option D, collective/focused, combine the instructions for B and C.

RECOMMENDED READING

The following list contains some of the shorter introductions to CA, in the sense used in this book; some have a methodological focus, others are more general: Boden (1990); Clayman and Gill (2004); Drew (2003; 2005); Goodwin and Heritage (1990); Heritage (1984a: 233–92; 1995); Heritage and Atkinson (1984); Peräkylä (2004b); Pomerantz and Fehr (1997); Psathas (1990b); Sacks (1984a); Zimmerman (1988).

Notes

1. Sometimes, especially in older sources, the expression 'conversational analysis' is used. I think this is a misnomer, since 'conversation' denotes the material object of analysis, while 'conversational' would suggest that the analysis is done in a conversational manner, which is nonsensical (compare 'discourse analysis' with a hypothetical 'discursive analysis').
2. On the art of transcribing conversations, see Chapter 5; for transcription conventions, see Appendix A. If you are not familiar with these, studying excerpts together with Appendix A might be a good way to learn to read transcripts.
3. A full history of CA still has to be written, but a major source would be the two introductions written by Emanuel Schegloff for the volumes of Harvey Sacks' *Lectures on conversation* (1992a; 1992b).
4. In Chapter 3, I make some remarks and provide some references on the complex relationship between Goffman and CA.
5. The 'story' of this discovery is told by Schegloff in his first introduction (Sacks, 1992a: xvi–xvii), while its content is available in the first lecture in the collection, 'Rules of conversational sequence' (Sacks, 1992a: 3–11), which is still a model of CA reasoning. See my discussion in Chapter 2.
6. Transcription will be further discussed in Chapter 6. A look at excerpt 1.1 already provides a sense of the complexities involved.
7. Cf. Sacks (1992b) and most of the CA papers from the early 1970s.

2

Three Exemplary Studies

Contents

In this chapter, I will provide a selective discussion of three 'classic' CA studies. The general purpose is to deepen readers' understanding of the argumentative structure of CA work. But along the way I also introduce some basic concepts and quote some interesting programmatic statements which were relatively frequently made in these early phases of CA's development.

Harvey Sacks' first lecture[1]

According to Schegloff's account (Schegloff, in Sacks, 1992a: xvi–xvii), a major moment in the emergence of CA as a discipline of its own was the 'discovery' by Harvey Sacks of some subtle ways in which callers to a Suicide Prevention Center managed to avoid giving their names. In the edited collection of Sacks' *Lectures*, this 'moment' is represented by the first lecture, given in the fall of 1964, posthumously entitled 'Rules of conversational sequence' (Sacks, 1992a: 3–11).

It begins as follows:

I'll start off by giving some quotations.

(1)   A: Hello
      B: Hello
(2)   A: This is Mr Smith may I help you
      B: Yes, this is Mr Brown
(3)   A: This is Mr Smith may I help you
      B: I can't hear you

A: This is Mr <u>Smith</u>.
B: Smith. (Sacks, 1992a: 3)

These are first utterances in calls to a psychiatric emergency service. According to Sacks, one important issue for the professionals answering calls was to get callers' names. The second case would be the standard form of solving this issue without raising it explicitly. By giving his own name, the call-taker made the caller's name-giving a 'natural' next action: '. . . if a person uses "This is Mr Smith . . ." they have a way of asking for the other's name – without, however, asking the question "What is your name?" ' (4). In case 3, however, a caller seemed to use 'I can't hear you' to avoid giving his name by filling the 'slot' designed by the call-taker for this purpose with a different object, one initiating what later would be called a repair sequence.

There are many interesting elements in this analysis – which, of course, can only be glossed here in a very rough manner. For our present purposes, it is important to note that at CA's very beginning, Sacks' strategy was to compare instances of sequences which were similar in terms of their institutional setting (the psychiatric emergency service), their structural location (a call's opening), and the basic procedures (paired actions), but different in the ways in which these were used. For analysing sequences, the notion of paired actions, later to be developed in the concept of 'adjacency pairs', is a basic one, although it should be noted already that the concept of 'sequencing' is not limited to it. In this first analysis, it is linked with a notion of structural location, as in the following:

> We can say there's a procedural rule here, that a person who speaks first in a telephone conversation can choose their form of address, and in choosing their form of address they can thereby choose the form of address the other uses. (Sacks, 1992a: 4)

And later:

> We can also notice that, as a way of asking for the other's name, 'This is Mr Smith . . .' is, in the first place, not an accountable action. By that I mean to say, it's not required that staff members use it and they don't always use it, but when they do, the caller doesn't ask why. 'This is Mr Smith . . .' gets its character as a nonaccountable action simply by virtue of the fact that this is a place where, routinely, two people speak who haven't met. In such places, the person who speaks first can use that object. [. . .] a call is made; the only issue is that two persons are speaking who presumably haven't met, and this object can be used. (5)

In the first instance of the three, an exchange of hellos, the issue of names does not appear at all. Sacks says that when callers started the call, after being connected with the agent by an operator, they invariably used 'hello' as their first utterance. 'Since such a unit involves no exchange of names, they can speak without giving their name and be going about things in a perfectly appropriate way' (6).

In contrast with these structurally specific issues, an object like 'I can't hear you' can be used any time, any place. Sacks calls it 'an "occasionally usable" device. That is to say, there doesn't have to be a particular sort of thing preceding it' (6).

With the wisdom of hindsight, we can say that this first lecture, even in the incomplete fashion I have discussed it here, has offered a starting point for analytic themes for much of latter-day CA. In its published form, the lecture has been given the title 'Rules of conversational sequence', and indeed, as I mentioned, the theme of paired actions, one creating a 'slot' for the next, later conceptualized as 'adjacency pairs', has proven to be a very fruitful one. A second theme opened up by this lecture is the complexity of the relation of conversational action to conversational form; 'asking' without using a 'question' to do so having implications of (non-)accountability. Thirdly, we encountered phenomena of repair, although here not yet analysed in those terms. Fourthly, I will just mention that the lecture has demonstrated that openings are a very useful place to study the negotiation of interaction formats – to be followed up in some of Sacks' later lectures, and especially in a number of papers by his 'first colleague' in CA, Emanuel Schegloff, as will be discussed in the next section. As Sacks mentions, some conversational phenomena are basically related to the place at which they occur, while others can be found 'anywhere'. Finally, at the most general level, this first lecture demonstrates what I consider to be CA's basic analytic strategy: take what people are doing, that is saying, not-saying, saying something in a particular manner, at a particular moment, etc., and try to find out the kind of problem for which this doing might be a solution.

Schegloff's 'sequencing in conversational openings'

Emanuel Schegloff's paper 'Sequencing in conversational openings' (1968) is, as far as I know, the first published paper that represented CA as it later would be known. Its first sentence reads:

> My object in this paper is to show that the raw data of everyday conversational interaction can be subjected to rigorous analysis. (Schegloff, 1968: 1075)

The analysis is based on some 500 instances of the openings of telephone calls to a 'disaster centre'. Overseeing his materials, Schegloff reports that he had formulated:

> A first rule of telephone conversation, which might be called a 'distribution rule for first utterances,' [which] is: *the answerer speaks first.* (1076)

Then he looked for exceptions:

> One case clearly does not fit the requirements of the distribution rule:
>
> #9 (Police makes call)
> Receiver is lifted, and there is a one second pause
> Police: Hello.
> Other: American Red Cross.
> Police: Hello, this is Police Headquarters . . . er, Officer Stratton [etc.]. (1079)

This one deviant case was used to trigger a deeper analysis of all cases in terms of a basic device called the 'summons – answer sequence'. In the routine case, the telephone ring functions as the summons, to which the opening utterance, such as a 'Hello' or an identification, is the answer. In the deviant case, this answer is not readily forthcoming, therefore the summons is repeated in a different form, the caller's first 'Hello' in case #9 above.

Schegloff focuses his subsequent discussions on various properties of the summons – answer (SA) sequence, including its 'non-terminality' (something should follow) and 'non-repeatability' (once a summons is answered, one shouldn't make another), and on its functionality in arranging the conversational interaction. Especially important for my purposes is his discussion of 'conditional relevance':

> By conditional relevance of one item on another we mean: given the first, the second is expectable; upon its occurrence it can be seen to be a second item to the first; upon its nonoccurrence it can be seen to be officially absent – all this provided by the occurrence of the first item. (1083)

Schegloff adds 'the property of immediate juxtaposition' to this, suggesting that the second item should be produced in 'next position', whatever 'next' will be in the circumstances, and for some type of sequences allowing other items to be 'inserted' between the two primary ones (cf. also Schegloff, 1972).

In the paper's last paragraph, Schegloff summarizes the general import of SA sequences as follows:

> [. . .] conversation is a 'minimally two-party' activity. That requirement is not satisfied by the mere copresence of two persons, one of whom is talking. It requires that there be both a 'speaker' and a 'hearer.' [. . .] To behave as a 'speaker' or a 'hearer' when the other is not observably available is to subject oneself to a review of one's competence and 'normality.' Speakers without hearers can be seen to be 'talking to themselves.' Hearers without speakers 'hear voices.' [. . .] SA sequences establish and align the roles of speaker and hearer, providing a summoner with the evidence of the availability or unavailability of a hearer, and a prospective hearer with notice of a prospective speaker. The sequence constitutes a coordinated entry into the activity, allowing each party occasion to demonstrate his coordination with the other, a coordination that may then be sustained by the parties demonstrating continued speakership or hearership. (1093)

In this paper, we again encounter the notion of paired actions. And again, we see it being tied to a specific structural location, the opening exchanges of a call. In contrast to Sacks' analysis, discussed above, the fact that all the calls were made to or from a specific institutional agency is not given any special attention in the analysis. It is, so to speak, an analytically arbitrary setting, as are, for the most part, the series of group therapy sessions, fragments of which are discussed throughout Sacks' *Lectures*.

For general interest, let me just mention here that in subsequent lectures (Sacks) and papers (Schegloff), several aspects of openings have been analysed in greater depth. Sacks has on several occasions discussed issues related to what he called 'the reason-for-a-call' as being quite often a primary topic just after the opening exchanges. Calling someone is, for non-intimates, an accountable action which has to be accounted for 'by and large on the first opportunity to talk after greetings' (Sacks, 1992a: 73; see also 773ff. and some later discussions in 1992b).

From Schegloff's later work on openings, I want to note his analysis of 'Identification and recognition in telephone conversation openings' (1979a) and some further work on the systematics of its sequential organization in 'The routine as achievement' (1986). These analyses have been challenged in terms of cultural variation, suggesting that Schegloff's cases were 'typically American', but this largely seems to miss their major analytic points.[2]

In Schegloff's 'classic' (1968) study also, the basic analytic strategy is taking what people are doing and finding out the kind of problem for which this doing might be a solution. The 'problem' here is a very fundamental one, how to start an occasion of talk-in-interaction, while the circumstances are more particular, that is restricted to two-party telephone conversations. The analytic ramifications, however, are very general indeed, having to do with issues of availability and initiative.

Schegloff and Sacks on 'opening up closings'

In 1973 Schegloff and Sacks published a paper together which can be seen to offer a nice complement to Schegloff's previously discussed one, in that it dealt with 'the other end' of conversations, closings. As they say, 'the unit "a single conversation" does not simply end, but is brought to a close' (289). What they try to do is 'to provide a technical basis' for this work of bringing 'a conversation' to a close. Although the paper was published in 1973, it takes the general concept of a 'turn-taking machinery' as a starting point, which was extensively discussed in another paper, published a year later, in 1974.

Although the authors start from the sequential organization of turns, they do note that a more complete solution of the closing problem 'requires reference to quite different orders of sequential organization in conversation – in particular, the organization of topic talk, and the overall structural organization of the unit "a single conversation"' (289).

The paper, therefore, offers an interesting 'bridge' between the turn-by-turn analysis of conversation, for which CA is best known, and considerations of more encompassing organizational levels.

In the introduction to the paper, Schegloff and Sacks make some general programmatic statements which are worth quoting at some length. They write:

> This project is part of a program of work [. . .] to explore the possibility of achieving a naturalistic observational discipline that could deal with the details of social action(s) rigorously, empirically, and formally. For a variety of reasons [. . .] our attention has focused on conversational materials; [. . .] not because of a special interest in language, or any theoretical primacy we accord conversation. Nonetheless, the character of our materials as conversational has attracted our attention to the study of conversation as an activity in its own right, and thereby to the ways in which actions accomplished in conversation require reference to the properties and organization of conversation for their understanding and analysis, both by participants and by professional investigators. This last phrase requires emphasis and explication. (289–90)[3]

One might say that this quote illustrates again, as some of the earlier cited ones, that in this early phase, CA was conceived by its originators as basically a sociological, rather than a linguistic, enterprise, concerned with the explication of action in organizational terms, rather than with 'language use'. In later phases, the articulation of CA in terms of a *grammar* has become more prominent, without, thereby, losing its interest in *action* (cf. Ochs et al., 1996). The statements following the ones quoted above emphasize a basic interest in the orderliness of action:

> We have proceeded under the assumption (an assumption borne out by our research) that in so far as the materials we worked with exhibited orderliness, they did so not only for us, indeed not in the first place for us, but for the coparticipants who had produced them. If the materials (records of natural conversations) were orderly, they were so because they had been methodically produced by members of the society for one another, and it was a feature of the conversations that we treated as data that they were produced so as to allow the display by the co-participants to each other of their orderliness, and to allow the participants to display to each other their analysis, appreciation and use of that orderliness. Accordingly, our analysis has sought to explicate the ways in which the materials are produced by members in orderly ways that exhibit their orderliness, have their orderliness appreciated and used, and have that appreciation displayed and treated as the basis for subsequent action. (290)

In other words, the orderliness studied by CA is conceived of as a produced orderliness and one produced by the interactants themselves. Therefore, CA's interest is with the local production of order and with 'members' methods' for doing so.

After some remarks on the data used, to which I will return later, Schegloff and Sacks develop a further specification of their 'problem'. At first, they locate the problem of closing work on the level of 'the overall structural organization of single conversations' (292), but they say that many features at that level, especially the organization of 'topic', are still unclear. The concept of 'a conversation' presupposes a concept of 'conversational activity', although not all conversational activities take place in single 'conversations'. Therefore, the specification of the closing problem starts from a discussion of the basic features of 'conversational activities':

> [. . .] two basic features of conversation are proposed to be: (1) at least, and no more than, one party speaks at a time in a single conversation; and (2) speaker change recurs. The achievement of these features singly, and especially the achievement of their cooccurrence, is accomplished by coconversationalists through the use of a 'machinery' for ordering speaker turns sequentially in conversation. (293)

They then give a summary account of the 'turn-taking machinery', stressing among other things its 'local' functioning, its 'normative' character, and the fact that it provides for the location and repair of occasions of 'failure' to achieve the two basic features. One kind of example of this last mentioned aspect is that a moment of non-speech can often be observed to be attributed by the participants as 'someone's silence'. The turn-taking machinery, then, provides for the orderliness of an indefinitely ongoing conversation, not for its orderly closing. On the basis of this argument, the authors propose 'an initial problem concerning closings':

HOW TO ORGANIZE THE SIMULTANEOUS ARRIVAL OF THE CONVERSATIONALISTS AT A POINT WHERE ONE SPEAKER'S COMPLETION WILL NOT OCCASION ANOTHER SPEAKER'S TALK, AND THAT WILL NOT BE HEARD AS

SOME SPEAKER'S SILENCE. [. . .] Again, the problem is HOW TO COORDINATE THE SUSPENSION OF THE TRANSITION RELEVANCE OF POSSIBLE UTTERANCE COMPLETION, NOT HOW TO DEAL WITH ITS NONOPERATION WHILE STILL RELEVANT. (294–5; capitals in the original)

The question, then, is how 'the transition relevance of possible utterance completion' can be lifted, for which 'a proximate solution involves the use of a "terminal exchange" composed of conventional parts, e.g. an exchange of "good-byes"' (295). Such a terminal exchange is presented as a member of a class of utterance sequences, which is called 'adjacency pairs'. Although Schegloff and Sacks do not provide an extensive discussion of this concept in general, the specifications they do give can still be considered to be the 'classic' treatment of this most important concept. I will, therefore, provide extensive quotations:

> Briefly, then, adjacency pairs consist of sequences which properly have the following features: (1) two utterance length, (2) adjacent positioning of component utterances, (3) different speakers producing each utterance.
>
> The component utterances of such sequences have an achieved relatedness beyond that which may otherwise obtain between adjacent utterances. That relatedness is partially the product of the operation of a typology in the speakers' production of the sequences. The typology operates in two ways: it partitions utterance types into 'first pair parts' (i.e. first parts of pairs) and second pair parts; and it affiliates a first pair part and a second pair part to form a pair type. 'Question–answer', 'greeting–greeting', 'offer–acceptance/refusal' are instances of pair types. A given sequence will thus be composed of an utterance that is a first pair part produced by one speaker directly followed by the production by a different speaker of an utterance which is (a) a second pair part, and (b) is from the same pair type as the first utterance in the sequence is a member of. Adjacency pair sequences, then, exhibit the further features (4) relative ordering of parts (i.e. first pair parts precede second pair parts) and (5) discriminative relations (i.e. the pair type of which a first pair part is a member is relevant to the selection among second pair parts). [. . .]
>
> A basic rule of adjacency pair operation is: given the recognizable production of a first pair part, on its first possible completion its speaker should stop and a next speaker should start and produce a second pair part from the pair type of which the first is recognizably a member. (295–6)

These quotes largely speak for themselves, but note especially the remarks on 'achieved relatedness' and 'the operation of a typology' which have a wider relevance than the concept of adjacency pairs by itself.

Schegloff and Sacks remark that adjacency pairs (APs) provide for a 'close ordering' of utterances which makes their use relevant for specific purposes, that is the creation of specific 'sequential implications', limiting what can orderly be done in next position, and for specific organizational tasks, such as opening or closing a conversation. 'Close ordering is [. . .] the basic generalized means for assuring that some desired end will ever happen' (297).[4] They further remark that two utterances are needed for such general organizational tasks, because:

> What two utterances produced by different speakers can do that one utterance cannot is: by an adjacently positioned second, a speaker can show that he understood what a prior aimed at,

and that he is willing to go along with that. Also, by virtue of the occurrence of an adjacently produced second, the doer of a first can see that what he intended was indeed understood, and that it was or was not accepted. Also, of course, a second can assert his failure to understand, or disagreement, and inspection of a second by a first can allow the first speaker to see that while the second thought he understood, indeed, he misunderstood. It is then through the use of adjacent positioning that appreciations, failures, corrections, etcetera can be themselves understandably attempted. Wherever, then, there is reason to bring attention to the appreciation of some implicativeness, 'next utterance' is the proper place to do that, and a two-utterance sequence can be employed as a means for doing and checking some intendedly sequentially implicative occurrence in a way that a one-utterance sequence can not. (1973: 297–8)

What we read here is another elaboration of what Heritage later called 'an architecture of intersubjectivity' (1984a: 254), an organizational template for the achievement of mutual understanding (see also: Heritage, 1995: 398; Sacks et al., 1978: 44; Schegloff, 1992a).

Schegloff and Sacks argue that although a 'terminal exchange' – like both speakers saying 'goodbye' – can be said to do the actual job of closing a conversation, this 'solution' is only a proximate one. It leaves open the issue of when such an exchange can be started. Therefore, they

> try to develop a consideration of the sorts of placing problems their use does involve. First, two preliminary comments are in order. (1) Past and current work has indicated that placement considerations are general for utterances. That is, a pervasively relevant issue (for participants) about utterances in conversation is 'why that now', a question whose analysis may (2) also be relevant for finding what 'that' is. That is to say, some utterances may derive their character as actions entirely from placement considerations. (1973: 299)

These observations are, of course, basic to the CA enterprise, with 'answers' being a most telling example – one only knows that a 'yes' does 'answering' by its placement following a '(yes/no-)question'. Terminal exchanges, it is suggested, may to a significant extent also depend on 'placement' for achieving their meaning as such. 'Answers', however, are placed in terms of a strictly 'local' level of organization, the one concerning adjacent utterances. The adequate placement of 'terminal exchanges' has to be considered on a more encompassing level, for which the authors use the concept 'section'; that is, 'their placement seems to be organized by reference to a properly initiated closing SECTION' (300; capitals in the original).

> The aspect of overall conversational organization directly relevant to the present problem concerns the organization of topic talk. [. . .] If we may refer to what gets talked about in a conversation as 'mentionables', then we can note that there are considerations relevant for conversationalists in ordering and distributing their talk about mentionables in a single conversation.[5] [. . .]
>
> A further feature of the organization of topic talk seems to involve 'fitting' as a preferred procedure. That is, it appears that a preferred way of getting mentionables mentioned is to employ the resources of the local organization of utterances in the course of the conversation. That involves holding off a mention of a mentionable until it can 'occur naturally', that is, until it can be fitted to another conversationalist's prior utterance, allowing this utterance to serve as a sufficient source for the mentioning of the mentionable [. . .]. (301)

Such a 'natural' occasion to mention something may, of course, not arrive at all:

> This being the case, it would appear that an important virtue for a closing structure designed
> for this kind of topical structure would involve the provision for placement of hitherto
> unmentioned mentionables. (303)

Against this background, Schegloff and Sacks develop the idea that by using
topically empty objects like 'We-ell. . .', 'O.K.. . .', 'So-oo', etc. (with downward
intonation), speakers may 'pass' their turn to contribute to further topical development and in so doing offer their conversational partner(s) a set of alternatives,
including further topical contributions, starting a new topic, or likewise passing
such opportunities, for example by reciprocating with a similar object. It is in the
last instance that the topic and the conversation itself may be said to be 'finished'.
Therefore, Schegloff and Sacks call such objects 'possible pre-closings'. They may,
if the participants 'agree', open up a proper 'closing section'. Whether they do may
depend, again, on their placement 'at the analysable end of a topic'. There are
several ways in which topic talk can be closed off: some depend on the type of
topic, such as 'making arrangements', others can be used more generally, such as
'Okay?', 'Alright', or 'one party's offering of a proverbial or aphoristic formulation
of conventional wisdom' which concludes the topic in an 'agreeable' fashion
(306). Furthermore, some encounters have an overall property of what Schegloff
and Sacks call 'monotopicality', which makes a closing of the conversation
relevant as soon as the major topic is closed, while for others the number of
topics is not so predefined.

The issue, then, is how the development of the conversation provides a
warrant for its closing, that is explaining the 'why that now', the exchange of
O.K.'s being one kind of such closing warrants:

> The floor-offering-exchange device is one that can be initiated by any party to a conversa-
> tion. In contrast to this, there are some possible pre-closing devices whose use is restricted to
> particular parties. The terms in which such parties may be formulated varies with conversa-
> tional context. (309–10)[6]

It is noted that closings are often proposed in reference to the other party's interests, which – in telephone conversations – are often different for callers and called,
and which may also be related to specific materials elaborated in the conversation
itself. Interest of the speaker may also be invoked, of course, as in 'I gotta go',
which does not need to be placed at an analysable topic end, but can be done as
an interruption ('I gotta go, my dinner is burning'). So, the option of closing the
conversation can be initiated at any moment, even at the very beginning, before
it really has been started, by using what the authors call a 'pre-topic closing offering' like 'Are you busy?' or 'Were you eating?'

In short, the solution of the closing problem requires not just a proper terminal exchange, but also an adequate preparation for such an exchange, that is a
properly initiated 'closing section'. That section can contain much more than a
minimal terminal exchange, including forward-looking 'making arrangements'
and backward-looking reinvocations and summaries of the conversation about to

be closed. That it is, for participants, a section with a recognized function, as 'collaboration on termination of the transition rule' (322), is demonstrated by the fact that 'new' topical material tends to be brought in using specific 'misplacement markers', like 'by the way'. These seem to claim that the 'porousness' of a closing section will not be abused to lengthen the conversation unduly. Finally, a closing section may also be so organized as to accommodate various practical actions related to departure, such as gathering one's belongings etc.:

> [. . .] to capture the phenomenon of closings, one cannot treat it as the natural history of some particular conversation; one cannot treat it as a routine to be run through, inevitable in its course once initiated. Rather, it must be viewed, as must conversation as a whole, as a set of prospective possibilities opened up at various points in the conversation's course; there are possibilities throughout a closing, including the moments after a 'final' good-bye, for reopening the conversation. Getting to a termination, therefore, involves work at various points in the course of the conversation and of the closing section; it requires accomplishing. For the analyst, it requires a description of the prospects and possibilities available at the various points, how they work, what the resources are, etc., from which the participants produce what turns out to be the finally accomplished closing. (324)

The above discussion has done no more than sketch the bare outline of an extremely rich argument. Moreover, the authors at various points remark that they can only offer a very restricted treatment of some of the issues they touch upon. In other words, rather than 'closing' the issue, the paper has really opened up some of the most important areas of conversational interaction for further research. Apart from the core issues of closing in relation to topic organization,[7] many other themes that are basic to the CA enterprise were elaborated, or at least put on the agenda in this paper. I would like to single out three of these for special attention: (1) the issue of 'placement' in relation to both local and more encompassing levels of organization; (2) the notion of alternatives chosen by participants or offered to their interactional partners; and (3) the continuous negotiability of (inter)action, or, more precisely, the interactional flow.

At the end of my earlier discussions in this chapter, I suggested that a 'problems and solutions' framework had been used in those studies. In those studies, the 'doings', the actual interactional phenomena, provided the starting point for the analysis. In the third classic CA study, the focus has shifted more to the 'problems' side of the argument, although data inspection has undoubtedly provided the starting point here as well.

Discussion

The purpose of this chapter has been to broaden the reader's understanding of CA through a summarizing discussion of some of its earliest achievements. I included quite a number of quotations, especially in the last section, to catch some of the flavour of this early work and to stress some of the basic methodological considerations and specific concepts of CA. Finally, I have presented here some of the fundamental resources I will use in the rest of the book.

What CA offers is an ability to elucidate the procedural bases of (inter)actions, in the sense that generalized 'organizations' and 'devices' can be used to analyse a field of local possibilities for action, depending on what happened before and various contextual particulars, and thereby to provide for the sense of the actions under consideration. As Schegloff has written in a later paper:

> [. . .] the locus of order here is not the individual (or some analytic version of the individual) nor any broadly formulated societal institution, but rather the *procedural infrastructure of interaction*, and, in particular, the practices of talking in conversation. (1992a: 1338)

A final comment will concern the use of data in these studies. How did Sacks use his data in his first lecture? The first three instances he quoted were his primary objects of analysis, which he discussed in a comparative fashion. I will call this his 'focal' observations. But he also referred to general regularities and possibilities that are not supported by concrete instances. He talked about how things 'regularly' happen (or rarely, or always, etc.), as regarding callers being reluctant to give their names. I would call these 'specific background observations', that is references to instances which the analyst knows of, could provide, but does not do so explicitly. Later in the lecture, Sacks also referred to some cases which he did cite, for instance to demonstrate that repair initiators like 'I can't hear you' are being used throughout conversations. This I would call 'supportive observations'. He also seemed to refer now and then to knowledge that any competent member is assumed to have on the basis of his or her own experience, for instance concerning non-acquainted persons exchanging names at the start of a call. I would call these 'general background observations'. Finally, he used some 'ethnographic' information, things he learnt from being in the field and talking with professionals, such as the importance of getting clients' names.[8]

The interesting thing about the choice of the three focal instances is that (1) and (2) are depicted as routine or regular, that is where the devices chosen are 'working' properly, while (3) is a deviant case in which these routines break down. It is the contrast between the routine and the deviant that does the trick here. It is used to open up the field for analysis. By comparing instances with each other, and with general experiences and expectations, their formatted properties, sequential placement, and local functionality can be related and explicated.

In Schegloff's analysis of openings, a similar strategy is used, in the sense that his 500-item corpus provides a strong basis for the formulation of his 'first rule', while the one exception to this rule occasions a deeper consideration of the *logic* of opening sequences, which has a much wider relevance than the cases under consideration.

In Schegloff and Sacks' 'closings' paper, finally, the argument starts on a 'theoretical' rather than data-based 'empirical' note. Data extracts are cited only later in the paper, when various 'solutions' to the closing problem are discussed. The authors refer to reasons of space to account for this, especially given the fact that it is not the short 'terminal exchanges' themselves that they are interested in, but rather the more elaborate exchanges that lead up to the possibility of closing the conversation.

In rough summary, in these papers, data excerpts have different functions: in the first two instances, to ground the problem to be discussed; in the last, to elaborate on some of the solutions available once a problem has been formulated in general terms.

EXERCISE

For this chapter, my suggestion is to read one of the classic CA papers, mentioned in the recommended reading section below, either one discussed in this chapter (marked with a *) or one not discussed in this chapter. Analyse the paper's argument in detail and pay special attention to its data treatment.

The specified suggestions for the different options are similar to the ones for Chapter 1 (page 13). For the collective options, C and D, again take care to select different papers. Compare the various papers in terms of whether they are based on a broad range of data, or one or a few fragments analysed in depth, and what this entails for the convincingness of the overall argument.

RECOMMENDED READING

The following titles represent a limited and personal selection of classic pieces in 'pure' CA: Button (1990); Goodwin (1979); Heritage (1984b); Jefferson (1985a; 1990); Pomerantz (1980); *Sacks (1992a: 3–11); *Schegloff (1968; reprinted in Gumperz and Hymes 1972: 346–80); Schegloff (1982; 1987a; 1988b); *Schegloff and Sacks (1973).

Note: The titles marked with a * have been discussed in this chapter.

Notes

1. For an accessible general introduction to Harvey Sacks' work, see David Silverman's *Harvey Sacks and conversation analysis* (1998).
2. For more extensive discussions and references regarding these issues, and telephone conversation generally, see Robert Hopper's (1992) book on the subject (openings are discussed on pages 51–91) and Luke and Pavlidou (2002), which has a reflective chapter by Schegloff.
3. They add a footnote here, with the text: 'Here our debts to the work of Harold Garfinkel surface. Elsewhere, though they cannot be pinpointed, they are pervasive.'
4. It may be noted that such a functionality of close ordering has been most clearly elaborated in later publications about 'repair', namely Schegloff (1979b; 1987b; 1992a) and Schegloff et al. (1977).
5. At this point, there is a short discussion about the special issues regarding 'first topics', often considered as 'reason-for-the-call'. For more extensive treatments, see Sacks (1992a; 1992b).
6. I will return to issues of 'interactions and their contexts' later in the book; see especially Duranti and Goodwin (1992).
7. Graham Button, in collaboration with Neil Casey, has published a number of thoughtful papers on the organization of closing (Button, 1987b; 1990; Button & Casey, 1984; 1985; 1989). See also Davidson (1978) and Jefferson (1973).
8. Cf. the section on 'ethnographic' information in Chapter 5.

3

Ideas and Evidence in CA Research

While in the first two chapters CA was mostly discussed 'in its own terms', in this chapter I will further explicate the basic methodological features of CA in terms of some of the general literature on qualitative enquiry. I hope that this 'externalist' approach will be helpful to locate the specific characteristics of CA more clearly.

CA's 'image'

Many people who take a look at CA 'from the outside' are amazed by a number of superficial features of CA's practice. It seems to them that CA refuses to use available 'theories' of human conduct to ground or organize its arguments, or even to construct a 'theory' of its own. Furthermore, it seems unwilling to explain the phenomena it studies by invoking 'obvious' factors like basic properties of the participants or the institutional context of the interaction. And finally, it seems to be 'obsessed' with the details of its materials. These impressions are not too far off the mark, but the issue is *why* CA refuses to use or construct 'theories', *why* it refuses interaction–external explanations, and *why* it is obsessed with details. The short answer is that these refusals and this obsession are necessary in order to get a clear picture of CA's *core* phenomenon, the *in situ* organization of conduct, and especially talk-in-interaction. So CA is not 'a-theoretical' but it has a different conception of how to theorize about social life. For the longer answer, I will use, as announced, some core notions from the current literature on 'qualitative social research' (cf. Ten Have, 2004a).

A 'dialogue of ideas and evidence'

I will start with some ideas taken from Charles Ragin. In his book *Constructing social research: the unity and diversity of method* (1994), he explores both what unites the various kinds of social research and the character of their marked differences. What unites social research is that it involves efforts to construct 'representations of social life' in a scientific way. He discusses various conventional ideas about the demarcation of social research from other kinds of 'telling about society', like journalism, or documentary film making, which he finds lacking in generality. Neither a special definition of its object, 'society' (or 'people doing things together' in Howard Becker's phrase), nor a special 'language' (the so-called 'variable language') or 'the scientific method' (i.e. testing hypotheses about relations between variables) seem to do the job of demarcation convincingly:

> The distinctiveness of the social scientific way of telling about society is most apparent [in] representations of social life produced *by* social scientists *for* social scientists [. . .].
> Briefly, social scientific audiences expect social scientific representations:
>
> - to address phenomena that are socially significant in some way,
> - to be relevant to social theory, either directly or indirectly,
> - to be based on or incorporate large amounts of appropriate evidence, purposefully collected, and
> - to result from some form of systematic analysis of this evidence. [. . .]
>
> Ultimately, it is their strong grounding in ideas and evidence that makes these representations especially relevant to social scientists. (Ragin, 1994: 23)

It is clear that CA is in the business of studying aspects of 'social life', in the sense of 'people doing things together'. That conversation analysts 'address phenomena that are socially significant in some way' may be a more contentious claim. Indeed, the study of the ordinary chit-chat of informal interaction is quite often considered to be 'irrelevant' from a societal point of view. And while many kinds of 'institutional talk' may be considered to be worth studying, the aspects chosen by CA may be not. Indeed, as a student of doctor–patient interaction, I have often heard that people considered this to be an 'important' topic, followed by the suggestion that my research might be 'useful' to teach doctors, or more generally to ameliorate medical care. I tend to react a bit hesitantly to such common-sense suggestions, but I will return to the issue in a later chapter. When CA researchers take a stand on the issue of 'social significance' at all, either they tend to refuse the implied assignment 'be significant', or they take it in a very general fashion, as the possibility to contribute to the basic understanding of social life. Emanuel Schegloff, for instance, has included the following statements in his World Wide Web presentation:

For me, direct interaction between persons is the primordial site of sociality. I am interested in exploring what we can learn about any of social science's traditional concerns through the detailed naturalistic study of interaction. In the course of pursuing this goal through the close study of (audio and/or video) recorded episodes of all manner of naturally occurring inter-action, it has turned out that we can also discover previously unrecognized concerns for social science, and ones which appear to be central to the organization of conduct in inter-action and of persons' experience of it. This mode of studying interaction ends up as an instrument for studying a broad range of topics in sociology and related disciplines.[1]

What is expressed here points at once in the direction of 'learning about social life' and in that of a kind of refashioning, or, as it has been called in current eth-nomethodology, a 're-specification' of 'social science's traditional concerns'. The latter hope or promise can be seen as a kind of fulfilment of Ragin's next 'expec-tation', quoted above, 'to be relevant to social theory, either directly or indirectly', although in an 'indirect' fashion. The issue of 'theory' in CA will be given a more extensive treatment in a moment.

The other two 'expectations', formulated by Ragin, 'to be based on or incor-porate large amounts of appropriate evidence, purposefully collected', and 'to result from some form of systematic analysis of this evidence', do not seem to pose serious 'problems' for CA. The 'large amount of evidence' requirement, in fact, is taken by Ragin to be satisfied for qualitative research by 'incorporating a lot of in-depth information about a limited number of cases'. CA's 'obsession with detail', then, can be seen to represent one of the legitimate choices a scientist has in fulfilling his or her obligations to ground the representation strongly in the evi-dence under consideration.

In his discussion of the variety of research types, Ragin concedes that social researchers pursue widely variant goals and follow very different strategies. A major part of his book is devoted to extensive discussions of three different 'research strategies', which are characterized as follows:

1 *Qualitative research* on the commonalities that exist across a relatively small number of cases.
2 *Comparative research* on the diversity that exists across a moderate number of cases.
3 *Quantitative research* on the correspondence between two or more attributes across a large number of cases (covariation). (Ragin, 1994: 33, cf. 48–50)

For instance, a qualitative researcher, like an ethnographer, might do an intensive study of the social life of a relatively small group of people, studying many aspects of it using a variety of methods with an eye on its uniqueness. Survey researchers, on the other hand, study tables based on simple answers to relatively superficial questions produced in thousands of standardized interviews, in order to disentan-gle the complex statistical relationships between variables like gender, education, and political preference. Intermediate between the two is Ragin's third type, com-parative research, which he defines in a specific way as studying 'configurations of similarities and differences across a limited range of cases', focused on patterns of causal conditions leading to specific effects (cf. Ragin, 1987).

Apart from its usefulness as an overview, I take it that the major point of this schema is that these various kinds of research should be discussed and evaluated in their own terms; that is, a survey should not be judged on grounds relevant to an ethnography and vice versa. CA can be seen as a kind of 'qualitative' enquiry, focused 'on the commonalities that exist across a relatively small number of cases'. In any case, it absolutely does not deal with 'the correspondence between two or more attributes across a large number of cases', with a focus on 'variables and relationships among variables in an effort to identify general patterns of covariation' (Ragin, 1994: 190).

Ragin's discussion of distinctions between various kinds of social research is embedded in a general conception, summarized in a useful 'Simple Model of Social Research' (cf. figure on p. 57; quoted and discussed in Ten Have, 2004a: 3). He starts off from the following observations:

> Social research, in simplest terms, involves a dialogue between ideas and evidence. Ideas help social researchers make sense of evidence, and researchers use evidence to extend, revise, and test ideas. The end result of this dialogue is a representation of social life – evidence that has been shaped and reshaped by ideas, presented along with the thinking that guided the construction of the representation. (Ragin, 1994: 55)

Because the 'distance' between abstract and general 'ideas' and concrete and specific 'evidence' tends to be a large one, his model specifies some mediating structures, called 'analytic frames' and 'images', between the two. 'Analytic frames' are deduced from general ideas and focused on the topic of the research, while 'images' are inductively constructed from the evidence, but in terms provided by an analytic framework. The researcher's core job is to construct a 'Representation of Social Life', combining analytic frames and images in a 'double fitting' process called 'retroduction' (a combination of deduction and induction, which has affinities with the concept of abductive reasoning as developed by Charles Pierce):

> Ideas and evidence interact through images and analytic frames. [. . .] Think of analytic frames as a detailed sketch or outline of an idea about some phenomenon. Ideas are elaborated through analytic frames. Frames constitute ways of seeing the things they elaborate. [. . .]
>
> Images, by contrast, are built up from evidence. [. . .] To construct images, researchers synthesize evidence – they connect different parts or elements of the things they study in order to create more complete portraits based on some idea of how these parts are or could be related. Initial images suggest new data collection paths. (Ragin, 1994: 58)

One can say that the various traditions in social research differ from each other in the kinds and contents of their leading ideas, in the character of the evidence used, and in the manner in which the dialogue of ideas and evidence takes form in their practices and public presentations.

Ideas

CA tends to be very sceptical of the existing repertoire of abstract and general ideas about human conduct, and especially of those about action, language use, and verbal interaction (cf. Heritage, 1995: 396–7). Established ideas in these areas are considered to be misleading, not doing justice to the complexities of human interaction, because they tend to be too individualistic and rationalistic, and in any case too simple. They do play a 'negative' role, however, as simplifications to be avoided.[2]

While in many traditions the starting point for any project is to deduce an analytic framework from the general repertoire of ideas, ideally codified in a systematic theory, such deductions are treated with suspicion in CA. This does not mean that CA does not have any 'ideas' or 'analytic frames', but rather that these are produced in a different, one could say more 'inductive', manner.[3] As I already indicated in Chapter 1, it makes sense, in this respect, to differentiate the early phase of CA, leading to a coherent research tradition, and its later, secondary, elaboration. It is clearly the work of Harvey Sacks and his co-workers, partially documented in Sacks' *Lectures on conversation* (1992a; 1992b), to have built CA's analytic frameworks, centred on basic concepts like turn-taking, sequencing, repair, preference, etc. Against the background of a wide-ranging reading in a number of disciplines, confronting the details of the evidence, Sacks et al. have constructed not only *images* of the interactions studied, but also the analytic *instruments* with which to make these constructions. Within a decade, a conceptual repertoire was formed that is still used today. Although Sacks and Schegloff were primary in developing this repertoire, their students, including especially Jefferson and Pomerantz, have also made important contributions, as have members of later generations (see the early papers collected by Lerner, 2004).

This general scepticism in regard to traditional conceptual ideas and distinctions is one of the main differences between Erving Goffman's work and CA, despite some obvious similarities. Goffman ultimately works to develop a broad conceptual schema that provides a neat ordering of the phenomena of interest. He does use various kinds of 'evidence', but in a rather loose, illustrative manner (as in Goffman, 1981; cf. Schegloff, 1988a; Lerner, 1996). His basic inspirations, however, tend to be found in the sociological tradition, especially Durkheim (cf. Burns, 1992; Manning, 1992, among others). Furthermore, Goffman's writings use a complex set of rhetorical 'tricks' to produce a curious mixture of surprise and recognition in his readers. As Rod Watson has noted:

> [. . .] Goffman's work is pattern-elaborative: It involves the subsuming of a huge variety of seemingly discrete phenomena under the aegis of, initially, a single metaphor. His work thus establishes a homologous pattern in an immense range of images. This approach capitalizes on an element of surprise and on the capacities of readers as active pattern detectors, in order to achieve a fresh view of what typically are overfamiliar phenomena. (1992: 4)

Indeed, a number of writers have commented on Goffman's literary style to the effect that he creates particular and, for sociology, rather unusual 'effects' by using 'incongruity', irony, etc. (cf. Fine & Martin, 1995; Lofland, 1980; Watson, 1992). Goffman's perspective, then, positions him as an onlooker, an outsider to the interactions he observes among ritually obsessed persons trying strategically to project a favourable image of themselves. CA, on the other hand, uses a rather 'flat' style to analyse the technology-in-use for talk-in-interaction, based on a detailed inspection, rather than an ironic gloss of talk's work. Some CA researchers, however, have used concepts derived from Goffman, such as 'involvement', 'participation framework', 'participation status', and the like, especially those who work with videodata (cf. Goffman, 1981; Goodwin, 1981; Goodwin, 1990; Heath 1986; 1988, etc.), as well as some of his observations. And all recognize their debt to Goffman in having opened up the field of interaction as a proper object of sociological study.[4]

The above contrasts and considerations should not be taken to imply that CA is indeed 'a-theoretical' in its overall orientation. I would maintain that it is, rather, strongly theoretical, but it deals with 'theory' in a different way compared with conventional social science. It is clear from the development of CA, as it can be traced in Sacks' *Lectures*, that its originators were widely read in a large number of disciplines, including not only various branches of social science, but also parts of philosophy, linguistics, the classics, literary studies, etc. (cf. Schegloff's introduction to Sacks, 1992a, and Silverman, 1998: Chap. 2). Although the aspect of CA as a critical dialogue with a wide range of theoretical approaches to human conduct is generally not stressed, it should not be denied either. In many ways, then, the major difference between CA and other efforts to understand human life is one of *theoretical style*. What CA tries to do is to explicate the inherent theories-in-use of members' practices as *lived orders*, rather than trying to order the world *externally* by applying a set of traditionally available concepts, or invented variations thereof.

Evidence

Various aspects of CA's approach come together in the way it deals with its evidence. The preference for recordings of natural interactions is, on the one hand, based on the experience that such evidence is extremely 'rich', 'inexhaustible' really, in the complexity of its details, which could never have been imagined (Sacks, 1992a: 419–20). On the other hand, CA's scepticism regarding established generalized ideas about human conduct leads to the rejection of evidence that is at least partly co-constituted by such ideas, as in observations, interview materials, or documents. The verbal accounts participants might produce regarding their own conduct are rejected also, at least as primary data on the interactions accounted for. Experience shows that participants may not afterwards 'know' what they have been doing or why, and furthermore tend to justify their behaviour in various ways. Such explanations may be interesting in their own right, as 'accounting practices', but are not accorded any privileged status in the analysis of the original interaction. CA tries to analyse conduct 'in its own setting', so to speak (cf. Heritage & Atkinson, 1984; Pomerantz, 2005, for a less strict discussion).

As I already indicated in Chapter 1, such recordings are not used on their own by just repeated listenings or viewings. What has been recorded is 'transcribed' using a set of conventions developed by Gail Jefferson (cf. Jefferson, 2004a). Transcripts are unavoidably incomplete, selective renderings of the recordings, focusing at first on the text of the verbal stream, and adding various kinds of particularities of the ways in which the words were spoken later. The purpose of a CA transcription is to make *what* was said and *how* it was said available for analytic consideration, at first for the analyst who does the transcribing, and later for others, colleagues, and audiences. Transcribing recordings gives the analyst a 'feel' for what has been recorded; it helps to highlight phenomena that may be later considered in detail. And, of course, transcriptions are used to communicate the evidence to an audience. In so doing, such an audience acquires a kind of 'independent access' to the data being analysed. But even when a recording is being played as well, transcripts help to highlight specific phenomena and create a 'shared focus' among audience and analyst. So, while the tapes contain the primary material on which the analysis is to be based, it is elaborated, clarified, and explicated by the transcripts.

When one compares the various conventions for transcribing verbal interaction (cf. Edwards & Lampert, 1993; O'Connell & Kowal, 1994), it is very clear that each system has its own theoretical and methodological 'bias'. For CA transcripts using the conventions developed by Gail Jefferson, the prime function is to note sequential phenomena in much more detail than is necessary for other kinds of approaches. The basic technique is to visualize on paper the timeline of the inter-actional stream, and to place each participant's contribution in relation to those of others. The space occupied by the letters in the printed words is taken as a visual image of the length it took to produce the corresponding sounds during the interaction. And the details added to the textual transcript serve to make this picture more complete and exact, noting pauses, overlapping, slower, faster, latched, or stretched speech. As Jefferson (1985b) makes clear regarding one particular kind of phenomenon (laughter), the system evolved in response to the emerging analytic needs and insights (cf. also Jefferson, 2004a).

For the vocal part, most conversation analysts follow the Jefferson conventions. Details not covered by that system, especially visual details when video recordings are used, can be added to that vocal 'baseline' according to the needs of the analyst (Heath & Luff, 1993). In this way, CA's transcription system, while recog-nizing Jefferson's foundational contribution, has become a kind of collective property, a 'language' that has evolved from the collectivity's experience (cf. also Psathas & Anderson, 1990, and the extensive discussion in Chapter 6).

Understanding

In terms of Ragin's overall model of research, one could say that transcripts function as a kind of mediation between the raw data, the recordings, and the to-be-constructed *images*. For the latter, no exact equivalent is available in CA, since the data are not combined or summarized before they are confronted with the analytic frames. What comes closest to Ragin's *images* are the 'understood' transcripts that are sometimes produced, with a column reserved for explicative *glosses* accompanying the transcript data themselves, as in the following example:

EXCERPT 3.1, FROM FRANKEL, 1984: 153; EARLIER QUOTED WITHOUT GLOSSES AS EXCERPT 1.2

[turn designed for agreement]	Pt:	This- chemotherapy (0.2) it won't have any lasting effects on havin' kids will it?
[silence]		(2.2)
	Pt:	It will?
[preference reversed]	Dr:	I'm afraid so

The point at this moment is not whether this method of adding 'glosses' to transcripts is useful, but to stress that an analyst works on a transcript in an 'understanding' fashion, before and during his or her more strictly 'analytic' elaboration. Inevitably, a member uses his or her 'membership competencies' to understand what the interaction may be all about and how the various details may function in that respect. As Sacks et al., in their classic paper on 'turn-taking' (1978: 44–5), have stressed, the interactants' own 'displays' of their understanding of the utterances, often discernible in their next uptake, are a preferred resource for checking those understandings. But the researcher's own comprehension, 'as a member', so to speak, is also and inevitably involved. This basic methodological insight has been very well expressed in an early paper by Roy Turner:

> As a solution to the vexed problem of the relation between the shared cultural knowledge (members' knowledge) that the sociologist possesses and the analytic apparatus that it is his responsibility to produce, I propose the following:
>
> A. The sociologist inevitably trades on his members' knowledge in recognizing the activities that participants to interaction are engaged in; for example, it is by virtue of my status as a competent member that I can recurrently locate in my transcripts instances of 'the same' activity. This is not to claim that members are infallible or that there is perfect agreement in recognizing any and every instances; it is only to claim that no resolution of problematic cases can be effected by resorting to procedures that are supposedly uncontaminated by members' knowledge. (Arbitrary resolutions, made for the sake of easing the problems of 'coding', are of course no resolution at all for the present enterprise.)
>
> B. The sociologist, having made his first-level decision on the basis of members' knowledge, must then pose as problematic how utterances come off as recognizable unit activities. This requires the sociologist to explicate the resources he shares with the participants in making sense of utterances in a stretch of talk. At every step of the way, inevitably, the sociologist will continue to employ his socialized competence, while continuing to make explicit what these resources are and how he employs them. I see no alternative to these procedures, except to pay no explicit attention to one's socialized knowledge while continuing to use it as an indispensable aid. In short, sociological discoveries are ineluctably discoveries from within the society. (1971: 177)

The ways in which these understandings and explications can be woven into the analytic process will be discussed more fully in the chapters on analytic procedures. For the moment, I just remark that 'understood transcripts' are the basic *images* a CA researcher works with, and that such 'understanding' involves the use both of members' knowledge and of analytic insights and concepts.

In Ragin's model, the ultimate analysis is characterized as a process of *double fitting* the images and the analytic frame, leading to a representation of (an aspect of) social life. In CA the analysis results in a collection of relatively abstract statements on the 'procedures' or 'devices' that participants have used in the specific cases analysed. This can be done on the basis of one case, in a *single case analysis*, or, more commonly, on the basis of a larger set of cases, in a *collection study*, but one can also use various kinds of combinations, such as one focal case and a series of less fully analysed supportive or contrastive cases.[5]

Ragin suggests that, especially in qualitative research, the process of *double fitting* involves changes in both the *images* and the *analytic frame*. For the analytic frameworks of CA, I have suggested above that these have developed, and continue to be developed, over the cumulative series of CA studies, rather than in just the individual studies on their own.

CA's *emic* interests

In anthropology, a distinction is often made between what are called *emic* and *etic* descriptions, concepts, or meanings. These terms were developed by Kenneth Pike:

> It proves convenient – though partially arbitrary – to describe behavior from two different stand-points, which lead to results which shade into one another. The etic viewpoint studies behavior as from outside of a particular system, and as an essential initial approach to an alien system. The emic viewpoint results from studying behavior as from inside the system. (1967: 37)

These terms were constructed by analogy with 'phonetic' and 'phonemic' from linguistics, but they have a wider relevance. *Etic* categories are in principle universal. They can be formulated prior to any particular analysis, to be applied afterwards to cases at hand. *Emic* categories, on the other hand, are focused on one culture in particular and are 'discovered' during investigation into that particular culture:

> Descriptions or analyses from the etic standpoint are 'alien' in view, with criteria external to the system. Emic descriptions provide an internal view, with criteria chosen from within the system. They represent to us the view of one familiar with the system and who knows how to function within it himself. (Pike, 1967: 38)

The last clause in this quote resonates with the notion of 'membership knowledge', inevitably used in an understanding of conversational materials, as discussed above. I would say, therefore, that CA is interested in an *emic* social reality. This does not exclude the use of a 'technical vocabulary', as in sequential organization, adjacency pairs, etc. What it does mean is that such a vocabulary refers to members' knowledge-in-use, that is members' methods or 'the procedural infrastructure of interaction'.

I should add, however, that the emic/etic contrast might be taken to suggest a rather particularistic version of 'culture' which tends to be disputed within CA.

A concept-like 'culture', if used at all, tends to be used in an 'enabling' rather than a 'limiting' fashion; that is, the competencies of 'members' are stressed, rather than any opaqueness to outsiders of 'a culture'.[6]

The actual terms *emic* and *etic* are rarely used in CA writing, but the repeated stress on taking a member's perspective can, I think, be fruitfully characterized in these terms. In a rare passage where these concepts are discussed in a CA context, Charles Goodwin (1984: 243–4) offers a critique of the way 'emic categories' are investigated in 'contemporary work in the ethnography of speaking, and disciplines such as folklore that draw from it', which depend on 'linguistic labels' used by participants or examples of a category produced at the request of the researcher. And he writes:

> Pike (1967), in his seminal expansion of the etic/emic distinction beyond the scope of phonology, defined emic analysis in terms of how phenomena are utilized within specific systems of action, not with labels recognized by informants. In the present chapter [Goodwin, 1984: 225–46], structures that participants attend to within a strip of talk (for example, 'background' as opposed to 'climax' segments of a story) have been specified, not by questioning the participants, but rather through study in detail of the actions they perform as the talk itself emerges. In addition to revealing some of the internal organization of multi-unit turns, such an approach embeds relevant structural units within the activity systems that give them meaning, and demonstrates how participants use this structure as a constitutive feature of the events they are engaged in. (Goodwin, 1984: 243–4)

In short, as I emphasized before, CA is interested in the procedural infrastructure of situated action, rather than in the categories of 'action-as-talked-about'. Therefore, CA's interest in an *emic* reality should be understood in this sense of implicated procedures of talk-in-interaction.

A 'specimen perspective'

In his *Researching culture: qualitative method and cultural studies* (1995), Pertti Alasuutari has made a useful distinction concerning the ways in which (qualitative) researchers conceive the analytic function of the data they use. When questionnaires or interviews are used, these are mostly put into what he calls 'a factist perspective'. In this view, data are taken to be statements about or indications of states of affairs, such as events or inner states, outside the data themselves. Such statements can, therefore, be more or less true.

It may be clear that CA is *not* taking a 'factist perspective' on its research materials. It represents, rather, the alternative perspective that Alasuutari discusses, the 'specimen perspective':

> What is meant by the specimen perspective? Unlike data seen from the factist perspective, a specimen as a form of research material is not treated as either a *statement about* or a *reflection of* reality; instead, a specimen is seen as *part of* the reality being studied. Therefore, honesty is an irrelevant concept to be used in assessing the material. A specimen may be badly representative of the whole, or it may be technically bad, but it cannot lie. (1995: 63)

As stated before, CA studies (transcripts of) recordings of episodes of naturally occurring interaction. These are, then, to be considered as *specimens* of their kind, and not, in a *factist* vein, as either *statements about* (as 'testimonies') or *reflections of* (as 'indexes') a reality 'out there'. It seems important to distinguish clearly these perspectives, both in discussions about CA and in one's own CA practice. From a CA point of view, one can indeed discuss whether an excerpt at hand is an 'instance' of a class, such as 'assessing non-present persons' or 'patients questioning physicians', but not whether the participants 'mean what they are saying', or even whether an action on display in the data is a 'reflection' or 'index' of, say, 'medical power'.

John Heritage has used a similar metaphor for CA's collection of data:

> [. . .] CA has adopted the naturalist's strategy of building up large collections of data from as many natural sites as possible. Like a good collection of naturalist's specimens, these growing data bases contain many variations of particular types of interactional events whose features can be systematically compared. Analysts constantly seek for new variants and may focus their searches on particular settings in the expectation of finding them. (1988: 131)

This image of CA research as a naturalist's hunt for interesting specimens suggests an attitude of a charming *naivety* not only as regards data collection, but also concerning data analysis, which has been disputed from an ethnomethodological point of view (to be discussed in the next chapter). I will return to this issue in the next section.

A logic of induction?

From Ragin's overall model, and the treatment of CA as a kind of qualitative enquiry which is distrustful of a priori 'theorizing', one might infer that CA's basic approach is an 'inductive' one. This has indeed been suggested in some publications, but it may also be disputed. In any case a clarification is in order.

Ragin characterizes induction in the following terms:

> Induction is the process of using evidence to formulate or reformulate a general idea. The process of constructing images (via the synthesis of evidence) is mostly inductive. Generally, whenever evidence is used as a basis for generating concepts, as in qualitative research, or empirical generalizations, as in quantitative research, induction has played a part. (1994: 188)

Heritage (1988), in the sequel to the quote in the previous section, gives the following overall sketch of CA's analytic treatment of its 'specimens', calling its procedures 'inductive':

> Once possessed of a corpus of data, CA operates in the first instance using inductive search procedures. An analyst who is interested, for example, in how invitations are accepted or rejected will begin by building up a collection of invitations and will attempt to establish regularities in the organization of positive and negative responses to them. At the core of this task is the demonstration that these regularities are methodically produced and oriented to by the participants as normative organizations of action. (1988: 131)

An essential part of this search for, and specification of, 'regularities' is the so-called 'deviant case analysis'. Within qualitative methodology in general, it is often stressed that 'negative' or 'deviant' cases should be treated seriously. This is especially so in the strategy called 'analytic induction' which was originally used to arrive at 'universal' statements, for which any kind of 'negative' finding was a serious challenge (cf. McCall & Simmons, 1969: 196–215). In more recent years, the concept of 'analytic induction' is used in a less strict sense 'to refer to any systematic examination of similarities that seeks to develop concepts or ideas' (Ragin, 1994: 93):

> Analytic induction is a technique used primarily by qualitative researchers to access commonalities across a number of cases and thereby clarify empirical categories and the concepts that are exemplified by the cases included in a category. It is a 'double fitting' of ideas and evidence that focuses on similarities across a limited number of cases studied in depth. (183)

A number of writers, including David Silverman (1985: 122; 1993: 128) and John Heritage (1995: 399), have used the concept of 'analytic induction' to describe CA's general approach to data. Silverman uses Schegloff's (1968) study of telephone openings as a major example of this strategy as used in CA. As will be recalled from Chapter 2, Schegloff first formulates a 'distribution rule for first utterances', and then finds that 1 case out of 500 does not fit, because it is the caller rather than the called who speaks first. He then reworks his analysis to come up with a 'deeper' one that fits with all cases at hand. So this is a clear example of 'deviant case analysis'. In Heritage's characterization, this general strategy is specified for CA in the following way:

> This means taking cases where the established pattern is departed from *and showing the ways in which the participants, through their actions, orient to these departures.* (1988: 131; emphasis added)

And he continues:

> If both dimensions of the analysis can be adequately accomplished, then the empirical task of showing that a particular normative organization is operative in interaction (that is, under-lying both the production of and reasoning about a particular social action or sequence of actions) will have been achieved. Beyond this point, there is the theoretical task of specify-ing the role which the organization that has been discovered plays in the communicative and social matrix of interaction. (131)

I take it that Heritage in this quote specifies three consecutive phases of an analysis:

1 establishing a regular pattern of (inter)action;
2 describing the normative orientations of participants, as demonstrated in 'deviant cases'; and
3 providing a functional specification of the organization, discovered in 1 and 2, in the wider matrix of interaction.

One could suggest, I think, that it is the first phase of this process that best fits with more traditional concepts of 'induction'. Recall that in his general definition of the concept, quoted above, Ragin mentioned two functions of induction: the generation of 'empirical generalizations', especially in quantitative research, or 'concepts' in qualitative investigations. Phase 1, establishing regularities, would be similar to the first of these, while phases 2 and 3 are more interpretive, analytic, or theoretic, rather than empirical, operations, although based on, inspired by, and referring to empirical materials. In other words, I am suggesting that there are two sides to a CA analysis, the first being more strictly empirical in a behavioural sense, the second oriented to what has been called the explication of the *endogenous logic* that provides for the sense of the (inter)actions, as part of a lived moral – practical order (Coulter, 1991: 38–9; Jayyusi, 1991: 242–3).

It will also be clear that the first, 'behavioural', phase is best served by a strategy of 'collection studies', while the second ultimately depends on intense 'single case analyses' of particular, 'telling' instances. The order of such phases in actual projects may vary, of course. One may, as Heritage's quote suggests, start with a collection, and later analyse the deviant cases in depth. But one may also begin with whatever one has at hand, or with what Gail Jefferson in a data session once called some 'virtuoso moments', episodes that strike the observer as being carried out in a particularly felicitous manner, or with two cases that seem to be instructively contrastive. In short, there is not one royal way to select instances (cf. related discussions in Chapters 5 and 7). In a certain respect, there is tension between the 'two sides' of CA. But I do think that both are needed to produce adequate findings. The art of CA is how to combine the two in one project, or over a series of projects.

In Ragin's overall scheme, 'induction' stands for a bottom-up move, from the evidence to the ideas, while 'deduction' refers to a top-down treatment of data in terms of pre-established ideas. I have earlier suggested that in its first phase CA's conceptual apparatus was developed in its originators' struggle with the data, while in its second phase this apparatus is generally available as an established repertoire. This means that in a general sense 'induction' has, to a certain extent, given way to 'deduction'. The danger in this situation is that less talented, insightful, or sensitive practitioners may be tempted to 'apply' the established concepts in a mechanistic fashion, as 'coding instruments'. The concept of 'preference', for instance, as developed by Sacks (1987) and elaborated by Pomerantz (1984) and others, has been codified in schemes like those of Levinson (1983: 332–45) or Heritage (1984a: 265–80) which may seem to suggest such a 'mechanistic' treatment. In other words, the temptation is to use CA's previously established concepts and findings as law-like or even 'causal' rules, whereas one should, I would maintain, see them as descriptions of possible normative orientations of participants, available for various usages as *they* see fit. Any instance of talk-in-interaction is built on routines of various sorts, but it is, at the same time, a unique achievement here and now. What is needed, then, is a continuous mutual confrontation of concepts and data, of 'ideas' and 'evidence', as rightly stressed by Ragin in his concept of 'retroduction', elsewhere known as 'abduction'.

CA's rationale

In order to understand CA's 'refusals and obsessions', referred to at the beginning of this chapter, one needs a solid understanding of CA's purpose in its own terms.

In an introductory booklet, George Psathas has provided a useful summary characterization of CA, which I quote below:

> Conversation analysis studies the order/organization/orderliness of social action, particularly those social actions that are located in everyday interaction, in discursive practices, in the sayings/tellings/doings of members of society.
>   Its basic assumptions are:
>
> 1   Order is a produced orderliness.
> 2   Order is produced by the parties in situ; that is, it is situated and occasioned.
> 3   The parties orient to that order themselves; that is, this order is not an analyst's conception, not the result of the use of some preformed or preformulated theoretical conceptions concerning what action should/must/ought to be, or based on generalizing or summarizing statements about what action generally/frequently/often is.
> 4   Order is repeatable and recurrent.
> 5   The discovery, description, and analysis of that produced orderliness is the task of the analyst.
> 6   Issues of how frequently, how widely, or how often particular phenomena occur are to be set aside in the interest of discovering, describing, and analyzing the *structures*, the *machinery*, the *organized practices*, the *formal procedures*, the ways in which order is produced.
> 7   Structures of social action, once so discerned, can be described in formal, that is, structural, organizational, logical, atopically contentless, consistent, and abstract, terms. (Psathas, 1995: 2–3)

This last point formulates the ultimate purpose of CA. It tries to provide analytic descriptions of the organization of (inter)action, abstracting from the 'contents' of those (inter)actions. Therefore, CA has been characterized by Schwartz and Jacobs (1979) as a kind of 'formal sociology', as have been the sociology of Simmel, ethnomethodology, and the approach taken by Erving Goffman. One might also speak of a procedural approach to social life. Note that Psathas' points 3 and 6 express CA's refusals regarding 'theory' and 'explanation', as discussed above. Point 4, order being 'repeatable and recurrent', grounds the search for 'regularities', but points 1 and 2 stress the notion that the order is produced *in situ* again and again. In short, even in this summary statement, CA's *creative tension* is discernible. The 'obsession with detail' noted in the first section of the chapter functions to keep this tension alive, and to ward off the temptations of a repeatable coding science.

EXERCISE

Design an exploratory CA study.
    Now that you have, hopefully, acquired a basic understanding of CA, think of a possible *project* in which you could try to get a hands-on acquaintance with CA's basic practices as these will be explicated in the later chapters. The project would have to be exploratory in nature,

(Continued)

(Continued)

that is provide you with opportunities to change it when you learn more from the book, additional readings, your own explorations, and, possibly, discussions with others. A first question would be what *kind of data* you want to record and why, audio or video, informal interaction or institution-based talk, etc. A second issue would be if you already have a *preliminary interest* in some aspect of the interaction, for instance discussions, stories, interruptions, or whatever. If you have certain *expectations* regarding the kinds of phenomena to be encountered in the kind of data you are planning to record, you might want to put these on paper, not as hypotheses to be tested, but as presuppositions to be 'bracketed', so to speak. This procedure is based on the assumption that if you formulate your expectations beforehand, it is easier to set those aside as issues to be dealt with later, while you first take a look at the data 'with fresh eyes'. Finally, you should think about ways in which you would *do* the analytic explorations themselves, what kind of *analytic strategy* you think would be useful. The overall purpose of the exercise is to ask you to *think for yourself* about these issues *before* you read my detailed suggestions in later chapters.

For the various options, I add the following specifications. For A, individual/open, the description above should suffice; for B, individual/focused, the overall interest has already been preselected. For C and D, collective/open and collective/focused, you might first have all participants make their own proposals, and then, in a group session, discuss these and decide the aspects on which you will make a collective choice and which aspects will be left open for individuals to decide. You might coordinate these individual choices in such a way that you have a range of related but still different individual projects. Remember that the overall purpose is to have a good learning experience, with a group setting providing opportunities to learn from others' experience as well as your own.

RECOMMENDED READING

Here are some longer introductions and overviews of CA: relatively short (about 80 pages), Psathas (1995); at full book length (about 260 pages), Hutchby and Wooffitt (1998); and a book centred on Harvey Sacks by Silverman (1998). An interesting discussion of CA methodology in terms of 'traditional' methodological concepts is provided by Peräkylä (1997). General sources on criteria for qualitative research are Seale (1999) and Silverman (2006).

Notes

1. The text hasn't been changed since I first read it in 1998; it is now (November 2005) at http://www.sscnet.ucla.edu/soc/faculty.php?lid=495&display_one=1.

2. Within CA, 'speech act theory' is often used as the chosen opponent (cf. Heritage & Atkinson, 1984: 5); in related work we find similar contrasts (cf. Button et al., 1995; Suchman, 1987).

3. The concept 'induction' is used here in a rather loose manner; I will return to its usability for CA later in this chapter.

4. These remarks do not suffice, of course, to draw a clear picture of a very complicated relationship. See especially Schegloff (1988a; in Sacks, 1992a: xxiii–xxiv), Lerner (1996), Watson (1992), and remarks in Psathas (1995: 9–11).

5. The issue of 'sampling', which might be raised in this context, is rarely dealt with in CA. This is defensible in the light of the 'exemplary' use of cases in CA, corresponding to the 'specimen perspective', discussed in the next section. I will take it up, however, in Chapter 5. See Benson and Hughes (1991: esp. 126–32) for a discussion concerning the irrelevance of established methodological considerations for ethnomethodological studies.

6. A core contribution to this debate is Michael Moerman's *Talking culture: ethnography and conversational analysis* (1988); see also Hopper (1990: chap. 4) and, on the related issue of 'foreign language data', Wagner (1996). I will return to the general issue in Chapter 5, page 75–6.

4

CA and Different Disciplinary Agendas

Contents

As noted in previous chapters, CA emerged within a sociological disciplinary matrix, with a strong input from the work of Erving Goffman and Harold Garfinkel's ethnomethodology. Over time it has developed into an endeavour that is relatively detached from its original disciplinary home base and has been adapted in various ways to rather different disciplinary settings and agendas. In this chapter I will discuss CA's relationships with some of these disciplines, including linguistics and (discursive) psychology. But first I raise some issues emerging from a confrontation of CA with its close allies: ethnomethodology (EM) and membership categorization analysis (MCA). Later, I will refer to debates on the usability or not of CA for different 'critical' agendas, prominently including feminism. As this book is meant to be a helpful introduction into CA-as-practised, my treatment of these interdisciplinary connections and debates will be relatively short and therefore superficial. It will be focused on possible 'lessons' for the actual practice of 'doing CA'. For more in-depth treatments I will refer to the relevant literature. In Chapters 9 and 10 I will return to this overall theme with a more extended treatment of some 'applications' of CA in studies of institutional interactions, work settings, 'disturbed' or 'handicapped' communications, and gender related issues.

CA and ethnomethodology

There is no dispute, I think, that Harold Garfinkel's ethnomethodology (EM) was a major influence in the emergence of the CA paradigm. There has been quite a lot of dispute, however, about the EM/CA relationship in later years. As I see it, there is a range of positions in these disputes. Some take CA to be an inherent part of the ethnomethodological movement, to the point of talking about 'ethnomethodological conversation analysis' to distinguish it from other kinds of analysis of talk-in-interaction. A variant of this position is the notion that CA can be used to 'do ethnomethodological studies'. At the opposite end of this range of positions are those who, while not denying that CA was originally partly inspired by EM, maintain that it has since been developed in a way that is at odds with (at least some) ethnomethodological principles. As they see it, current CA aspires to be a 'science' in a sense that is not compatible with the phenomenological and/or Wittgensteinian inspirations in and of ethnomethodology.

As Garfinkel's writings are notoriously difficult to understand, there is a wide choice of writings 'about' ethnomethodology (see the recommended reading list). A recent one is *An invitation to ethnomethodology* written by David Francis and Stephen Hester (2004). Their treatment offers some useful characterizations for the present overview. Let me start with their succinct description of what ethnomethodology is all about:

> Its concerns are with the 'observability' of ordinary social life, and its principle method of investigation is that of observation. Its focus is upon the methods by which observable social activities are produced. It seeks to investigate how social activities are accomplished by members of society (or 'members' for short). (20)

In outlining later developments in ethnomethodology, they mention three different approaches: 'sequential analysis' and 'membership categorization analysis', stemming from the initiatives of Harvey Sacks, and the so-called 'studies of work programme' which emerged in the 1970s from Harold Garfinkel's teachings. These three differ both in their concern and relatedly in their favoured data sources and data treatment. The point is always how to gain access to the procedural foundations of the activities of interest, their 'observability' and 'accountability'. It requires that everyday sense-making practices are transformed from resources of analysis into topics for analysis. As Francis and Hester say:

> [I]t is important to grasp that ethnomethodology means starting out with what anyone can observe about some situation or activity and then turning 'what is observably the case' into a topic for analysis, where the observable features of social life are treated as 'productions' of the parties to them. Accordingly, doing ethnomethodology involves taking three methodological steps:
>
> 1 Notice something that is observably-the-case about some talk, activity or setting.
> 2 Pose the question 'How is it that this observable feature has been produced such that it is recognizable for what it is?'
> 3 Consider, analyse and describe the methods used in the production and recognition of the observable feature. (26)

In their book they explicate three different 'modes' of this 'three-step method of ethnomethodology': 'self-reflection', 'analysis of recorded talk and action', and what they call 'acquired immersion'. The common basis of these modes is 'the presumption that analysis is premised upon immersion in the activity under study' (26). In other words, as explicated in my Chapter 3, in order to analyse an activity, one has to understand it *as* a participant in such an activity. This is the essence of what Harold Garfinkel has called the 'unique adequacy requirement', which means that the analyst must be 'vulgarly competent' in the activity studied (Garfinkel & Wieder, 1992: 181–2).

In the first of these modes, 'self-reflection', the ethnomethodologist's 'own understandings and activities provide the phenomena for analysis'. The researcher's own experiences and activities are turned into objects of analysis. In their book, Francis and Hester use their own sense-making and understanding of a newspaper headline and a television news story as objects of an ethnomethodological analysis. At the same time, their treatment of this mode offers an introduction to membership categorization analysis, which is their main analytic resource for self-reflection (see my discussion below).

In the second mode, 'analysis of recorded talk and action', ethnomethodologists rely again on their own competencies, this time specifically as 'conversationists and speakers of natural language'. This is, of course, the preferred mode of conversation analysis, as explicated throughout the present book., which can also be described using the three steps outlined above. It is important to note (again) that the presupposition here is that the conversation analyst is indeed 'vulgarly competent' in doing and understanding the conversational activities being studied.

When this is not the case, the third mode, which is called 'acquired immersion', becomes relevant. As Francis and Hester argue:

> Where conversation analysis focuses upon structures of talk, our third mode of application of our method involves the study of complex activities where talk and physical behaviour both play a part. More specifically, we seek to analyse activities that are removed by some distance from ordinary conversation. To understand such activities requires 'acquired immersion', because such understanding demands that the analyst possess something of the particular knowledge and competence taken for granted by practitioners. (2004: 27)

This mode is specifically required for the study of specialized activities, often professional ones like those of laboratory scientists, auctioneers, or plumbers. It is when discussing the study of such specialized activities that Garfinkel talks about the 'unique adequacy requirement'.

Francis and Hester note that the three modes 'are not mutually exclusive, nor are they unrelated'. Instead, 'they can usefully be combined. Indeed, the separation of them into distinct modes is somewhat arbitrary' (27). However, it has been on the issue of combining these modes that various discussions about CA in relation to ethnomethodology have emerged.

One issue concerns the combination of membership categorization analysis and sequential analysis (as practised in CA). It seems useful, therefore, to present here an overview of what MCA involves and of the various arguments in this debate.

Membership categorization analysis (MCA)

An important interest in Sacks' earlier work was the organization of knowledge as used, relied on, and displayed in actual interactions. He noted that a large part of such knowledge is organized in terms of categories of people, either in general terms (as in 'children') or in reference to the speaker (as in 'my husband').[1] These insights and their elaborate explication was at first based on his PhD research on calls to a *Suicide Prevention Center* (cf. Sacks, 1967; 1972a; also a number of lectures in Sacks, 1992a) in which callers explained their life situation and their feeling that they had *No one to turn to*. What Sacks noted, among other things, was that people use person-categories as part of *sets* of categories, which he called *Membership categorization Devices* (MCDs; Sacks, 1972a; 1972b). For instance, within the MCD 'sex' (or as we now say, 'gender') there are two basic categories, 'female' and 'male', while within the MCD 'age' there is not a fixed number of categories, as their use depends on situational considerations; sometimes two suffice, 'old' and 'young', but often more subtle differentiations are called for. Categories are not just named or implied, they also carry a number of different associated properties, later called *category predicates*, like the one that Sacks used a lot: *category-bound activities*. So, for instance, he noted that the activity 'crying' may be considered bound to the category 'baby', while the activity 'picking up (a child)' is typical of the category 'mother' (Sacks, 1972b). Other kinds of predicates might involve properties like rights and responsibilities, specialized knowledge and competencies. Sacks (1972a) also made an effort to explicate 'rules of application', such as an 'economy rule' (one category is often sufficient) and a 'consistency rule' (once a category from a specific MCD is used, other categories from that device tend to be used also). When describing a medical situation, for instance, one participant may be identified as 'the physician', which is quite often enough as a practical indication, although that person might also be called 'a man', 'an adult', or 'Friso de Haan'. While many different categories may be *correct*, there are most often only a few that are also *relevant*. This relevance criterion also accounts for the consistency rule: once one person in an encounter is identified as 'the physician', others may get called 'the nurse', 'the assistant', or 'the patient'. Within the MCDs mentioned so far, we can discern a difference between those that may be relevantly used on any population, like 'gender' and 'age', while others have more specific fields of application. Furthermore, a subset of MCDs has a 'team' or 'relational' implication. Sacks used the expression 'duplicative organization' to refer to cases like 'the chair opened the meeting, the secretary read the minutes' and 'standardized relational pair' (SRP) for 'husband and wife', 'doctor and patient', etc. So *Membership Categorization Analysis* (MCA) offers a useful entrée to start analysing the social knowledge which people use, expect, and rely on in doing the accountable work of living together.

It is remarkable, as can be seen by reading Sacks' *Lectures* (1992a; 1992b) in chronological order, that his interest in these matters became less prominent after about 1967, being more strongly focused on turn-taking and sequential matters. He did, however, publish some of these mid-1960s', explorations of categorization much later (1972a; 1972b), so apparently he did not disavow them. In his introduction to the first volume of the *Lectures* (1992a), Schegloff has commented on this shift as mainly a methodological one. While the work on membership categorization tended to stress the 'recognizability' of expressions such as category terms, for any member of the culture, Sacks later sought to demonstrate such claims in terms of the demonstrable understanding by the participants, as visible for instance in their uptake. On the notion of 'category bound activities', Schegloff writes:

> In my view, Sacks abandoned the use of 'category bound activities' because of an incipient 'promiscuous' use of them, i.e., an unelaborated invocation of some vernacularly based assertion (i.e., that some activity was bound to some category) as an element of an account on the investigator's authority, without deriving from it any analytic pay-off other than the claimed account for the data which motivated its introduction in the first place. (Sacks 1992a: xlii)

And later:

> There is a shift here in analytic stance and procedure, from the analyst's understanding as initial point of departure on the one hand to the coparticipant's understanding as initial point of departure on the other. (xliii)

While MCA more or less declined in general interest and as a method from the CA enterprise as such, it was later taken up again by more ethnomethodologically inclined authors, including: Peter Eglin, Stephen Hester, Lena Jayyusi, and Rod Watson. As noted above, Francis and Hester (2004) use MCA as a method in their first mode of ethnomethodological enquiry, 'self-reflection', in which the researcher investigates his or her own activities and understandings as an example of what 'any member' could do. In other words, they recover Sacks' early analytic stance as described by Schegloff in the quote above, as a legitimate 'initial point of departure'.

In their introduction to a volume collecting some of these later MCA studies, Stephen Hester and Peter Eglin (1997: 11–22) have, however, commented on an ambiguity in Harvey Sacks' observations on 'membership categorization'. Some of his formulations suggest a 'decontextualized model' of membership categories and collections of categories as 'pre-existing' any occasion of use, while at other times he stresses the occasionality of any actual usage. Hester and Eglin stress that for ethnomethodology 'membership categorization is an *activity* carried out in particular local circumstances'. It should be seen as 'in situ achievements of members' practical actions and practical reasoning':

> Categories are 'collected' with others in the course of their being used […] this means that the 'collection' to which a category belongs (for this occasion) is constituted through its use in a particular context; it is part and parcel of its use *in that way*. Its recognizability is part of the phenomenon itself. What 'collection' the category belongs to, and what the collection is, are constituted in and how it is used *this time*. (Hester & Eglin, 1997: 21–2)

In other words, when a researcher is dealing with materials in which particular categories and categorical systems are being used, he or she has a choice in how to analyse these data. On the one hand, one can take a 'culturalist' tack and talk about the availability in 'the culture' of particular categories and categorization devices, such as 'age' or 'sex' (gender). But, as Hester and Eglin suggest, a more purely ethnomethodological analysis would focus on the particularities of any occasioned use of the categories and categorization devices, *this time*. As the title of their book reminds us, MCA is concerned with *Culture in action*, and furthermore, 'categorization' is an activity and analysable as such.

An interesting contrast in the actual use of MCA can be made between categories that are purely 'occasioned' and others that are 'available for that person' but now actually 'in play'. For instance, the categories of caller and called in a telephone conversation, or speaker and recipient in considering a spate of talk are what I call 'purely occasioned'. When someone makes a phone call, he or she takes on the occasioned category of caller-in-that-conversation. And similarly, when someone tells a story or a joke, he or she 'becomes' the (primary) speaker (Houtkoop & Mazeland, 1985).

Emanuel Schegloff has elaborated his 'critical' assessment of MCA that he made as if in passing in his introduction to volume 1 of Sacks' *Lectures*, noted before, in a later essay (2007b). After a penetrating overview of Membership Categorization as formulated by Sacks, he goes on to stress again the point that the actual orientation to categories and the category-boundedness of particular activities has to be demonstrated. He noted earlier that quite often MCA has been used to analyse texts and interview responses, in which an uptake by other participants is not available, and – in the latter case – the categories used are often brought in by the researcher, so that their relevance to the respondent remains opaque. So the methodological and practical issue is how the local relevance for participants of particular categorization devices and the category-boundedness of some activities can be *demonstrated* rather than just asserted as (common-sensically) obvious:

> The 'obviousness' of it is not the investigator's resource, but the investigator's problem. And this, the subsequent literature – especially in so-called membership categorization analysis – has too often failed to notice, has failed to take seriously, has failed to be constrained by. It can thereby become a vehicle for promiscuously introducing into the analysis what the writing needs for the argument-in-progress. To avoid this, there must be analysis to show the claim is grounded in the conduct of the parties, not in the beliefs of the writer. (Schegloff, 2007b: 476)

Schegloff suggests, then, that much of current MCA work selectively takes up an aspect of Sacks' early work, conceived 40 years ago, but fails to incorporate Sacks' later stress on methodological rigour, as well as the achievements of CA in some 35 years since then.

Ethnomethodological critiques of CA

Switching back to Francis and Hester's three 'modes of ethnomethodological research', I will now discuss the other combination of 'modes', 'sequential analysis' and 'acquired immersion'. The issues arising from this combination are a persistent theme in the critiques of those who think that latter-day CA fails in terms of ethnomethodological principles.

I will begin my discussion of these critiques with a short treatment of some remarks by Michael Lynch in a series of publications under his own name as well as in collaboration with others (Bjelic & Lynch, 1992; Lynch, 1985; 1993: 203–64; 2000; Lynch & Bogen, 1994; 1996; cf. also Bogen, 1992; 1999). In the earlier writings, his critique of CA is often expressed by contrasting the more general aspirations, findings, and concepts of CA with the more specifically local and specialized interests of the so-called *ethnomethodological studies of work* programme. In his well-known book on laboratory practices (Lynch, 1985), for instance, he acknowledges that CA has provided him with very useful resources for his studies of 'shop talk', but he also writes:

> This resource, however, is of double-edged usability for studies of specific settings of locally organized conduct.
>
> Conversational analysis offers an ostensive general relevance for studies of work wherever work is achieved in persons, use of verbal commands, requests, orders, questions, agreements/disagreements, and announcements as constituent features of their occupational practices. These recognizable conversational actions are abstractable as "materials" employed in getting work done in specific settings. [...] I speak of this resource as "double-edged," however, since the wholesale application of results from studies of conversation to investigations of specific work situations provides an easy way to produce analytical findings while leaving the specific and substantive character of the work being done in-and-through the conversation unexplicated. (8–9)

Using CA's *general* findings and concepts, he suggests, would lead to taking an analytical distance from the work's detailed accomplishment as a *specific* feature of those settings, or what he calls, following Garfinkel, 'the "just what" of the work':

> The "just what" of the work specifically eludes any account which subsumes an analysis of shop talk within a general conversational analytic. This is not a fault of conversational analysis, *per se*, since conversational analysts study those occasions of concerted speaking which are visibly "having a conversation," "asking a question," "doing a greeting," and so forth. However, the application of those findings to work settings cannot fail to generate further analytical specifications which *do* address the work as it actually appears, but which do not specify how the work is uniquely *that* work and not some other instance of "conversation." (Lynch, 1985: 9)

In other words, while CA insights can be based on a generalized conversational competence that all 'members' are supposed to share and count on, the analysis of specialized activities, like doing laboratory work, require a relevant specialized competence, based on the third mode, 'acquired immersion', in order to fit the 'unique adequacy requirement'.

This kind of critique seems to be related to another one, which can be glossed as the 'scientism' critique. The ethnomethodological critique of CA's 'scientism' tends to differentiate between an early phase of Sacks' thinking oriented to a notion of a 'primitive science' based on what every member can see and recognize, and a later one, when CA became a shared professional endeavour. This latter phase is often discussed with reference to the 1974 paper on turn-taking (Sacks et al., 1978), as an exemplar for all later work based on *collections* of particular, technically identified instances. In a paper on 'The ethnomethodological foundations of conversation analysis', Michael Lynch (2000) writes:

In its developed professional form, conversation analysis exhibits a unique mixture of empiricist and phenomenological tendencies. Although Sacks's earliest writings and lectures exemplify this mixture, the 'empiricist' tendencies became predominant (though never exclusively so) with the development of the professional discipline of conversation analysis. (525)

And, after referring extensively to Schegloff's discussions of the development of CA in his introductions to the two volumes of Sacks' *Lectures* (1992a; 1992b), he adds:

In my view the most problematic aspect of conversation analysis's ethnomethodological foundations is the developing split between the constitutive 'analysis' that, in principle, produces any actual instance of conversation, and the disciplined 'analysis' of conversational data. The split arises, and gradually deepens, when an insightful, contextually sensitive way of explicating the situated production of singular talk – an anti-method that takes its 'critical' initiative from the prior existence of formal academic programs – itself becomes a technical, professionally situated program of formal analysis. (Lynch, 2000: 529)

Lynch's problem with CA, in other words, is that explications of contextual achievements tend to give way to formulations of organizational systematics. For Lynch, talking about ethnomethodological foundations 'has to do with the way ethnomethodology derives its "solution" to the problem of social order not from an academic literature but from the study of commonplace activities' (528). In the case of CA, it refers to CA's insistence to study participants' observable orientations as a required 'first step', which I discussed in Chapter 3 as *understanding* (pages 32–4). He regrets that this first step of explicative understanding tends to be 'attenuated' in later-day CA, but he appreciates CA's continued insistence on participant understanding as its primary object:

Aside from providing a 'ground' for conversation analysis's findings, the repeated demonstration of how intersubjective order is achieved relentlessly at the surface of communicative actions remains conversation analysis's most important lesson for the social sciences. (529)

Lynch's position, then, is one partly of appreciation, and partly criticism. As I understand it, it issues a useful warning against any 'mechanical' use of CA's findings, for instance 'coding' instances as belonging to one or another CA category, without explicating in detail one's understanding of those instances in terms of the category that is being used (cf. my discussions in Chapter 8, pages 162).

The problem of and for CA as raised by Lynch and other ethnomethodologists can be formulated in terms of what I have called elsewhere 'the problem of generalities' (Ten Have, 2004a: 174–6). Let me quote a few sentences from an author who effectively 'uses' CA to 'do' ethnomethodological studies, namely Douglas W. Maynard. In the introductory chapter of his book *Bad news, good news* (2003: 11), he refers to 'Garfinkel's (1996) continuing preoccupation with the 'what more' of everyday structures' and he adds:

In briefest terms, this translates into a fascination with the in situ *procedures* that participants use in their talk and social interaction for delivering (notifying, forecasting, announcing, reporting, pronouncing, elaborating, explicating) and receiving (obtaining, responding to, affirming, admitting, accepting, evaluating) bad and good news. Such procedures are generic – participants employ them methodically and universally because they are known in common. At the same time, the use of these procedures in concrete situations is singular and particular (Sacks 1984a). Each episode of bad or good news has generic properties *and* a unique, distinctive quality. (Maynard, 2003: 11)

The observation in the last phrase of this quote, I would suggest, is not limited to the specific kind of episodes being discussed, but seems to be true of *any* episode of talk-in-interaction. So, in order to do justice to the phenomena we study, we should always seek a balance between the general and the specifics of the case at hand. And it deserves repeating that in these things we are after the participants' displayed orientations. This means that the generalities that we may formulate should target generalities-in-use, not just our constructions of what we fancy to be general in how people interact.

I would like to add a final remark on the 'combination' of the three modes, which does not directly involve CA. The first mode, self-reflection, can also be combined with the third one, acquired immersion, when a researcher observes him- or herself during the process of acquiring a specialized competence, as I did when I learnt to write HTML for constructing the *Ethno/CA News* website (Ten Have, 1999; cf. Ten Have, 2004a: 151–72 for other examples), or more forcefully in David Sudnow's writings on his learning to play jazz piano (Sudnow, 1978; 2001).

Returning to the general theme of this section, it can be noted that the ethnomethodology-CA relationship has not been discussed intensively from the CA side, although there is a collection of 'comparative' remarks and publications (cf. Heritage, 1984a, Maynard & Clayman, 1991; Clayman & Maynard, 1995). In the introduction to a ground-breaking collection on the topic of my next section, Schegloff produces a rather pointed remark on the ethnomethodology–CA confrontation.

> Although there is much which differentiates CA from many central features of ethno-methodology […], the local determination of action and understanding has ethnomethod-ology as its most substantial and proximate source. However, […] the emphasis in ethnomethodology […] was on the uptake, interpretation and understanding of apperceiv-able elements of the surround, and much less on their production. […] The practices it brought to attention […] were most likely to be *interpretive* practices, leaving under-addressed the contingencies by reference to which the conduct to be interpreted had come to have the features and character which it did. (Schegloff et al., 1996: 15; original emphasis)

In other words, it would be the emphasis on the (inter)active *production* of conduct that constitutes CA's most pointed contribution to the human sciences.

CA and linguistics

The story of CA's relationship with linguistics differs from the previous one, although it is also filled with ambiguities and ambivalences. While Sacks and Schegloff studied what might be called 'linguistic phenomena', language-as-used, their interests were different from those of the linguists of their time: social interaction rather than sentence structure. In fact, they claimed that while their 'attention has focused on conversational materials', this was 'not because of a special interest in language' (Schegloff & Sacks, 1973: 289–90). Despite such claims, some of the most important early papers were published in linguistically oriented journals, such as *Semiotica* and *Language*. One reason for this was probably a negative one: lack of interest from most social science journals. But a positive reason may have been that at least some linguists realized that it was indeed interesting work, exploring an area of language that had not been studied in any depth before.

Perhaps the most important theme in these ambivalences and affinities was the critique of a linguistics limited to structural explications of well-formed sentences in terms of grammatical rules. Although Sacks was willing to formulate 'rules' that might be thought to produce observed linguistic forms, these were interactional ones, related to utterances and sequences rather than isolated sentences, and more interestingly, processes like sequencing and turn-taking. It is understandable, therefore, that the linguists who were interested in CA's findings and methods were those who were similarly 'critical' of structural and sentence-based linguistics: those in functional linguistics, discourse-oriented linguistics, (interactional) sociolinguistics, pragmatics, and linguistic anthropology.

Over time, the split between CA and linguistics has been replaced by selective mutual affinities, collaborations, and inspirations. At least since Schegloff's (1979b) paper 'The relevance of repair to syntax-for-conversation', published in a volume titled *Syntax and semantics 12: Discourse and syntax*, it has been recognized that CA indeed offers a contribution to a 'syntactical' study of language-as-used. This contribution enlarges the scope of syntactical study in various directions: in the study of sequences and larger discursive units as well as in the (functional) study of smaller units like particles. But it does more than that: it places the study of 'syntactical' phenomena on an entirely different footing than the ones accepted as obvious in most of linguistics. In slogan form, it is data-driven rather than theory-based, and the data being used are 'naturally occurring' rather than invented or experimentally produced ones. These differences have become less marked over the last decades, as many linguists have turned to natural data of various sorts.

In their introduction to the volume called *Interaction and grammar*, Schegloff et al. (1996) stress three aspects of this importance: temporality, activity implication, and embodiment. The running of the tape in the machine and, less forcefully, the visual depiction of it in the transcript point to the actual *temporality*, including pace and pauses, of the original event, and open up these aspects for analysis. Temporality also means directionality and thereby projectability. The flow over time of the interactional production of language allows the participants to 'project' what might be coming next, which is a major resource for both the production and understanding of language *in situ*.

Concerning *activity implication*, Schegloff et al. (1996) write:

> Once we register that language figures in the actual, practical activities of the lives of people and societies, and that how the language is configured is more than incidentally related to its involvement in those activities, it is readily apparent that, at the very least, attention must be paid to what the relationship is between activity, action and the orderly deployment of language called grammar. (21)

Embodiment plays a part, of course, in the vocalization of language, but also in the mutually implicative relations between talk and various forms of bodily conduct, such as pointing 'that' for instance (cf. page 165).

The point of the volume to which Schegloff et al. offer an introduction is the idea 'that grammar and social interaction organize one another'. This involves three distinctive kinds of arguments: '(1) grammar organizes social interaction; (2) social interaction organizes grammar; and (3) grammar is a mode of interaction'. 'These arguments vary in the conceptualization of grammar and its vulnerability to the exigencies, potentialities, and architecture of social interaction' (33).

Grammatical forms that are available in the specific language system used offer participants a range of *resources* to organize various aspects of their interaction, concerning, for instance, turn construction, turn-taking, repair, and even the significance of past and future turns. CA was originally developed using American English-language materials, but was later applied to interactions using language systems with more or less different grammatical properties such as German, Finnish, or Japanese. Similar interactional functions can, in different languages, be enacted using different grammatical features available in those languages.

The second argument, of the three mentioned above, suggests that grammar can be conceived as 'an *outcome* of lived sociality'. Social interaction is the 'home environment', so to speak, of the emergence, acquisition, and change of language. In other words, language systems can be seen as the institutionalized outcome of interactional practices.

A more radical version of this gets us to the third argument that grammar *is* a mode of social interaction. It says that 'Grammar is not only a resource for interaction and not only an outcome of the interaction, it is part of the essence of interaction itself' (38). CA stresses the 'moment-by-moment, evolving interactional production' of linguistic structures. They 'can be understood as collaborative achievements of different interlocutors' (39), as is the case when a speaker changes the design of an utterance in mid-turn reacting to the responsive displays produced by the recipients (Goodwin, 1979; 1981; see the discussion below). 'The meaning of any single grammatical construction is interactionally contingent, built over interactional time in accordance with interactional actualities' (Schegloff et al., 1996: 40).

However one might conceive the linguistics/CA relationship, it is clear that the mutual influence and collaboration have contributed to the sophistication of both disciplines. Originally, the conception within CA of particular linguistic constructions and other phenomena of language production were relatively 'basic'. In the classic turn-taking paper, for instance, the linguistic elements that might be used to produce a 'turn' were described in an open manner:

> There are various unit-types with which a speaker may set out to construct a turn. Unit-types for English include sentential, clausal, phrasal, and lexical constructions. (Sacks et al., 1978: 12)

The interest, at the time, was in the functional property of 'projectability' of a possible ending of the turn, a 'transition-relevance place' (TRP), rather than the structural resources for it. Later this issue became the focus of a lot of work by linguists and conversation analysts with a non-linguistic background alike (cf. the recommended reading section for some of the sources on this issue). The most important points in these explorations seem to be that:

- the projectability of a possible completion point depends on a multitude of properties, which include most prominently syntactic structure and prosody or intonation, but pragmatic or (inter)action considerations also play a part;
- different language systems provide different resources within these categories for users of those systems;
- in face-to-face situations the organizations of visually available bodily action and hearable vocal activity, talk-in-interaction, are closely intertwined.

The first point is supported, for instance, by a study by the functional linguists Cecilia Ford and Sandra Thompson (1996) who investigated the use of syntactic, intonational, and pragmatic resources for the management of turns. They found a high degree of coincidence of syntactic, intonational, and pragmatic points of completion in what they call 'complex transition relevance places' or CTRPs. They write:

> A major finding of this study is the fact that speaker change correlates with CTRPs. This is evidence that the units defined by the convergence of syntactic, intonational, and pragmatic completion are real for conversationalists; speakers and hearers orient to, and design their own turns in response to, these units. Participants in these conversations treat CTRPs as the basic points relative to which they take and yield turns. (Ford & Thompson, 1996: 172)

For support of the second point, I like to refer to a number of studies by Hiroko Tanaka. In her paper 'Turn projection in Japanese talk-in-interaction' (2000), for instance, she notes that 'the grammatical structure of Japanese permits incremental transformability of a turn in progress and overwhelmingly results in a later arrival of the point at which the emerging shape of a turn can be known'. This 'delayed projectability' is, however, 'to a large extent compensated by a potentially greater degree of certitude with which participants can localize turn endings through devices that mark possible transition-relevance places'. The devices include 'utterance-final elements (such as copulas, final verb suffixes, and final particles) or marked prosodic endings' (Tanaka, 2000: 1, 4; see also Tanaka, 1999).

On the third point, the work of Charles Goodwin is of paramount importance, as are the contributions of Christian Heath and others. In his first published paper, 'The interactive construction of a sentence in natural conversation' (1979), Goodwin showed that a speaker in a conversation produced his turn in accordance with shifts in the availability of different active recipients, available through their gaze, while he spoke. In later studies he analysed the connections of talk with various visually available aspects of interaction including pointing and gesture, as well as the manipulation of different artefacts. Christian Heath has done similar studies in settings of medical interaction and technologically complex work settings (e.g. Heath & Luff, 2000).

Finally, some of the most important collaborations and cross-fertilizations between linguistics and CA have occurred on the theme of prosody. As linguists Elisabeth Couper-Kuhlen and Margaret Selting write in the introduction to their edited volume *Prosody in conversation: interactional studies* (1996), prosody involves 'auditory parameters such as pitch, loudness and duration' (1). They characterize the interactional perspective as follows:

> In contrast to previous approaches to prosody, [it] attempts to reconstruct prosodic categories 'from within' as participant categories, showing how speakers use prosody as a resource for the management and negotiation of interactive meaning. The demonstration that participants do indeed orient to the prosodic features in question is used as a warrant for the analytic decisions made. (3)

The papers in the collection demonstrate the importance of prosody in interaction very well. In some cases prosody functions in the organization of turn-taking, in others prosodic differences can be shown to differentiate activity types. The late Clare Tarplee, for instance, demonstrates that adults in a picture-book session with a child often repeat the attempts by the child to label the picture, but do so in prosodically different ways. These differences, in timing and/or intonation, are constitutive of the interactional meaning of the repeat as affirmative or as inviting another attempt at labelling.

These indications of the possibilities for a fruitful 'collaboration' of CA and linguistics should suffice for the moment (but see the recommended reading list for further overviews and examples).

CA and discursive psychology

In a chapter on 'Discourse analytic practice', Alexa Hepburn and Jonathan Potter (2004: 180–1) start by noting that the label 'discourse analysis' (DA) is used in many different ways and that 'part of the complication' has been that different kinds of discourse analysis 'have emerged in different disciplinary environments'. And they add that these often 'are structured by, and against, the basic issues of the parent discipline'. It therefore makes sense to differentiate styles of DA according to their disciplinary home base. In the present section I discuss the one that seems, for many of its practitioners, to have become closest to CA: discursive psychology.

The label 'discursive psychology' (DP) collects a range of approaches within psychology which locate the phenomena which they study – cognition, emotions, attitudes, psychotherapy, etc. – as 'discursive' rather than 'mental' in the conventional sense of the term. Some authors within this range are rather 'critical' of CA, as we shall see in the next section on CDA, while others are mostly positive, to the point of using CA methods in their own studies. This latter kind of discursive psychology is most strongly associated with people like Derek Edwards and Jonathan Potter at Loughborough University in the UK.

Looking at the history of discursive psychology (cf. Wooffitt, 2005), one can note a set of distinctive although related trends. Many of today's DP practitioners started their work by digesting a wide range of approaches to discourse, including highly theoretical and 'critical' ones (Foucault, Derrida, etc.), science studies (Gilbert, Mulkay), and to a lesser extent ethnomethodology and CA (cf. Potter & Wetherell, 1987). As they integrated these various influences in their own work, especially their empirical studies, CA became more influential. Originally, they tended to use texts and interviews, but later they turned to 'naturalistic data': recordings and transcripts (cf. arguments in Hepburn & Potter, 2004). In its early phases, discourse analysis in its UK shape, as it emerged in the sociology of scientific knowledge and later was used in social psychology, was developed 'in opposition to' conventional methods and theories. In other words, its orientation was quite strongly polemic. Over the years, however, this polemical accent seems to have become less strong.

In overviews of discursive psychology (Edwards & Potter, 2001; Hepburn & Potter, 2004), the approach is characterized as 'highlighting three core features of discourse': an 'action orientation', the idea that discourse is 'situated', as well as 'constructed and constructive'. The notion of 'action orientation' is characterized in ways compatible with the CA approach. Contrasts are drawn from both a 'speech act' approach, which might suggest a correspondence of particular words, like 'promise' and specific acts like 'promising', and from conventional 'mentalistic' psychological conceptions, like cognition for instance. 'Instead of cognitive entities and processes being the principal *analytic* resource, as they are in mainstream psychological research, they are approached empirically as participants' *ways of talking*' (Edwards & Potter, 2001: 14). DP takes a 'non-cognitivist' and empirical stance towards 'psychological' phenomena, talk about those phenomena, as well as their more or less covered 'invocation' (cf. Edwards & Potter, 2005).

The notion that discourse is 'situated' is taken up in somewhat variant ways. Like CA, DP is interested in the ways in which talk is 'occasioned', both in its immediate sequential environment and in larger, for instance institutional, settings. But furthermore, 'DP considers discourse to be pervasively *rhetorical*': 'claims and descriptions offered in talk are often designed to *counter* potential alternative versions, and to resist attempts (whether actual or potential) to disqualify them as false, partial or interested'. 'That is, they can have both a defensive and offensive rhetoric' (Edwards & Potter, 2001: 13).

Finally, there is the idea that discursive psychology is 'constructionist'. This is a rather complicated (if not confusing) notion which is broken down into two components: discourse is considered as both *constructed* and *constructive*. It is constructed in the sense that it is built from various resources, including words, metaphors, idioms, categories, etc. And it is constructive in the sense that 'versions of the world' are constructed in discourse. DP 'studies how versions of inner life, of local circumstances, of history and broader social groups are produced to do particular things in interaction' (14–15). It is stressed, however, that DP's 'constructionism' differs from other approaches under that name, as it is not ontological (what is) but epistemological and methodological (what can be known and studied empirically),

In a more extensive overview, Derek Edwards and Jonathan Potter characterize discursive psychology in a different manner, by specifying three closely related ways in which DP works (2005: 241–2). The first of these is given as 'respecification and critique'. The idea is that standard psychological topics are 're-worked in terms of discourse practices'. This implies a 'critical' stance towards mainstream psychology's treatment of cognition and other mental states and processes, attitude measurement, etc. The second is labelled 'the psychological thesaurus'. 'DP explores the situated, occasioned, rhetorical uses of the rich common sense psychological lexicon or thesaurus: terms such as angry, jealous, know, believe, feel, wand, and so on.' The idea is 'to explore the ways in which' such 'concepts are used interactionally and rhetorically, with regard to specific locally relevant alternative descriptions'. The third kind of work that DP intends to do is called 'managing psychological implications'. This means that 'DP examines discourse for how psychological themes are handled and managed without being overtly labelled'. For instance, they 'explore how agency, intent, doubt, belief, prejudice, commitment, and so on, are built, made available, or countered 'indirectly', through descriptions of actions, events, objects, persons, and settings'.

In a way, then, discursive psychology has travelled a long way, from theoretical reflections, often with a 'critical' or at least polemical twist, to a strongly empirical enterprise with a focused topical agenda, in which CA has offered the main methodological inspiration. Not all discursive psychologists have taken this road, however, as we shall see in the next section. Within the overall programme, sketched above, a wide range of topics and kinds of materials have been chosen. For instance, Alexa Hepburn and Jonathan Potter (2004) provide a down-to-earth sketch of their way of working in investigating the practices used in talks to a child protection helpline, as reported in various papers, notably one called '"I'm a bit concerned": early actions and psychological constructions in a child protection helpline' (Potter & Hepburn, 2003). A special issue of *Discourse & Society*, edited by Alexa Hepburn and Sally Wiggins (volume 16/5, September 2005), offers a range of examples of current DP studies, covering such diverse topics as prejudice, body size, noise in neighbour disputes, responsibility and blame in email discussions on veganism, narrative reflexivity in sex offender treatment, and creating us/others in talking about books in a school setting.

Returning now to the DP – CA relationship, a first observation can be that this is a strongly asymmetrical one. This can be seen from even a superficial glance at the lists of references in recent DP and CA publications. Current DP is clearly indebted to CA for conceptual and substantive inspiration and this is abundantly acknowledged by quoting the CA literature. In CA books and papers, on the other hand, DP authors and titles are not too often mentioned, although recently more often than before. Furthermore, it is clear that DP is becoming more and more a particular branch of what I have called 'applied CA': it 'uses' CA concepts and methods for accomplishing its own particular agenda, on the one hand a 'respecification' of psychology as a science of the mental, and on the other hand a close study of situations in which one or another kind of 'psychology', lay or professional, is relevant, as can be seen in the topics just mentioned.

In essence, to summarize it again, CA focuses on the organization of 'talking together', whether done 'just for fun', to exchange information, or to transact some kind of business. Anything said in interaction can be understood as doing this vis-à-vis the other participants and as designed for that purpose. The task that CA sets for itself is to explicate the means and methods used for the organization of talk-in-interaction. On any occasion, participants display an orientation to the specifics of the situation, including who they *are* in relation to each other.

Nonetheless, at the same time, they use means and methods which are, to a large extent, shared and conventional.

As we saw before, CA's unique perspective developed in the 1960s from two kinds of considerations and experiences. On the one hand, Sacks and his colleagues were dissatisfied with the then current ways of doing social science, both methodologically and theoretically. On the other hand, they were amazed by the intricate ways in which people could handle various kinds of situations. In order to 'see' such intricacies, one had to set aside or 'ignore', however, the presuppositions and methods of the then current social sciences and be willing to consider seriously the full details of what people were doing. This setting aside of current presuppositions, which was summarized in the slogan 'unmotivated looking' (which I will discuss more fully in Chapter 7, pages 120–1), has clear affinities with 'bracketing' in the phenomenological tradition and 'ethnomethodological indifference', as defined by Garfinkel and Sacks (1970: 345–6; see also Lynch, 1993: 141–7). This amounts to the obligation to 'bracket' all pre-conceived notions and evaluations of the practices being studied. In the case of talk-in-interaction, the material means of facilitating this setting aside has become the making of detailed transcripts of audio and/or video recordings. As the same time, this meant that most CA researchers lost interest in (debates about) conventional theories and methods, except in some rare 'asides'.

In other approaches to discourse, including DP in its earlier phases, it seems that these were much less radical in setting aside conventional conceptions and methods. Rather than 'just dropping' conventional methods, theories, and agendas as CA has done, these other approaches seem to be struggling with various conventions, although in different ways. As can be seen in Wooffitt's (2005) treatment of DA, as it emerged in the sociology of scientific knowledge and later was used in social psychology, it was developed 'in opposition to' conventional methods and theories. In other words, its orientation was quite strongly polemic. DP researchers may have had to struggle harder to loosen the grip of their 'home discipline', academic psychology. This might account for the relatively large amount of polemical publications as well as the tendency to choose more 'socially/ politically relevant' themes and materials, while CA often works on very 'mundane' issues and data and, at least in 'pure CA', is engaged in developing its 'technical' insights in the organization of interaction. In other words, while CA preserves its distance from convention (generally, but not always) by avoiding materials of obvious social importance, DP on the other hand tends to concentrate on such materials.

CA and 'critical' approaches to discourse and interaction

I characterized the relation of CA and ethnomethodology as one of ambivalence and the one with linguistics as selective affinity and collaboration. A similar characterization could be used for DP. With what I will call 'critical' approaches', the relationship, as far as it exists at all, is polemical. Such approaches have the ambition to do more than 'just' produce knowledge about (discursive/interactional aspects of) social life; they take a 'critical' stance towards current arrangements in society. Key terms are power, oppression, inequality, and ideology. In other words, they think it is essential, when studying discursive practices, to take into account various contextual features, especially those that can be related to crucial social and political issues. And while CA does not want to take off from grand social and political conceptions, as exemplified in the idea of 'unmotivated looking', proponents of 'critical discourse analysis' (CDA) maintain that taking an a priori stance is both unavoidable and desirable (Fairclough, 2001; Wodak, 2004; see also: Wooffitt, 2005).

I will, in this section, discuss aspects of this relation as they surfaced in polemic exchanges between, on the one hand, two critically minded discursive psychologists and, on the other, Emanuel Schegloff. Margaret Wetherell (1998) and later Michael Billig (1999a; 1999b) took issue with aspects of a paper by Emanuel Schegloff, called 'Whose text? Whose context?' (1997), to which Schegloff (1998, and, respectively, 1999a; 1999b) responded again. In his paper, Schegloff made the point that for any consideration of a 'text' and its 'context' (whether academic or 'critical' in one or another respect), one should first analyse that 'text' *on its own terms*. By doing this, any form of 'critical discourse analysis' of an interactional episode would then require a technical, CA type of analysis as a *first step*. This involves attention to the details which are demonstrably relevant for the participants and which constitute practices that have been observed in other contexts. A basic analysis along these lines, focused on the participants' own relevancies, he suggests, could serve 'as a buffer against the potential for academic and theoretical imperialism which imposes intellectuals' preoccupations on a world without respect to their indigenous resonance' (Schegloff, 1997: 163).

In other words, Schegloff makes an 'at least' argument: when analysing interactional data – one should 'at least' consider these in terms of their local organizational features. His opponents, however, argue for a 'not enough' stance. Margaret Wetherell (1998), for instance, while accepting the value of a CA-type approach for an analysis of interactional materials, says that the CA perspective is 'too narrow'. She writes: 'Conversation analysis alone does not offer an adequate answer to its own classic question about some piece of discourse – why this utterance here?' (Wetherell, 1998: 388). For her, one should use a more eclectic set of approaches, including CA, but also some 'post-structuralist' concepts and interests. She demonstrates her preferences with a discussion of a stretch of talk involving three boys and an adult interviewer talking about some sexual activities of one of the boys. For her, such an analysis would be 'incomplete' if it did not include the various 'interpretative repertoires' used to 'place' the boy's activities in various ways. In other words, she would prefer to include some wider and supposedly pre-existing cultural resources in an analysis of a particular stretch of talk.

In his response, Schegloff (1998) limits himself to two issues. Firstly, he explicates the intended meaning and import of the question 'why that now' (note the different formulation!), as included in his classic paper with Sacks (1973). It was meant as *a member's question*, and furthermore an indexical one. In other words, it is a question to which participants themselves can be shown to be oriented and it can refer to any aspect of talk, or more generally action. It is, then, a crucial question for CA in so far as it can be demonstrated to be a crucial one for the parties to the interaction. In itself it is not an analytic question for CA to which CA could be held accountable, as Wetherell seems to suggest. The second point raised in Schegloff's response is that in the analysis of Wetherell's materials she completely ignores the fact that these materials were produced in an interview context. The statements which she analyses were 'provoked' by an adult, male academic for research purposes, while she refers them to the adolescent community at that particular boy's school. As he concludes:

> Obviously some may wish to proceed differently (than CA, PtH), but it is worth recognizing that the enterprise is different and the payoffs are likely to be different in kind and in groundings as well. For CA, it is the members' world, the world of the particular members in a particular occasion, a world that is embodied and displayed in their conduct with one another, which is the grounds and the object of the entire enterprise, its sine qua non. (Schegloff, 1998: 416)

In his book on *Conversation analysis and discourse analysis*, Robin Wooffitt (2005: 168–79) offers a more extensive treatment of Wetherell's paper, including a 'critical' reanalysis of her data. Again, from a CA point of view, analyses like the one promoted by Wetherell run the dangers of ignoring the interactional context as it is relevant for the participants and of rushing to see in localized utterances the manifestation of presupposed cultural themes, 'interpretative repertoires', or 'discourses.'

Michael Billig's criticism targets Schegloff's (1997) paper in a different way. He discusses what he calls the 'rhetoric' of CA as exemplified in that paper as well as its supposed ideological neutrality. He suggests that CA in using terms like 'conversation' and 'member' would suggest 'a participatory view of the world, in which equal rights of speakership are often assumed'. He also objects to various other aspects of CA's claims and practices, such as its claim of naivety in 'unmotivated looking' and its 'naming practices' (pointing to Watson's 1997 critique to be discussed on page 97). Referring to the way in which Schegloff has distinguished CA and CSA, he writes:

> I would prefer the distinction between CA and CDA to be drawn differently, although a firm distinction would be misleading because CDA, like CA, encourages the close examination of spoken interaction; indeed, CDA often uses the methods and findings of CA. However, there are differences between CDA and 'traditional' CA. The specific tasks of CDA are frequently part of a wider analysis of social inequality. Moreover, CDA wishes to theorize the presuppositions that must be brought to the micro-analysis of interaction. CDA does not claim epistemological naivety in the fulfilment of its methodological tasks, but explicitly wishes to incorporate insights from social theory and other social sciences, including macro social science, into the analysis of particulars. (Billig, 1999b: 576)

Schegloff, in his final contribution, quotes himself from the paper that set off the debate:

> I understand that 'critical' discourse analysts have a different project, and are addressed to different issues, and not to the local co-construction of interaction. If, however, they mean the issues of power, domination, and the like to connect up with discursive material, it should be a serious rendering of that material. And for conversation, and talk-in-interaction more

generally, that means that it should at least be compatible with what was demonstrably relevant for the parties [...] Otherwise the 'critical' analysis will not 'bind' to the data, and risks ending up merely ideological. (1997: 183)

CA and feminist concerns

The rise of feminism in the 1960s and 1970s has been a challenge to all social and human sciences, and therefore also to CA. It has raised the issue of whether CA's principles and practices can be (made) compatible with feminists' concerns with gender and gender-related inequalities and oppression. The polemic between on the one hand Schegloff and on the other Wetherell and Billig, discussed above, has been one important moment in the struggles over this issue, which deserves a more elaborate treatment. Wetherell has not been the only feminist who voiced critical evaluations of CA in relation to gender issues (cf. Kitzinger, 2000, and more extensively Speer, 2005, for overviews). However, a first thing to note is that neither 'feminism' nor the different ways in which CA has been or can be 'applied' are unitary. Instead, both are rather diverse. This implies that we cannot discuss the theme of this section as involving two 'camps' (cf. Kitzinger, 2000). We should, rather, see it as a field with many different and complex relations of incompatibilities and affinities. Furthermore, it was noted a few years ago that 'the partnership of "CA and feminism" is still in its infancy' (Tanaka & Fukushima, 2002), suggesting that more empirical work is needed before one could really judge its fruitfulness. In this section, I will discuss some of the theoretical and methodological themes that are discernible in the relevant literature, while I will go into some exemplary studies in Chapter 10 (pages 206–9).

Probably the first published attempt to use CA in a feminist framework was a paper by Don Zimmerman and Candace West, 'Sex roles, interruptions and silences in conversation' (1975). They analysed segments of informal two-party conversations recorded in a variety of settings, which were chosen for the occurrence of noticeable silences and/or simultaneous speech. In same-sex conversations (male–male and female–female), they found that 'both overlaps and interruptions appear to be symmetrically distributed between speakers' (115). In cross-sex conversation (male–female), however, 'the pattern [...] is dramatic: virtually all the interruptions and overlaps are by male speakers (98% and 100%, respectively)' (115). They also investigated 'silences', lapses in continuous speech, which were also distributed asymmetrically.

In the years following its publication, this paper has served as a springboard for more extensive researches, in which not only interruptions and silences, but also more complex aspects of conversational actions were related to the sex of the speakers (Fishman, 1978; West & Garcia, 1988). This kind of work later became the object of various criticisms. A common theme in these is that the study 'reified' its topics, on the one hand gender itself and on the other the conversational 'facts' being studied. Susan Speer (2005) collects the Zimmerman and West study with a range of other early feminist writings under the heading of the 'sex difference' approach, and criticizes them on a number of points. A central objection is that such studies 'share an *essentialist* understanding of gender identity', which means that it 'conflates sex with gender, and treats gender as a relatively fixed trait or "essence" that resides in male and female selves' (45). Sex categories are treated as an unproblematic independent variable, to be correlated with features of language use. In this way a 'natural' and causally effective difference between men an women is presupposed, which reinforces what has been called 'gender dualism' and 'a two genders agenda' (Stokoe & Smithson, 2001).

It should be noted that in later publications, Don Zimmerman and Candace West have changed their position, in the sense that they shifted their focus to the activities that may be said to be 'doing gender'.[2] In this later work, gender is seen as being produced or accomplished, rather than being a given fact. This accords with the general ethnomethodological slogan: 'treat facts as accomplishments' (Pollner, 1974). There are some similarities with feminist writings with a different background, such as post-modernism or more generally constructionism. In principle gender is presented as 'performed', 'constructed', or 'achieved', but some critics of this kind of work still see 'essentialist' leanings in it, for instance in suggesting that some topics or speech styles are female or male (cf. Speer, 2005, for more on this).

With his 1997 paper, Schegloff has revived reflections on the (in)compatibility of feminist concerns and CA. Quite a number of feminist researchers, many with a background in discursive psychology, have taken up the challenge that his paper offered to see how far they could get in taking CA seriously, while keeping their feminist agenda alive (cf. Speer, 1999: 476–7). These include Hannah Frith, Celia Kitzinger, Susan Speer, Elizabeth Stokoe, and Sue Wilkinson. The large number of papers by these authors prohibits an extensive discussion of their variant viewpoints regarding the ways in which CA might be useful for the pursuit of a feminist agenda. So I will limit my treatment here to just a few of the themes that emerge from some programmatic statements, while I will return to a consideration of empirical work in Chapter 10.

Celia Kitzinger, on her own or with various other authors, has probably made the most influential contributions to this literature. In a core piece, 'Doing feminist conversation analysis' (2000), she argues for the compatibility of CA and at least some versions of feminist research. A major issue, however, is 'the difficulty of reconciling CA's emphasis on "participants orientations" with the analyst's own preoccupations with gender, class, sexuality and power when these are not apparently attended to by participants themselves' (165). '[I]t raises difficulties for the analyst who "hears" in the data oppressions and power abuses not "oriented" to by the participants' (169). There may be occasions on which issues of gender, or worse, of gender-based oppression, harassment, or 'heterosexism' (taking heterosexuality for granted), are not oriented to by the participants in any noticeable way. She notes that most CA researchers seem happy to restrict their analyses to orientations that are visible 'on the surface' of the talking, but she takes a different position which she introduces as follows:

> Feminists, by contrast, have been quite concerned about the relationship between their (feminist) analysis of their participants' actions and the (generally non-feminist) way in which

participants themselves interpret the same behaviours [...] the desire to present politicized analyses of non-politicized participants, while still somehow 'validating their realities', has led to unresolved dilemmas in feminist work. [...] From my own perspective, it would be unbearably limiting to use CA if it meant that I could only describe as 'sexist' or 'heterosexist' or 'racist' those forms of talk to which actors orient as such. Indeed, it is precisely the fact that sexist, heterosexist and racist assumptions are routinely incorporated into everyday conversations without anyone noticing or responding to them that way which is of interest to me. How is it, for example, that an unquestioned set of mundane heterosexual assumptions regularly surface in talk in which participants do not notice (or orient to) their own heterosexual privilege, and how does precisely this failure to orient constitute and reconstitute heterosexist reality? (171–2)

In later work, to be discussed in Chapter 10, Kitzinger made several efforts to pursue such questions. From it we can conclude that Kitzinger takes at heart Schegloff's overall advice to 'critical' analysis of talk-in-interaction: *first* analyse the materials in their own terms as talk-in-interaction, that is by observing the displayed orientations of the participants, *before* you turn to your own 'critical' agenda. As Kitzinger writes: 'We can harness CA's careful and sophisticated description of the methods people use to do things in talk, and use them as resources in developing our own feminist analyses' (174).

Maria Wowk (2007) has written a 'critical' reaction to Kitzinger's proposal as formulated in the paper that I discussed above from a rather strict ethnomethodological point of view. Her major complaints regard Kitzinger's quite loose arguments to the effect that CA and ethnomethodology are perfectly compatible with at least some kinds of feminism. She maintains, to the contrary, that 'feminist CA', as conceived by Kitzinger, is a 'chimera', a monster composed of the parts of different animals. She specifically argues that feminism's presupposition of gender-based oppressions and power abuses is incommensurable with the requirements of 'ethnomethodological indifference', mentioned before (page 57). As Wowk says: 'This indifference is required as a *methodological* move in order to topicalize the local and practical objectivity and recognizability – local accountability – of particular settings and actions within them.' In other words, Wowk argues that Kitzinger is trying to mix two different approaches which are incompatible, the one starting from particular assumptions and the other which should commence only from the data-at-hand as a rendering of members' practices.[3]

It should be noted, of course, that Wowk's conception of CA as a strictly ethnomethodological enterprise may not be shared by all who consider themselves conversation analysts. I think it is fair to say that Kitzinger's proposal for a 'feminist CA' can be subsumed under the label 'applied CA': that is, as an effort to 'use CA' for purposes that are not, strictly speaking, intrinsic to the CA project as such. In other words, what she proposes is to combine the two agendas, CA and feminism, as far as these seem to be compatible. And while she is quite explicit in saying that feminism is not a unitary project, especially methodologically, she seems to imply that CA is. This can be disputed, however, as I tried to make clear in the section on CA and ethnomethodology.

If I understand Schegloff's position in these matters correctly, as voiced in the debates discussed before, he argues for a two-step procedure: firstly apply a CA analysis uncontaminated by theoretical and political assumption, and then use the results of that analysis in theoretical and/or political arguments. Whether it would be possible in any concrete instance to keep one's theoretical and political convictions at arm's length is another matter, of course.

In a chapter called 'Gender and sexuality in talk-in-interaction', Elizabeth H. Stokoe and Janet Smithson (2002) formulate some ideas for a 'feminist CA' that can be seen as in part an alternative to Kitzinger's proposals. They also present an overview of previous research in the field of feminist studies of language use and consider the value of CA for feminist purposes. A remarkable difference is that they argue explicitly for a combination of CA with *Membership categorization Analysis* (MCA): 'These methodological traditions (ethnomethodology, CA and MCA), although often discussed quite separately, may be used fruitfully together to investigate the procedural consequentiality of categories-in-interaction' (81). They suggest that MCA could offer a way out of the problems associated with CA's reliance on members' orientations as demonstrated in the data, versus feminism's invocation of 'external' relevancies.[4] From an overview of the relevant literature, they conclude that MCA does allow an analyst to a larger extent than most of CA to use his or her background knowledge to infer what speakers using or suggesting the relevance of particular categories 'talk about', as for instance regarding gender and sexuality.

Using MCA in this way seems to be compatible with the proposal by Francis and Hester (2004), mentioned earlier (page 44), that MCA could be used as a kind of 'self-reflection' to investigate how 'any member' might conceive of particular categorizations and their associated predicates. Used in such a way it might be part of the first step in the analytic process, which I have called *understanding* (pages 32–4). In the second phase, *analysis* proper, the 'methods' used in achieving understanding should then be explicated. This returns us to the issue of whether feminist methods of understanding would be sufficiently similar to those of the participants in the scene being analysed. This should, of course, not be assumed but demonstrated or at least made plausible (cf. Schegloff, 2007b). Whether this could be successful cannot be decided on the level of a general discussion; it has to be tackled in actual cases. The proof of the pudding is in the eating! I will return to this issue when I discuss some examples of feminist CA in Chapter 10.

EXERCISE

I would suggest that you select one of the shorter pieces from the list of recommended reading, below, one that appeals to your interests in terms of your own disciplinary background or 'concerns'. Read it and then check the design of an exploratory CA study which you wrote as an exercise for the previous chapter.

RECOMMENDED READING

On CA and Ethnomethodology: Francis and Hester (2004); Ten Have (2004b).

On membership categorization analysis (MCA): Hester and Eglin (1997); Schegloff (2007b).

On ethnomethodological critiques of CA: Lynch (2000).

On CA and linguistics: Ford et al. (2002; 2003); Ochs et al. (1996); Schegloff et al. (2002).

On CA and discursive psychology: Hepburn and Potter (2004); Hepburn and Wiggins (2005); Wooffitt (2005).

On CA and 'critical' approaches to discourse and interaction: Schegloff (1997).

On CA and feminist concerns: Eglin (2002); Kitzinger (2000); Stokoe (2006); Wowk (2007).

Notes

1. Some later authors have proposed to extend MCA to include various kinds of other 'entities' than persons, such as places or collectivities; I will not follow that proposal here.
2. Written in 1977, published in 1987, reprinted together with later elaborations in a book by Fenstermaker and West in 2002.
3. The rendering of Wowk's critique given in this paragraph covers only a small proportion of her paper.
4. Stokoe has defended the use of MCA for feminist studies in a number of her publications (cf. 2006). In her later work, to be discussed in Chapter 10, Kitzinger has incorporated MCA in her analyses.

Part 2

Producing Data

5

Collecting/Producing Recordings

Contents

As has become clear in the previous chapters, it is essential for the CA enterprise to study recordings of natural human interaction in detail. In the present chapter, I will first discuss some general aspects of the 'research design' of CA studies. Included are discussions of sampling issues, naturalness, and the question whether any additional information, apart from recordings, should be collected or not. Then there follows a treatment of some of the practical problems of producing CA data. A general discussion of 'consent' is followed by a detailed review of three overall strategies of getting recordings: copying radio and TV broadcasts; using existing recordings; or making one's own recordings. In the next chapter, I will proceed to the subsequent issues in the production of data: making transcriptions.

Research design

Although CA projects, like most qualitative enquiries (cf. Ragin, 1994), do not, in general, have a strictly predefined 'research design', as is recommended for quantitative research, they are being 'designed', in a way, even if this design is not explicated. As Ragin says:

> Research design is a plan for collecting and analysing evidence that will make it possible for the investigator to answer whatever questions he or she has posed. The design of an investigation touches almost all aspects of the research, from the minute details of data collection to the selection of the techniques of data analysis. (1994: 191)

For CA, the general outline for research projects would at least involve the four phases of:

1 getting or making recordings of natural interaction;
2 transcribing the tapes, in whole or in part;
3 analysing selected episodes;
4 reporting the research.

As is usual for qualitative enquiries, these phases are not strictly separated. In fact, it is often advisable to proceed in a 'spiralling fashion', where earlier phases are 'inspired' by tentative efforts at later-phase work. The division of chapters in this book should not, therefore, be taken as suggesting that one first has to do all recording activities before one starts transcribing etc. In any phase, one should at least anticipate what is to follow, and if at all possible try to do some exploratory work for the later phases.

Interwoven in the four-phase schema given above is a gradual elaboration of analytic 'questions' and 'answers'. Some projects will start with a general interest – how is talk-in-interaction organized? – which will be elaborated as one goes along, especially in the analysis. Others will start off with some quite specific questions, but even these will often have to be specified when one struggles to find good answers through an analysis of the data.[1] For the moment, these issues will only interest us as they are to be taken into account in the decisions one has to make regarding data collection.

'Naturalism'

The general CA recommendation for making recordings is that these should catch 'natural interaction' as fully and faithfully as is practically possible. The term 'natural' in this expression refers to the ideal that the interactions recorded should be 'naturally occurring', that is 'non-experimental', not co-produced with or provoked by the researcher. This preference contrasts with Harold Garfinkel's 'breaching experiments' in ethnomethodology, which produced hilarious dialogues like:

EXCERPT 5.1, FROM GARFINKEL AND SACKS, 1970: 350

HG: I need some exhibits of persons evading questions. Will you do me a favor and evade some questions for me?
NW: [Oh, dear, I'm not very good at evading questions.]
Note: Square brackets do *not* indicate overlap here.

In other words, the ideal is to (mechanically) observe interactions as they would take place without research observation, but one can never really verify this (cf. Labov's remarks on the Observer's Paradox, 1972). Therefore, many researchers try to make the observation, including recording activities, as unobtrusive as possible. I will later discuss some tactics for making the activity of recording at least less imposing on the interaction being recorded. For the moment, let me just suggest that, in many cases, there does not seem to be a sharp line separating 'naturally occurring' from 'experimental' data (in the broad sense of 'researcher-produced'). The following excerpt, for instance, can be seen as presenting a piece of 'non-natural' speech, since Pam is referring to the activity of being recorded, and in so doing characterizes the situation as being an 'experimental' one, in a way.

EXCERPT 5.2, FROM SCHEGLOFF, 1996A: 59 [AUTOMOBILE DISCUSSION 1: 01–12]

```
Carney:    (... hear the same story),
Pam:       ˙hh Oh yeah you've gotta tell Mike tha:t. Uh-cuz they
           [want that on fi:lm.
Carney:    [Oh: no: here we go ag(h)[(h)ain o(h)o(h)o     ] ·hh=
Curt:                                [Huh huh huh huh.]
Gary:      =I[dont thin[k it's that funny.
Carney:      [O h :    [:,
Pam:                   [I gotto go t'the
           joh[n before I hear tha[t again.
Carney:       [You'll like it, you' [Il rilly like it.
Curt:                               [You do too y[ou laugh leke hell you
           Hhuh!                                 [
Phyllis:                                         [°ejjej huh
```

Schegloff does analyse aspects of this episode, however, *as* natural talk. In fact, the speakers do seem to talk in a, for them, ordinary fashion. So, whether some piece of talk can be treated as 'natural' or not depends not only on its setting, but also on the way it is being analysed. Data that seem to be 'artificial', in terms of their content being provoked by the researcher, or the situation of being recorded, may be considered 'natural' in terms of the ways in which the participants interact while responding to this provocation.

In various types of 'applied CA', the data may 'in themselves' be 'experimental', for instance as part of a research project based on interviews, while for a CA researcher, with an interest in the social organization of interview talk, these are 'natural' specimens of the phenomenon of interest.[2]

Sampling issues

In many types of social research, a major aspect of research design is to draw a useful sample of cases from a 'population' of possible cases to investigate. Ragin, for instance, defines sampling as follows:

> Sampling is the process of selecting a representative set of cases from a much larger set. Researchers sample because they often confront a wealth of potential cases and do not have the time or resources to study them all. (1994: 191)

Most often, methodological discussions of 'sampling' presuppose a 'factist perspective', rather than a 'specimen' approach (cf. Alasuutari, 1995, and Chapter 3 above). That is, data are sought in order to represent a reality that is not directly observable. Therefore, the sample should provide a set of indicators for the population parameters to be estimated. When the evidence is used in a 'specimen perspective', however, the reality to be studied is seen to be directly observable in the specimens at hand. So, for instance, if a naturalist would like to study some aspects of the life of *Passer domesticus*, observing a few specimen sparrows will do. The investigator might take care to select cases that are not markedly exceptional, for example by observing sparrows in some places where they are quite common, but no effort at statistical sampling would seem to be needed. The specimens have to be representative not of the population of sparrows, but of the category *Passer domesticus*. In a similar fashion, instances of 'story-telling' or 'repair', or whatever, are analysed in CA in terms of their category, not of a 'population' of stories or repairs.

In his lectures, Harvey Sacks (1984a; 1992a; 1992b; for instance 1992a: 483–8) has repeatedly discussed these matters in terms of their presuppositions regarding the phenomena one studies. If, as the corpus of CA studies suggests, the way people organize their talk-in-interaction is 'orderly', that is based on a set of formal procedures of immense generality,[3] then it does not matter very much which particular specimens one collects to study that order. As a member of a culture, one has been exposed to a very limited and arbitrary 'selection' from the culture, which still allows one to develop the required competencies to deal with other members one encounters in a large variety of settings in an orderly fashion (on these processes see Wootton, 1997/2005).

In the quote below, already used in Chapter 3, John Heritage adds an important note to these ideas:

> [...] CA has adopted the naturalist's strategy of building up large collections of data from as many natural sites as possible. Like a good collection of naturalist's specimens, these growing data bases contain many variations of particular types of interactional events whose features can be systematically compared. Analysts constantly seek for new variants and may focus their searches on particular settings in the expectation of finding them. (1988: 131)

The sparrow example is based on the assumption that the category *Passer domesticus* refers to a collection that is basically invariant, but this may not be the case for 'stories' etc. Therefore, a 'maximum variation strategy' is often proposed, as does Heritage in the quote: selecting specimens 'from as many natural sites as possible'. Sparrows may feed their young in different ways, depending on certain properties of their biotope, for instance. In a similar fashion, 'stories' may be told differently in a peer group, a doctor's office, or a radio talk show. A maximum variation strategy may be specifically fit if one is interested in story-telling as such, that is in 'pure CA', while in some kinds of 'applied CA' one might rather prefer a deliberately restricted set of instances, for example to a specific circumstantial category. In such a strategy, the interest is not in the activity-as-such, but in specific kinds of category- or context-bound activities. In both strategies, comparing cases is an essential operation (to which I will return). The issue here is whether the data set will allow for direct comparisons, or whether the analysis will focus on one core category or setting, while other categories or settings will of necessity only be used in an indirectly comparative fashion, for instance by reference to presuppositions and/or findings about that category or setting. The *logic* of CA, however, in terms of data selection suggests that *any* specimen is a 'good' one: that is, worthy of an intense and detailed examination. It is focused on the specific ways in which that particular specimen has been produced as an 'orderly product'. As Sacks has suggested:

> It may be that we can come up with findings of considerable generality by looking at very singular, particular things. By asking what it takes for those things to have come off. (1992a: 298)

When you are interested in 'greeting', for instance, you may not need to examine '100,000 random greeting sequences' to do that.

In short:

- When you are interested in a particular class of interactional phenomena that can happen anywhere, you might select a varied set of data sources to collect instances of your phenomenon.
- When you are interested in a class of interactional phenomena that you expect to be particularly prominent in a, or some, specific setting(s), you might collect recordings from that or those setting(s).
- When you are interested in a particular setting, you will, of course, have to collect recordings made in that setting, but you might consider catching some variation within that setting, and you might also consider data from other settings for comparative purposes.
- When you are interested in a class of interactional phenomena as it functions in a particular setting, your choice will tend to be even more restricted, but you might still strive for some variation and/or data from other settings as well.

In any case, however, and in particular if your project is an exploratory one, you might use whatever data you can lay your hands on, especially at the start of the project. Whatever choice you make, you should take the particular possibilities of a setting into account, and look for any indications of 'setting sensitivity' that the participants might demonstrate in their talk and other activities.

Audio or video

As was noted before, CA was originally developed on the basis of audio recordings only, either of telephone conversations or of face-to-face interactions. In the latter case, the analysis was inevitably 'incomplete', in the sense that the recorded interaction might have involved non-vocal exchanges, or non-vocal accompanying activities, that would not be accessible to the analyst of the audio tape. This handicap did not prevent CA's originators from developing the enterprise in a way that is still valid today. Later students of interaction, who used video materials, were able to supplement these early findings with insights concerning visual aspects of verbal interaction. In face-to-face situations, who is addressed by an utterance, or, more generally, where a participant's attention is directed to, is routinely inferable (and inferred) from the direction of his or her gaze. As far as I am aware, Charles Goodwin initiated this line of CA research, in close collaboration with Marjorie Harness Goodwin. Apart from CA's originators, Sacks, Schegloff, and Jefferson, he was most strongly influenced by Adam Kendon, who had already started to study 'gaze' in natural interaction in the 1960s (cf. Kendon, 1990), and Erving Goffman, who had been his teacher (see, for instance, Goffman, 1981). It is, as I noted before, remarkable that 'the video branch of CA', which also prominently includes the work of Christian Heath, uses many of Goffman's concepts (cf., for instance, Goodwin, 1981; M.H. Goodwin, 1995; Heath, 1988).

Apart from the visual aspects of the interaction, a special argument for using video over audio applies to those settings in which core aspects of the action relate to the physical environment, the use of objects, technological artefacts, and/or the body or bodies of one or more of the participants (cf. especially Jordan & Henderson, 1995; also Heath, 1997; 2004; Heath & Luff, 2000: 20–1; Suchman & Trigg, 1991). As Christian Heath remarks:

> The emergent and sequential organization of interaction is also relevant to how we might consider the contextual or *in situ* significance of visual conduct and the physical properties of human environments. Gestures and other forms of bodily conduct arise in interaction, people not infrequently use artefacts when talking to each other, and it is not unusual for aspects of the physical environment to become relevant within the course of social activities. (1997: 187; 2004: 270)

He further adds, however, that while visual conduct is part of what I would call the interactional stream, it tends not to have a neat turn-by-turn organization, as talk has been found to have overwhelmingly. This may be one reason why video analysis seems to be less used than one might expect, given its obvious importance.

However, even if one's analysis is not focused on the intricacies of the interweaving of vocal and visual conduct, it may be advisable to use video, because video recording provides a wealth of contextual information that may be extremely helpful in the analysis of interactional talk-as-such, especially in complex settings with more than a few speakers, like meetings of various sorts.

The choice between audio or video recording can also be influenced by considerations of costs, availability of equipment, and relative ease of access. As Heath and Luff explain:

> There can be additional problems associated with video recording, particularly since it is more difficult to preserve the anonymity of the participants. However, it has been found that people in a wide variety of settings are often willing to allow researchers to record both the audible and visual aspects of their conduct if they are guaranteed a final veto on whether the recordings should be preserved. (1993: 308)[4]

Recordings and other sources of information

It has become clear, by now, that conversation analysis requires access to recordings of talk-in-interaction. The question remains, however, whether these would be the only sources of information used, or whether additional data should also be collected. This is an issue that has been, and continues to be, widely and hotly debated, between CA and its critics, as well as within the CA community. This is not the place to review, let alone evaluate, these debates extensively. Therefore, the discussion below is limited to a summary of the various arguments and standpoints, and an enumeration of some possibilities of additional data gathering and its possible analytic usefulness.

CA's insistence on the use of audio or video recordings of episodes of 'naturally occurring' interaction as their basic data is, indeed, quite unique in the social sciences and means that some of the most common data sources are not used, or at least not as 'core data'.

These include:

- interview data, as expressions of opinions and attitudes or descriptions of scenes not witnessed by the researcher;
- observational studies, relying on field notes or coding procedures;
- idealized or invented examples, based on the researcher's own native intuitions; and
- experimental methodologies.

All of these kinds of data are seen as too much a product of the researcher's or informant's manipulation, selection, or reconstruction, based on preconceived notions of what is probable or important (Heritage & Atkinson, 1984: 2–3). Recorded data, instead, are indefinitely rich in empirical detail, which could never be produced by the imagination of anybody (Sacks, 1992b: 419–20). As Heritage and Atkinson say:

> [...] the use of recorded data serves as a control on the limitations and fallibilities of intuition and recollection; it exposes the observer to a wide range of interactional materials and circumstances and also provides some guarantee that analytic conclusions will not arise as artifacts of intuitive idiosyncrasy, selective attention or recollection or experimental design. The availability of a taped record enables repeated and detailed examination of particular events in interaction and hence greatly enhances the range and precision of the observations that can be made. The use of such materials has the additional advantage of providing hearers and, to a lesser extent, readers of research reports with direct access to the data about which analytic claims are being made, thereby making them available for public scrutiny in a way that further minimizes the influence of individual preconception. (1984: 4)

So recordings are CA's basic data, but, as noted above, CA researchers differ amongst themselves as to the extent to which it makes sense to use additional data as 'background information' in addition to recordings, which serve as 'focal data'. In 'pure' CA, as originally developed, even the general setting in which the recordings were made was hardly considered. Either it was left in the dark, or the data source was only mentioned in general terms, as in 'tape recorded phone calls to and from the complaint desk of a police department in a middle-sized Midwestern city' (Schegloff, 1968: 1093, n. 1).

This reliance on such a 'restricted' database has sometimes been seen as a severe limitation of the validity of CA's findings. Critiques on this point can take a variety of forms. Reference has been made to 'missing data' concerning participants, such as the usual macro-sociological variables (socio-economic status, age, gender), institutional position, and personal background. Often, critics tend to complain that the institutional context of the interaction is neglected analytically in CA (Cicourel, 1981; 1992). And others wonder why sources like interviews with participants, their comments on recordings ('member checks'), or interpretations of taped material by panels of 'judges' are not used.

To put it bluntly, explanations of what happens in any kind of interaction, institutional or not, that make reference to 'fixed' givens such as institutional identities and functions, institutionalized resources or relationships, or whatever, are not acceptable to CA until their local procedural relevance is demonstrated (cf. Schegloff, 1987c; 1991; 1992b). And even then, what may be said concerning such interactional moments is only that those properties or relationships are 'talked into being' then and there. For example, in my own work on medical consultations, I think I can show that a 'medical consultation' is only constituted during specific parts of the encounter, and by analysable means, while at other moments something like a 'conversation' or another kind of interaction is going on (Ten Have, 1989; 1991b). The same kind of reasoning may then apply to certain properties and identities that are, by members, considered to be stable within settings, such as being a patient or a physician, and also to those that are thought of as constants to any setting, such as age or gender (cf. Garfinkel, 1967: 116–85).

Given these ideas and findings, any preconceptions of properties, relationships, and occasions that are used as taken-for-granted realities in other branches of the social sciences are to be 'bracketed' in an analysis such as CA aspires to. In that sense, CA is a member of the family of 'foundational sciences', examining the pre-givens of everyday life (cf. Lynch et al., 1983: 208). It should be noted that one might even object, on these grounds, to mentionings of the institutional identities of speakers (such as 'Dr' and 'Pt'), as was done in some transcription fragments quoted earlier in this book, and massively elsewhere. The existence and relevance of such identities are, strictly speaking, to be discovered in the analysis, as products of the local practices of participants (cf. Watson, 1997, and my discussion in Chapter 6).

Similar kinds of arguments can be raised against criticisms that accuse CA of unwisely neglecting other sources of data, in addition to recordings. When, for example, I present my own work on medical consultations to a non-CA audience, I am often questioned why I do not use various other kinds of information, such as interviews with participants, case records, or interpretations made by a panel of 'judges', to support my findings. My answer to the question of why I do not interview the doctors and patients who are represented in my corpus of recordings is as follows. There is no way of knowing how an interpretation of an action by a participant, produced in a setting different from the original one, relates to the action so interpreted. It might make more sense to connect such interpretations to the setting in which they are made, the sociological interview, the viewing or hearing session, than to the setting referred to. It may be very hard for participants to reconstitute after the fact the moment-by-moment interweaving of meanings in interaction. They may be prone to present rather partial accounts, putting their actions in a favourable light (see Pomerantz, 2005, for a more extensive discussion, and a more 'liberal' stance on this issue). Furthermore, the attention of CA is directed not at uncovering hidden meanings, strategic projects, and the like, but at the meanings that actually and observably are produced in and through the interaction, in order to describe the 'technology' used to bring those about.

Similar arguments could be raised against the use of case records as a source of information on patients' backgrounds or medical careers, and against the use of panels of lay interpreters of the recordings, to ground or confirm the researcher's interpretations. Again and again, the CA practitioner will feel that those other sources could be analysed in terms of their own productive processes (cf. Garfinkel, 1967: 186–207; Heath, 1982; Heath & Luff, 2000: 31–60), but that the information which they provide should not prejudge the detailed analysis of the interactional data themselves, and should not be considered more valuable than those data on a priori grounds.

During the last few decades, however, this 'the data are enough' perspective of 'pure CA' has been criticized from positions closer to its centre than before. One general critique of CA that is relevant here starts from what may be called a 'culturalist' and 'humanist' perspective. It is most prominently represented by Michael Moerman in his book *Talking culture: ethnography and conversation analysis* (1988) and some subsequent papers (1990/1; 1992), who argues for a 'culturally contexted CA'. While already an anthropological fieldworker, Moerman encountered CA almost at its beginning. It seemed to resonate with some of his misgivings about traditional fieldwork methods, but the following quote expresses his ambivalence:

> But to know conversation analysis is not necessarily to love it. Its high-powered lens sacrifices range, breath, and *mise-en-scène*. Moreover, the world it has discovered is startling and strange. There are general, powerful, and intricate abstract structures and processes of human conversation that do not correspond to the social order we commonly recognize or to the cultural worlds that we admire. This can make conversation analysis seem bloodless, impersonal, and unimportant to anthropology's central concerns. Few [CA] publications connect the technical organization of conversation to richly experienced human reality. (Moerman, 1988: x)

The general idea seems to be, on the one hand, that analysing talk-in-interaction on the basis of recordings presupposes and requires a thorough knowledge of the culture shared by the participants and taken for granted in their actions. Such membership knowledge can be acquired as a lay participant in the culture involved, or through participant observation using the well-known techniques of anthropology. On the other hand, the suggestion is also that one has to know the local circumstances, the interlocutors themselves even, in order to get at the meanings and intentions involved. Moerman's interests, then, go beyond 'the technology of conversation' (Sacks, 1984b: 411; 1992b: 339), because, as he says 'we never merely exchange turns of talk. In all conversation, people are living their lives, performing their roles, enacting their culture' (Moerman, 1988: 22). In his proposals for a 'culturally contexted conversation analysis', Moerman wants to combine the methods and objectives of ethnography and CA, as he sees them. His conception of CA, as John Heritage (1990/1: 302) has remarked, seems, however, to be rather limited, as an arid form of 'sequential analysis', to which ethnography should add the 'blood' it lacks:

> All actions are socially situated and all situations structured. Sequential analysis delineates the structure of social interaction and thus provides the loci of actions. Ethnography can provide the meanings and material conditions of the scenes in which the actions occur. Culturally contexted conversation analysis thus permits a description that while never complete, is sufficient for showing the nexus between cultural rules and individual intentions. (Moerman, 1988: 57)[5]

Moerman's book has stimulated a lot of debate, which I will not summarize here.[6] Instead, in the spirit of the present book, I now turn to some more practical considerations.

A second 'internal' position of critique on CA's traditional reluctance regarding non-recorded data can be found among people engaged in so-called 'workplace studies', who work with video recordings to analyse local work practices in technologically complex environments. They suggest that in order to study talk-in-interaction as part of the work in those settings, the analyst should acquire at least some knowledge of the organizational and technical purposes and procedures that the workers studied use as a matter of course. Christian Heath, who earlier undertook video-based studies on medical consultation (1986; 1988; 1992), and more recently studied a variety of technologically complex workplaces (Heath & Luff, 1996; 2000), writes in an introduction to video analysis:

> As studies of talk and interaction have become increasingly interested in more specialized forms of human activities, often arising within particular organizational or institutional domains, it has been recognized that it is necessary to augment recorded materials with extensive fieldwork. So, for example, our own studies of general practice involved a long period of non-participant observation before any recording took place in order to begin to assemble a sense of the organization of certain specialized tasks such as diagnosis, treatment and using medical records. (Heath, 1997: 190; 2004: 273)

Switching to his recent activities, he adds:

> With the emergence of more wide-ranging studies of workplace interaction, especially those concerned with the use of tools and artefacts in complex technological environments such as control rooms and emergency centres, we have witnessed an increasing commitment to undertaking wide-ranging fieldwork alongside more focused interaction analyses (Whalen, 1995). [...] It is not unusual in such studies to delay gathering recorded materials until researchers have a passing understanding of the activities in question and the various tools and technologies which feature in the accomplishment of even the more mundane activities in such settings. (1997: 190–1; 2004: 273)[7]

Jack Whalen, for instance, mentions in the report to which Heath refers in the quote above:

> My resources for developing this analysis include extensive field observations undertaken while working as a call-taker and dispatcher at a police and fire communications facility [...] for fifteen months, as well as video recordings of call-takers at work that were collected at [...]. The discussion is also informed by field work at other public safety dispatch facilities. (Whalen, 1995: 187)

The paper itself presents a detailed analysis of the work of call-taking by analysing a single case using both the audio recording of a call and a video recording of the computer screen on which is visible the call-taker's work of filling in the computer-based 'form'.

My own position in these debates is a balanced one (I think!). For 'pure' CA, in the sense explained in Chapter 1, as an examination of 'the institution *of* interaction as an entity in its own right' (Heritage, 1997; 2004), gathering additional information does not seem to be required in most cases, especially if one studies interaction 'from within' one's own culture and if one has enough recorded data from the same or similar participants to acquire a sense of their *emic* competencies and understandings. For studies of talk-in-interaction from a less familiar culture, one might indeed require deeper understanding of that culture, based on an extended period of 'living in' or 'immersion', as a kind of unfocused ethnographic research.

For studies in 'applied CA', such as studies of 'the management of social institutions *in* interaction' (Heritage, 1997; 2004, again), the methodological situation seems to be quite different. For studies of certain relatively routine and standardized situations, the CA researcher might not need much more background knowledge than what he or she has as a member of society at large, depending, of course, on one's research objectives. In my own research on doctor–patient interaction in the setting of general practice, for instance, I did not gather any particular information on the setting, the doctors, or the patients. I did not seem to need such information to study the 'obvious' structures, strategies, and devices that I analysed. Had I been interested, however, in particular professional aspects of the doctor's questioning, such as the use of 'protocols', the additional data would have been necessary. In his study of calls to a 'poison centre', Frankel (1989) needed information on the bureaucratic 'form' the call-taker was using in order to understand the particular questioning strategies observed, which seemed illogical when limiting oneself to the tape alone (cf. Whalen, 1995, for similar observations). Maurice Nevile collected his core data for his studies of 'talk-in-interaction in the airline-cockpit', by videoing the activities of flight crews on scheduled flights by commercial airlines. But before he even approached the airlines to ask for their cooperation, he prepared his research by extensively reading whatever he could find about the operation of commercial airlines, training and operations manuals, official accident reports, etc. He also watched available information videos showing pilots at work, visited conferences, and talked to research psychologists working with flight crews and accident investigators. In this way he developed what he calls a 'disciplinary competence' in his field of interest, without which he could understand barely anything of what was happening in the cockpit (Nevile, 2004: 21–2). In short, ethnographic research in addition to CA can be helpful to build up a knowledge base that is sufficiently similar to what a member knows to understand what is going on. One could speak of a 'virtual membership' require-ment, which does not compete with the primacy of recorded data, but rather supports it.

In a chapter in a book on qualitative research, Anssi Peräkylä (1997; revised as 2004a) raises the issue of what he calls the 'inclusiveness' of tape-recorded data:

> Although tape-recorded data have intrinsic strength in terms of accuracy and public access, spe-cial attention needs to be paid to the *inclusiveness* of such data. Video or audio recordings of spe-cific events (such as telephone conversations, medical consultations or public meetings) may entail a loss of some aspects of social interaction, including (a) medium- and long-span tem-poral processes, (b) ambulatory events and (c) impact of texts and other 'non-conversational' modalities of action. The potential loss can be prevented with appropriate arrangements in the data collection. (1997: 203–4; cf. 2004a: 286–7)

He mentions, among other things, for (a) temporal processes, the possibility of recording a series of events, such as consultations, but one could also think of meetings (cf. Boden, 1994), where one builds on previous ones and anticipates later ones, for (b) ambulatory events, the possibility of using multiple cameras or recorders in different parts of a work setting,[8] while (c) is mentioned with refer-ences to studies by Firth, Frankel, Maynard, and Whalen:

> In sum, by appropriate research design, conversation analytic studies of institutional interaction can be made more inclusive in terms of different layers of the organization of interaction. (1997: 205; 2004a: 287)

In the end, then, the choice of whether one needs additional data apart from the recordings does seem to depend, on the one hand, on one's theoretical-methodological outlook, and, on the other, on the kinds of activities one wants to study. No 'fixed' answer seems to be available, but any choice one makes should be accounted for in terms of debates and considerations like the ones given above.

Hunting for data

Like a late eighteenth-century medical researcher looking for corpses to dissect, a conversation analyst is an habitual 'data hunter'. Using a less gruesome metaphor, Bill Davey and Karsten Gramkow Andersen, of Aalborg University, Denmark, write in a paper on 'Some practical and legal aspects concerning the collection of empirical data':

> It is of paramount importance that the analyst goes about his everyday life like a photogra-pher. Just as the photographer looks at the world through an imaginary camera lens assess-ing potential shots, so the analyst must look for potential data sources in the world around him. (1996)

In short, any option for procuring data should be considered, but practical, ethical, and legal considerations should also play a part.

When one considers the possibilities for procuring data for 'doing conversation analysis', the most obvious way of getting data would seem to be to make one's own recordings of 'natural interactions', either audio or video. There may, however, be other, less cumbersome ways of obtaining data. I will distinguish three overall strategies of procuring useful recordings:

1   copying radio and TV broadcasts;
2   using existing recordings;
3   making one's own recordings.

Before I discuss these three strategies in greater detail, I will present a general discussion of issues of consent.

Consent

Whatever one's data source, one should always consider issues of consent. This means that one needs to consider the rights of the participants in the interaction, and/or those responsible for the situation, and/or the owners of the recording. These rights concern three basic, often mixed, but distinguishable, rights to refuse:

1   to be recorded or to give access to the situation for recording purposes;
2   to grant permission to use the recording for research purposes;
3   public display or publication of the recordings in one form or another.

If one uses the first or second of the three strategies mentioned above, the issue of the right not to be recorded has already been faced, explicitly or implicitly, by the person who was responsible for the original recording. It can be considered to be settled, for all practical purposes. What is still open, however, is, firstly, the issue of using the recording for detailed consideration in a CA research project, and, secondly, the possible 'publication' of the recording in one way or another.

It is a fact that many people dislike the idea that known or unknown aspects of their spontaneous actions will be considered in great detail. This is clearly evident from the reluctance of many to have their actions recorded for research purposes, as well as the mirror reluctance of many researchers to request or even admit that they want to record their conversations, or have them recorded. And even if people do consent to being recorded, they quite often offer nervously hilarious comments on possible exposures etc.[9] There seems to be a common-sense association, then, between a detailed consideration of actions and an unpleasant exposure, or critical assessment, of those actions. People seem to be afraid of being 'caught' off-guard. It depends on one's interests and inclinations how one handles such resistances, but they should at least be noted.

One strategy is to restrict one's data to people one does not know personally, which seems to make detailed study easier to accept for both parties, the researcher and the researched. This may be one advantage of using the first or second of the three strategies. How one goes about these things in the third strategy will be discussed in detail in the section on making recordings oneself.

As to the issue of 'publication', there are, of course, many modalities in which recordings can be made 'public' (cf. the suggestions in Appendix C). For the sake of the present discussion, I will consider the following:

- the use of transcripts in a restricted setting;
- the public use of transcripts;
- the use of recordings in a restricted setting;
- the public use of recordings.

When one uses transcripts, it is advisable *always* to change identifying details, such as names, addresses, etc. One might think this is unnecessary in restricted settings, ranging from informal 'data sessions' to presentations at conferences, but I have experienced some quite embarrassing situations when this was not done and someone 'recognized' one or more of the interactants. Therefore, I have made it a routine to change identifying details as part of the transcribing process (see next chapter). In so doing, the distinction made above between restricted and public use of transcripts is no longer relevant.

With recordings, whether audio or video, the situation is different. It may be very useful, in a data session or paper presentation, to play an audio or preferably a video tape, together with showing a transcript (see Appendix C). It can help to make the phenomena under discussion more vividly 'present' as a support for the analysis. This is what I call 'use in a restricted setting', for instance among professionals, who may be supposed to be able and willing to handle any 'recognition' discreetly. There is still a risk, however, of embarrassing situations when a person is recognized. Furthermore, it is possible, especially when considering the activities of public figures like politicians, that the reception of the analysis itself is somehow contaminated by pre-existing evaluative images of those figures.

Until recently, it was hardly possible to make recordings used for CA research available with an 'unrestricted' publication of the analysis. With current advances in information and communication technologies, however, this is becoming a real issue. 'Sound bites', 'frame grabs', and 'video clips' can now be added to a research report made available to an unrestricted public on CD-ROM or the World Wide Web. When using such possibilities, the issues of privacy and consent can become especially acute.

The practical upshot of these considerations is that gaining the required consent for making and using recordings of natural interactions may be quite complicated. It may involve differentiating the recording process itself, the use of the recording for detailed research, and the public use of data excerpts in one way or another. For this last phase, one can negotiate various restrictions, whatever is necessary to gain consent. As I mentioned, making transcripts unrecognizable by a process of anonymization should be a routine procedure, which can be explained as part of the consent-gaining process. Furthermore, one can promise to confine public showing to restricted, professional audiences. In cases of real, that is unrestricted, publication, one probably should procure separate consent, possibly by showing the relevant excerpts to the interactants themselves.

In the discussion above, I have treated the issue of 'consent' as one that should be on the agenda in the negotiations between researcher and researched. But of course these relationships are embedded in a larger arena. There is a general tendency now, most prominently in the United States, for universities and even governments to *require* formal consent procedures. Universities have 'Internal Review Boards' (IRBs) and require all research projects that involve humans to be reviewed. In other countries, such requirements tend to be especially enforced in medical settings, such as hospitals. Their ethical committees will usually demand the use of consent forms for any audio or video recording (an exemplary consent form is available at http://www.paultenhave.nl/CF.doc).

With these considerations in mind, I will now discuss the three strategies in more detail.

Radio/TV broadcasts

The use of radio and TV broadcasts as a data source may seem strange at first, since the interactions recorded in such a way are generally considered to be rather 'artificial'. Not only may the interactions themselves be prepared or rehearsed, but the recordings may also have been edited in ways which are not discernible to the lay observer. There still may be good reasons, however, to consider such a source, depending on one's overall research goals and the characteristics of the broadcast under consideration. Using this kind of material is obviously sensible if one is interested in a particular form of 'mass media talk', as in studies of news interviews (for instance, Clayman, 1992; Greatbatch, 1988; Heritage, 1985; Heritage & Greatbatch, 1991; and esp. Clayman & Heritage, 2002a), or aspects of the interaction in televised political debates (Atkinson, 1984a; 1984b; 1985; Clayman, 1993; Heritage & Greatbatch, 1986), TV talk shows (Hopper, 1995) or 'talk radio' (Hutchby, 1996, and other publications). But since people do not shift to a completely different set of interactional procedures when they know their talk is broadcast, mass media recordings can also be used for studying talk-in-interaction as such (see, for instance, Schegloff, 1978). In fact, I think that for beginning CA researchers, the mass media are a real data goldmine. At a nominal cost, one can have access to professionally recorded interactions occurring in a wide range of situations and in all major languages. One should, of course, be aware that the material may be edited in various ways, and that the fact that people know they are being recorded may influence their interactions. But at least for exercise materials, this should not be too much of a problem.

When I started doing CA research, I recorded a long series of weekly call-in radio shows, broadcast live in the Netherlands in the late 1970s, which featured informal counselling conversations between the hostess and callers about 'problems with sex and relationships'. Of course, this material had special features, some of which were more or less 'visible', such as the speakers' orientation to the fact of broadcasting, while others were hidden, such as alerts for fake calls, sometimes passed on to the hostess in the studio. But for me, the material offered an excellent training opportunity, and it helped me gain a first overall conception of how such problem-oriented talks might be organized, and some of the detailed ways in which this could be done.

Existing recordings

Another simple way of getting useful recordings is to copy existing ones. This may, again, be done if one does not have a specific interest, but would like to have 'any' recordings of natural interaction. But this strategy may be particularly useful if one does have such a special interest and if the interactions one wants to study are being recorded 'naturally', as part of routine procedures. Both Harvey Sacks and Emanuel Schegloff used existing recordings, routinely made in a suicide prevention centre and a police department, respectively, for their first systematic investigations. Similarly, Alan Firth (1995b; 1995c; 1995d) has used routine recordings to study business negotiations. As he explains:

> The data reproduced in this paper were collected over a four-month period in 1989–90. The source of the data is 'Melko Dairies,' one of the largest dairy conglomerates in Denmark. As a matter of policy, the company audio records all international telephone calls made to and received from foreign clients. Invariably, international calls within the company are conducted in English. [...] In order to protect the anonymity of the parties concerned, all personal names, company names and public places have been changed. (1995c: 169, n. 5)

And again, Harrie Mazeland asked a varied set of qualitative researchers who had done interviews for copies of some of the recordings of such interviews, in order to study question/answer sequences in such settings (Mazeland, 1992; Mazeland & Ten Have, 1996). For my own research on doctor–patient interaction (as in Ten Have, 1989; 1991b; 1995a), I relied entirely on recordings made for teaching purposes or other research projects, copied from tapes made by colleagues. Apart from the practical benefits, this fact also served as an extra barrier, so to speak, to protect the privacy of the participants.

Making field recordings: social issues

Making one's own recordings, or having them made at one's request, is quite often the only way to get precisely the kind of data one wants. This may be less urgent when one has a general interest, but is quite often required if one has a specific interest. In other words, for those engaged in 'pure' CA, as previously defined, making recordings is often less a problem than for those in 'applied' CA. There are a number of issues related to making recordings, some strategic or tactical, others practical, technical, ethical, and legal. In this section, I will focus on the choice of the setting, the problems related to gaining access and consent, and some general practical issues. I will not go deeply into the technical aspects here, such as brand names and types of devices, etc., because these would probably be out of date once this book is published. And I will also only roughly gloss the legal issues, since these are bound to vary from country to country, as well as from situation to situation.

As I suggested, if you are interested in talk-in-interaction in a general way, you can make recordings in 'any situation'. So you could just pick a setting that is accessible to you, and where you can either gain consent from the parties present, or get away with it without getting such consent. The most important consideration for you would probably be to set up the recording device and manage the consent in such a way that it does not interfere with the parties speaking in a 'natural' way (but see my earlier remarks on 'naturalness').

At the very start of my CA work, I recorded quite a number of my own telephone calls. This at least provided me with what is called 'one-party consent', since I was consenting to my own recording, which seems to be sufficient in many situations.

Here is the start of the very first call I recorded, in which I called my father-in-law (Schrama), who offered to make enquiries about the gadget I needed to tap the phone:

EXCERPT 5.3, START OF A TELEPHONE CONVERSATION[10]

```
 1       ((telephone ring))
 2   O:  Schrama
 3   B:  dag met Paul
 3   B:  hi Paul speaking
 4   O:  ja Paul
 4   O:  yes Paul
 5   B:  ik kom even melden dat ik eh geslaagd ben in het kopen van een
 5   B:  I just called to tell you I uh succeeded in buying a
 6   B:  telefoonspoel
 6   B:  telephone coil
 7   O:  HA hh hh
 8   B:  du[s daar hoeft u uw best niet meer voor te doen
 8   B:  so you don't have to make any more efforts for that
 9   O:     [goed
 9   O:      Okay
10   O:  oh (.) oh (.) oh (.) 'h goed gelukkig voor je
10   O:  oh (.) oh (.) oh (.) 'h okay I'm happy for you
11   B:  ja hoor[11]
11   B:  yes okay
12   O:  dus ik kan nou eh alle (.) akelige dingen op dit gesprek kun je-
12   O:  so I can now uh all (.) nasty things on this conversation you can-
13   O:  ik moet dus meer oppassen wat ik zeg
13   O:  I have to be more careful about what I say
14   B:  ja ik [neem het inderdaad op om te kijken of het lukt
14   B:  yes I [do indeed record it to see whether it works alright
15   O:        [als ik het goed begrijp
15   O:        [if I understand it rightly
16   O:  juist
16   O:  right
```

Details of this excerpt can be seen as a demonstration of some of the points I raised earlier concerning the 'feelings' people may have about being recorded. My father-in-law's cautiously formulated remarks in lines 12 and 13 clearly indicate that his awareness that I might record the call made the situation a different one for him. In 12 he starts twice with an utterance that he does not finish, only to make a full statement of the consequences hinted at in the last try in 13. Similarly, my account for making the recording, in 14, as an exercise to check whether the device worked all right, can be heard as a kind of 'mitigation' of my act of making the recording, pretending that this was not a serious attempt, but just a preparatory, throw-away one. When I later showed him the excerpt in my first published CA paper, he did not comment explicitly, but his wry smile seemed to indicate his surprise rather than pleasure.

As with many other kinds of 'deviance', later recordings produced less awkward feelings, at least in me. I stopped the habit later, however, because the fact that I was one of the participants, and that I had a lot of background knowledge on many of my interlocutors, tended to influence my analysis of such data too much and in ways that were hard to control. Some of these data have been used by others, though. Indeed, most CA researchers seem to avoid data in which they themselves participate.

There are several ways in which the making of recordings can be arranged: one can ask a participant to do it; one can arrange to have some technician make the recordings; or one can make them oneself, but then without participation, or at least only minimally. In the first option, one often does not have, or even seek, personal access to a setting, resulting in a database that consists mainly, or practically only, of the recorded interactions. The second option is mostly chosen in well-funded projects using technically complicated video equipment. When one selects the third option, one has a chance, and often the intention, to acquire a more extensive database, including personal experience in the setting, field notes of observations, and possibly formal interviews with participants as well. As discussed in a previous section, researchers differ in their preferences in this matter, some arguing for a pure form of CA, uncontaminated by any knowledge external to the recorded data, while others prefer analysing the data within a framework informed by ethnographically acquired knowledge. To put some flesh on the bones of this abstract debate, it may be useful to provide some examples. I therefore turn now to a summary description of two 'cases', illustrating the first and the last options, respectively. Both concern varieties of 'applied CA', where quite specific kinds of data were needed.

As an example of the first procedure, I quote and paraphrase parts of the PhD thesis of Patricia Haegeman, on 'Business English in Flanders: a study of lingua franca telephone interaction'. For this project, she needed recordings of telephone conversations made in a business setting in Flanders, with native speakers of Dutch, graduates in economics, speaking English for business purposes. She describes that it was quite difficult to get the right kind of people to cooperate in such a project. She started out with graduates in applied economics from her university, but relatively few graduates agreed to cooperate and had the permission from their superiors to do so. Notwithstanding our promise to leave out confidential data, a huge number of potential subjects were lost for this reason. (Haegeman, 1996: 78)

Therefore, she had to search in a wider network of candidate participants. She succeeded, finally, in constructing a corpus of 49 calls recorded in seven companies, more than three hours of talk, rendered in about 6,500 lines of transcript, or 148 pages. The actual process of having the recordings made is described by her as follows:

> For each tape we went to the company to hand to the participant a recorder, usually walkman-size, plus a tape and a small suction cap microphone which could be stuck to the receiver of their own phone. This procedure was chosen to disturb the normal course of affairs as little as possible. In the following days or weeks the participants recorded their English calls and contacted us when the tape (usually only one side) was full or when they thought they had recorded enough. We then collected the materials at the company. No money or presents were given: only a thank you letter was sent afterwards and the people interested received an article about other parts of the research (a questionnaire study). (78)

Referring to the debate between what she calls 'hardcore CA' and a 'more ethnographic trend', she adds that she refrained from collecting additional 'background data':

> Never did we collect any ethnographic information about the company, products, (co)participants etc., nor did we conduct any post data interviews. We only know what we could not avoid getting to know: since we went to the company to take and bring back the recorder, we know the location and had some impression of the company in general. We saw the recording participant and spoke with him for five or ten minutes, mainly to show how to handle the recording equipment. All we know and wanted to know is based on the recorded conversations, some of the unavoidable facts mentioned above and the equally unavoidable knowledge we have of the world as a member of a culture. (79)

Interestingly, she went so far as to seek professional legal advice on her liabilities 'for the sake of completeness and, admittedly, just to be on the safe side' (81). She submitted her 'case' to lawyers who applied the then relevant Belgian law, which, of course, may differ from laws elsewhere. I will selectively render her summary of the 10-page report she received:

> The facts are split up into the recording and the transcribing, each of which involves a discussion of criminal law and one of civil law. [...] In any criminal charge it would be difficult to define the interaction recorded as 'private communication' on the one hand and difficult or impossible to prove that there was any 'criminal intent' on the other. [...] As for civil law, any plaintiff would have to prove fault, damage and the causal relation between the two. Fault: since the researcher has taken all possible measures to avoid any infringement on privacy and since the recordings were made voluntarily and free of charge by people who were informed beforehand about the aim and who decided themselves what was recorded, it would be far from simple to find the researcher guilty of any fault. Damage: since no identification is possible it will be difficult to prove that there ever was any damage suffered

by any party. Thirdly, it would have to be proved that the possible infringement on privacy was the cause of the possible damage suffered.

Conclusion: as long as the tapes, which may contain (ab)usable data, are safeguarded from access by any third party and as long as the transcripts delete any data which could identify any party involved, there can in principle be no problem. (81–2)

These findings and suggestions may not be taken as guidelines for other situations and countries, of course, but they may serve as an indication of the sort of issues that may be involved.

My second example refers to work by a team formerly based at the University of Giessen, Germany, including Michaela C. Goll and Christoph Meier, and their study of what they call 'telecooperation', which includes *teleconferencing*. In one of their papers,[12] they write:

An alternative to the established procedures for investigating telecooperation [...] is to penetrate the 'skin' of an organization, inject a probe and actually look at how collaborative work is performed in situ. In the case of our research, the probe is our videorecording equipment, which allows us to analyze authentic and contextualized work processes in much more detail than any other procedure would afford. Where observational notes or interviews would give us accounts based on 'after-the-fact' sense-making and interpretation, audiovisual recordings provide us with a real-time version of participants' conduct and procedures. Repeatedly viewing particular episodes and rendering them as transcripts on paper in order to literally compare them side by side are powerful resources for reconstructing the systematics underlying participants' actions.

And coming to the topic of this chapter, they explain:

However, often no attempt is made to obtain permission for audiovisual recordings of authentic work processes for fear of being rejected immediately or for fear of losing whatever rapport has been gained with representatives of an organization. We have made the likelihood of eventually gaining permission for such videorecordings the central criterion in pursuing access to various organizations. Of course we were not granted permission to do so right away. However, we have made clear from the very beginning that audiovisual recordings are a central component of our research procedures and that we eventually will want to make such recordings. In the case of the organization where we have observed the videoconferencing interaction reported on [in the paper], contact was pursued during a 'trial period' of three months involving participant observation in the meetings before permission to record interactions was finally obtained. Proceeding in this way we have been able to gain permission to record interactions involving various telecommunications technologies in three organizations.

In fact, Christoph Meier was sitting in on the meetings that were recorded on tape, making notes on what was happening. He was, indeed, keeping a low profile in the interaction, but he unavoidably was part of the events, looking at the points where the action was, laughing with the jokes, etc.

The recordings were made under strict conditions regarding confidentiality concerning the identity of each company and the participants, and pseudonyms were used throughout the transcripts and the analysis. Meier had to sign a contract on the protection of participants' rights and the use of materials with the company at which he recorded the videoconferencing sessions. The paper, however, does contain 'frame grabs' from the video tape, from which the participants might be identified, although the images are in fact rather vague. All publications, however, have been checked with Meier's 'sponsor' at the company, and have been agreed with.

As these examples make clear, there are many ways of organizing 'access' to data and 'consent' with recordings being made. 'Gaining access' and 'managing field relationships' are widely discussed in the older literature on ethnographic methods (cf. Bogdan & Taylor, 1975: 25–78; Douglas, 1976: 133–80; Hammersley & Atkinson, 1983: 54–104; Lofland & Lofland, 1984: 13–45; Schatzman & Strauss, 1973: 18–33). Getting consent for, and managing the making of, recordings seems to be just a special case of that general problematic. From that literature, my own experiences, and that of my colleagues and my students, I would say that one should try to design a strategy and develop tactics which serve to weaken negative motivations and to strengthen positive ones for whoever has the power to keep you from making the recordings, or whose cooperation you may need to influence the disinclined, and to normalize and naturalize the recording situation. The major negative motivation one encounters is that people want to avoid 'trouble', of whatever sort.

The major troubles expected are the fear of some kind of 'exposure' (as discussed in the section on consent), disturbance of established work processes, and resistances from other parties in the field. The major strategy, then, is to neutralize these fears, by providing guaranties of anonymity, minimal disturbances of work processes, and the willingness to face other parties' resistances. The major positive motivations one can hope for include the possibility of helping nice people such as the researcher who deserve such help and of facilitating a research project which may have some practical pay-offs, or social research in general. In this respect, students have some advantages: they seem 'innocent', or at least not too 'dangerous', and they obviously need help to finish their study obligations.

Pointing to possible practical benefits may be dangerous, since this may be seen as making promises which may turn out to be hard to fulfil. Sometimes, however, organizations may ask researchers for some kind of advice on 'communication problems' and the like. In such cases, the making of recordings of the routine handling of whatever the organization deals with can be requested as a prerequisite for such assistance. Those tapes, then, can serve the purposes of both informing the advisor and providing materials for detailed CA research, either as part of that process or independently of it. In general, whenever some kind of interaction is felt to be 'problematic', in one sense or another, it may be easier to find people willing to have it recorded for research.

In the paper quoted earlier, Davey and Gramkow Andersen suggest exploiting any 'existing networks, e.g. family and friends or clubs and associations to which you may have access'. They continue:

> When approaching companies or institutions, try to approach them through an existing contact. Often people you know will be eager to help by recording meetings or phone calls, and they are generally prepared to overcome potential difficulties. In such cases, the informant

> will probably be willing to persuade the co-participants that the data will be treated confi-
> dentially. Implicit in this is that the informant obtains the consent of the co-participants and
> that they 'know' of the recording. (1996)

When no such contacts exist, a different approach is needed:

> When approaching an area, a company or an institution with which there is no initial
> contact, it will be necessary to keep a higher level of formality. The approach we use can be
> described in three main steps. First you must present yourself and your work, then overcome
> any objections from potential informants and the company, and finally there is the actual
> recording of data. (1996)

The presentation is best done in writing, using official (university) paper, (co-)
signed by someone clearly identified as a person of authority, like a professor. The
actual negotiations are probably best done during a personal visit, arranged by
telephone. One could start the conversation by presenting oneself and explaining
the purpose of the research in general terms, to be followed by a more detailed
sketch of the research process, including the making of the recordings. The reassurances regarding routine anonymization and minimal disturbance, mentioned
before, should be emphatically stressed. Any objections raised should be taken
seriously, and it depends on one's circumstances and interests which concessions
should be made if the reassurances do not do the job of gaining consent.

Davey and Gramkow Andersen add a very sensible suggestion:

> After arranging for the recording to take place, it is useful to send a resumé of the agreements
> reached. This gives both parties to the recording agreement something they can refer to in
> the future, in case of uncertainty about the conditions of data collection and use of the data.
> (1996)

The negotiations quite often will result in various conditions which limit the
future use of the data, as suggested in the section on consent. It seems best to be
quite reluctant in this respect, but to respect any conditions agreed upon, since
one may be taken to be legally responsible for any use not agreed beforehand.

Making field recordings: technical issues

As to the technical details of making recordings in 'natural settings', I will limit
my discussion to a bare statement on basic requirements and a few suggestions.
For any recording, whether audio or video, an obvious requirement is that the
recorded talk is transcribable. It does not need to be superb hi-fi, but the words
spoken should be clear and the interactional details that have been proven to be
important for CA (see next chapter) should be discernible. This may be quite
difficult to realize over bad telephone lines or in noisy environments. What helps,
in the case of field recordings of face-to-face interactions, is to have good microphones, independent of the recorder, and placed as close to the sound sources as
is practically possible. As Charles Goodwin writes:

Tests [...] showed that the main influence on sound quality, even more important than the quality of the microphone used, was the distance of the microphones. The closer the microphone, the better the sound. The best sound is obtained by actually attaching the lavaliere microphone to the speaker. Because of the quality obtained, this method is regularly used by linguists to obtain samples of speech. (1981: 38)

This is often cumbersome and intrusive, however, therefore Goodwin decided to do it differently:

I recorded speech by positioning a stationary microphone with the participants but not attached to them. The microphone was centrally placed and located as close to the participants as possible without being excessively intrusive. The placement that produced perhaps the best results was over the center of the group, slightly above the heads of the participants. (1981: 39)

Note that the microphone should be hanging rather than standing, in order to avoid picking up too many noises through a table etc.

Technically, almost perfect recording is possible, but how much of this ideal can be realized depends on local technical and financial resources, and interactional circumstances. Many researchers will make concessions in terms of recording excellence, in order to have a less obvious and imposing recording situation. For this it helps to acclimatize the participants to the situation, for instance in recording regularly held meetings. Then the impact of the recording situation will in all probability be less strong, and the recorded interaction quite natural.

Marjorie Goodwin, for instance, reports on the data gathering for her research on 'talk as social organization among black children', based on audio recordings, in the following terms:

My actual method of working consisted of travelling with the children as they went about their activities while I had a [brand name and type] cassette recorder with an internal microphone over my shoulder. I began recording two months after I started fieldwork and continued for sixteen months. The children knew they were being taped, but talked directly to the machine only in the early days of recording. Because I used only the internal microphone, I never had to actively point something at the children in order to record them but could get good records of their conversations simply by staying with them. Indeed, the recorder became a natural part of my appearance, almost like a purse. Strapped over my shoulder in its black case, often over my black trenchcoat, it was seldom commented upon after the first weeks of use. (1990: 22)

In many cases, however, such extended periods of fieldwork, in which recording activities can become almost 'natural', are not feasible, or maybe not even desirable (cf. the earlier discussion). In such cases, when there are only a limited number of recording situations, extensive pre-testing of the equipment is desirable, unless one is willing to accept the risk of a beautiful 'recording' resulting in a useless tape.

There are various techniques for capturing telephone sound, some based on induction, with a coil attached to the telephone externally, while others use a direct connection to the telephone wires. Davey and Gramkow Andersen discuss the possibilities for Danish telephones, which suggest that the technical possibilities strongly depend on local technical circumstances. Therefore one should make one's own local enquiries and test the device on each connection to be taped.

For video taping, one should select such a position for the camera that the recording will show not only all the participants in the required detail, but also whatever is important for understanding what is going on, such as various objects handled or referred to, computer screens viewed, etc. This may be quite a puzzle, possibly requiring more than one camera and 'split-screen' techniques for transcription and presentation purposes. Years ago I saw a tape, for instance, made by Richard Frankel, for a study of physicians' note-taking during medical consultations. If I remember correctly, it had a side view of the two parties sitting together, but, in addition, one could see, in a small 'window', the doctor's writing hand on the paper, taken by a camera above the desk looking down. In this fashion, one could study in detail how the talk and the writing were coordinated.

Try to use a fixed camera, on a tripod, whenever that is possible. A handheld camera gives you more flexibility, but that introduces an element of selectivity that may frustrate you in the analysis. Furthermore, a stable image is much more comfortable to look at, especially when you have to watch a scene repetitively. And finally, a stable image is easier to handle for compression programs when you digitize the data, which is now becoming the common procedure.

Heath and Luff suggest that although one might think that a camera is an intrusive element in the setting, it may in the end influence action less than would a human observer:

> Thus, where possible, the researcher should set up the equipment prior to the events being recorded and try to avoid focusing and operating the camera equipment during the events. Of course it will be necessary to change cassettes, but normally it is possible to manage these practicalities between events. (1993: 308)

As this chapter has tried to make clear, the process of collecting recordings, or making them oneself, needs a CA researcher's careful attention. In some cases, it can be quite simple, but in others rather complicated. This depends on circumstances, opportunities, and especially research purposes. No easy recipes can be given. One needs to adapt the considerations and suggestions provided to one's own circumstances.

EXERCISE

Make at least one audio recording of naturally occurring verbal interaction and write a detailed account of your choice of the recording strategy, the equipment and set-up used, the experience with it, including any reactions from the participants and the ultimate sound quality of the record. Alternatively, if it suits your purposes, you can choose to make a copy from the mass media (radio or TV) or to use an existing recording. In this

(Continued)

case, you should write an account for that particular choice, referring to issues of naturalness and sampling, the particularities of the recording situation, any possible editing, etc. Conclude with an evaluation in methodological terms.

For the four options, I add the following suggestions. For A, individual/open, the above seems enough, while for B, individual/focused, you should, of course, select a situation in which some 'questioning' is likely to occur; you might record a larger episode and afterwards select a part with questioning activities to focus on. For C, collective/open, and D, collective/focused, each participant should make or select his or her own recording, while care should be taken to make these as varied as is practical and/or as fits your overall project. For D, a similar restriction as specified for B should be taken into account.

RECOMMENDED READING

As noted, the practical aspects of 'producing data', in the sense of collecting or making recordings, are hardly discussed at length in the CA literature, especially as concerns audio recordings. Therefore, I cannot provide a long list of recommended reading on this topic. Of the titles mentioned below, the paper by Davey and Gramkow Andersen is probably hard to get hold of, and quite strongly oriented to the Danish situation. The Goodwin pieces are very good, and – although focused on video recording – recommended for reading by researchers using audio as well. Maynard has an inspiring chapter on the selective use of ethnography as support for CA.

Davey and Gramkow Andersen (1996); Goodwin (1981: 33–46; 1994a; Maynard (2003: 64–67).

Notes

1. These issues will be discussed more fully in later chapters on analysing data.
2. Cf. Mazeland (1992) and Mazeland and Ten Have (1996) on qualitative research interviews, and Houtkoop-Steenstra (2000), Maynard and Schaeffer (2000), and Maynard et al. (2002) for examples of CA studies of standardized survey interviews; Roulston (2006) provides an overview of this kind of work.
3. Cf. the characterizations of CA by George Psathas (1995: 2–3), quoted in the last section of Chapter 3.
4. Cf. discussions of consent and access later in this chapter.
5. I am indebted to John Heritage (1990/1: 302) for locating this quotation.
6. Cf. a collection of papers by Robert Hopper (1990–91) for further information.
7. Cf. Heath (2004); for an updated version and Heath and Luff (1993: 309) for a similar statement.
8. David Frohlich has done some experiments with 'electronic shadowing' that also seem to offer a promising solution for this problem.
9. Excerpt 5.3, to be given later, provides an illustration of this phenomenon.

10. As in all non-English transcriptions, an English gloss, printed in italics, is provided in the line below the one representing the original speech (see discussion of data translation in the next chapter).

11. Any translation of a particle like 'hoor' seems to be problematic. Cf. 'demonstration 4' in Chapter 7.

12. The paper, called 'Interactional dynamics of electronically mediated collaborative work: local solidarity in videoconferencing', was, at the time of writing, available on the World Wide Web on the home page of the project at http://www.uni-giessen.de/~g312, but has been withdrawn; other reports have been made available at the site.

6

Transcribing Talk-in-Interaction

Contents

The unique core activity of conversation analytic work is the careful, repeated listening to (and viewing of) recorded interaction in order to make detailed transcriptions of it, using some version of a set of conventions originally developed by Gail Jefferson. This chapter will provide an extensive discussion of methodological and practical aspects of using this style of transcribing verbal interaction.

What is involved in 'transcription'

Transcribing recorded talk might be seen by some as a relatively simple matter, a secretarial task. One 'just' writes down what is said by the parties to the interaction. In fact, this is only the starting point for a transcription adequate for a detailed analysis. But even this task may be quite difficult when the recording is not of the highest quality, when people are not articulating very well, when more than one person is talking at a time, when they are laughing, etc. A conventional secretarial transcription will tend to clean up the mess a bit, by leaving out 'noise' considered inessential, and by 'correcting' obvious mistakes. This will be the way 'verbatim protocols' of meetings or interviews will be made when one is only interested in the contents of what has been said. For analysing talk-in-interaction, however, one wants to write down not only *what* has been said, but also *how* it has been said. And that is why transcription is so important and difficult for a research tradition like CA.

For contrast, one may think of a kind of transcription that only catches the 'sounds' on the tape, as in a *phonetic* transcription, independent of the speech's meaning, or of the particular language spoken by the interactants. Such a transcript will provide a certain kind of access to *how* things were said, but *what* was said will be inaccessible to most readers. Therefore, transcription systems used in the various varieties of 'discourse analysis', largely conceived, tend to offer a practical *compromise* between the interests of faithfulness to the original, recorded sounds, and of readability of the final transcribed product. As Heritage and Atkinson write:

> [. . .] the transcripts result from and represent an attempt to get as much as possible of the actual sound and sequential positioning of talk onto the page, while at the same time making this material accessible to readers unfamiliar with systems further removed from standard orthography. (1984: 12)

In other words, a transcription might best be seen as a *translation*, made for various practical purposes, of the actually produced *speech* into a version of the standardized *language* of that particular community, with some selective indication of the actual speech production.[1]

As noted, most, if not all, transcripts used in CA, as conceived in this book, employ a more or less close variant of the transcription 'system' devised by Gail Jefferson in her work for Harvey Sacks, first, and on her own, later. Therefore, I will limit my discussion to this particular style of work. There are, of course, other systems (cf. Edwards & Lampert, 1993), but as this book is designed to help those who are beginning to work *within* the CA tradition, it is best to stay on the path that has been taken before. No transcription system is perfect, of course, since it represents the result of a series of compromises between heterogeneous considerations. It has not been 'designed' on the basis of a set of worked-out principles, but evolved in the course of doing CA's work. It has been criticized on a number of points, including its inconsistency (O'Connell & Kowal, 1994), but as a working instrument it seems to be generally sufficient for most CA purposes. Furthermore, it can be extended with special ad hoc features if required for a particular purpose (cf. Atkinson, 1984a; 1984b, for the 'transcription' of applause, for instance). The disadvantages of continuing to work with the system seem to be less than those of designing a new system that nobody else uses or knows how to read (cf. Psathas, 1995). In fact, it takes time and practice not only to learn to *make* transcriptions according to a specific system, but also to learn to *read* them. Alessandro Duranti (1997: 142) stresses 'the fact that the process of transcribing implies a process of socialization of our readers to particular transcribing needs and conventions'. Probably the best strategy is to combine the two processes of learning to make and to read transcriptions.

Although the basic system was devised by Gail Jefferson, it has become a kind of 'common language', with various dialects, so to speak. There is not *one* clearly defined, canonical way of making and formatting CA transcriptions, but Gail Jefferson is still considered to be the best transcriber and something like the final authority on matters of transcription. Therefore, her most recent statement on the topic (Jefferson, 2004a) deserves close study! One can discern, however, among other CA transcribers, minor variations in the conventions that are actually used. Compared with Jefferson's work, these are often simplifications. What I will describe, then, is just 'my' version, and indeed a simplified one (see Appendix A), rather than something like *the* officially endorsed system.

The functions of transcripts

The activity of transcribing a recording can be conceived in various ways, as rendering the sounds on the tape, as describing the verbal interaction, or, as I did above, as translating 'speech' into 'language'. These conceptions have different consequences for the methodological status conferred on transcripts, as 'data', 'observations', or 'versions'.

It is often stressed that transcripts are not the 'data' of CA, but rather a convenient way to capture and present the phenomena of interest in written form. An obvious reason for using transcripts in publications is that most publication outlets until recently did not allow any other way to 'represent' the data. It is also a common experience, however, that at a first hearing/viewing of a recording, the phenomena of interest to a particular researcher are not at all obviously available. It is only after repeated listening/viewing, and quite often only after repeated efforts at transcription, that certain phenomena 'present themselves' to the ears, eyes, and minds of the tape's audience.

As various writers, including Heritage and Atkinson (1984) and Psathas and Anderson (1990), have noted, transcriptions should not be taken as a substitute for the recordings. They are selective, 'theory-laden' renderings of certain aspects of what the tape has preserved of the original interaction, produced with a particular purpose in mind, by this particular transcriptionist with his or her special abilities and limitations. Therefore, it is generally recommended that an analyst makes his or her own transcriptions. Even if the work is tedious, and just because it is tedious, it gives one a kind of access to the 'lived reality' of the interaction that is not available in any other way. In other words, because, for making a transcription, a researcher is forced to attend to details of the interaction that would escape the ordinary listener, transcription works as a major 'noticing device' (see Jefferson, 1985b; 2004a, for telling examples of the analytic yield of detailed transcripts).

> The process of transcription is an important analytical tool, providing the researcher with an understanding of, and insight into, the participants' conduct. It provides the researcher with a way of noticing, even discovering, particular events, and helps focus analytic attention on their socio-interactional organisation. (Heath & Luff, 1993: 309)

Furthermore, once made, transcripts provide the researcher with quick access to a wide range of interactional episodes that can be inspected for comparative purposes. Transcription, therefore, allows the analyst to build an accessible data archive. As I will explain at greater length in Chapter 9, this 'archival' function of transcripts can be supported by various additional techniques.

In short, making transcriptions helps one to take note of particular phenomena, it serves to build an accessible data archive, and it provides an audience with a limited but useful access to the phenomena discussed in an analysis.

Elements in constructing transcript files

Transcriptions, then, are always and necessarily selective. The system used in CA is specifically designed to reveal the *sequential* features of talk. As it has developed over the years, more and more details of the actual sequential production of talk-in-interaction have been added to the basic 'text', written in standard orthography, or a modified version of it. From its inception in the work of Harvey Sacks in the 1960s, this development has mainly been the work of Gail Jefferson, whose sensitivity and precision in the rendering of interactional details seems to be unmatched by anyone in the field.[2] Occasionally, other analysts have added particular features in which they had an interest to the system:

> [...] conversation analysts do *not* claim that the transcription system captures the details of a tape recording in all its particulars, *or* that a transcript should (or even could) be viewed as a literal representation of, or observationally adequate substitute for, the data under analysis. Like all transcription systems, the one used [in CA] is necessarily selective [...] and indeed this system is particularly concerned with capturing the sequential features of talk. (Heritage & Atkinson, 1984: 12)

In order to give some substance to my discussion of the transcription system, I quote an example of a transcript by Jefferson.[3]

EXCERPT 6.1, FROM JEFFERSON, 1989: 171–2
[SBL:1:1:12:R:15–16:SO] ((TELEPHONE))

```
[line numbers added]
  1  Maude:    I says well it's funny: Missi:z uh: ↑Schmidt ih you'd
  2            think she'd help<·hhh Well (.) Missiz Schmidt was the
  3            one she: (0.2) assumed respo:nsibility for the three
  4            specials.
  5            (0.6)
  6  Bea:      Oh↓*::. °°M-hm, °°=
```

```
 7  Maude:    =Maybe:lle ↑told me this.
 8  Bea:      Ah ↓hah,
 9                        (1.2)
10  Bea:      °Uh-hah, ° ·hh Isn't ↑her name ju:t plain Smi:th?
11                        (0.7)
12  Maude:    Schmidt.h
13                        (1.2)
14  Bea:      Oh I thought it was just S-m-i-t-h:.
15  Maude:    No I think it's S-c-h-m-i-d-t, something like that it's just
16            Sch↑mi↓:dt.
17                        (0.3)
18  Bea:      Ah hah.
```

Following Psathas and Anderson (1990: 80–4), I will discuss the following kinds of information available in a transcript file:

- Time, date, and place of the original recording.
- Identification of the participants.
- Words as spoken.
- Sounds as uttered.
- Inaudible or incomprehensible sounds or words.
- Spaces/silences.
- Overlapped speech and sounds.
- Pace, stretches, stresses, volume, etc.

I will take up these elements one by one in the same order.[4]

Time, date, and place of the original recording

As an essential part of the research *archive*, one should note the details of the recording occasion. When making a recording public, however, it is usual to use a coding system that is opaque to outsiders, as in the example above.

Identification of the participants

Participants are identified in the left column by a letter code. Psathas and Anderson (1990: 80) suggest that within the CA framework 'the respective membership categories of the participants are not deemed relevant, except as they appear/are accomplished in the course of the interaction'. So in transcripts of 'ordinary' conversations, you see either letters or names being used (as in excerpt 6.1). For studies of institutional interactions, however, most transcribers use some sort of categorical identification. Rod Watson has, in a challenging essay on the relation between sequential analysis and *membership categorization analysis* (MCA), made some critical remarks about this practice. He notes (Watson, 1997: 51–3), for instance, that CA studies of medical interaction are in the habit of presenting their data in a format like the one below in excerpt 6.2:

EXCERPT 6.2

```
Dr:  Did y'feel sick.
          (0.6)
Pt:  A little bit. Yes
```

He argues that such a presentation seems to be 'instructing' the reader to 'hear' the utterances transcribed as being produced by 'the doctor' and 'the patient', respectively, without providing or inviting an MCA of the utterances under consideration. This critique is part of a general argument that pleads for a re-involvement of MCA in the CA enterprise generally.[5] Watson suggests that in later CA 'categorical' aspects tend to recede to a background status, while sequential organization is 'foregrounded'. This, he suggests, impoverishes the analysis and may lead to a 'constructive analytic' reification and stabilization of the categories involved. Analysts would do better, he thinks, to 'combine' categorical and sequential analyses and include the interactional relevance of various categories into their analytic problematic (cf. Schegloff, 1991: 49–52). A similar argument can be developed regarding the habit to use gender-specific first names for speaker identification. So even this minute technical detail of what kind of identification to use in a transcript can be seen to have analytic consequences, or at least carry analytic suggestions. As Psathas and Anderson note, it ultimately depends on the analysts' purpose, doing 'pure' or 'applied' CA, for instance what kind of identification code is most useful.

Words as spoken

Under this heading Psathas and Anderson write that 'a first effort is directed toward capturing (in written form) the actual words as spoken'. And they continue saying: 'The assumption here is that the interactants are engaged in the use of conventional linguistic forms grounded in a common language with semantic and syntactic conventions' (Psathas and Anderson, 1990: 80–1).

This suggests that one starts the transcription by rendering the words spoken in standard orthography, which seems sensible. It does, however, already 'translate' stretches of sound into strings of discrete units, 'words', which in fact may not be audible as such on the tape. While this translation seems unavoidable, it should not be ignored that it is being used (cf. Duranti, 1997: 123–6).

The assumption of 'a common language' may be even more problematic, however. Contemporary sociolinguistics seems to undercut this kind of assumption for many if not most communicational situations. One may think of situations in which speakers with different linguistic backgrounds talk with one another in a lingua franca, or in the language of one or the other (cf. Wagner, 1996). And one should also recognize the fact that even 'within' a language there may be more or less marked linguistic variations related to various sub-communities. *Black English* is probably the most noted and best researched example of this (cf. Erickson & Shultz, 1982; Labov, 1972). Well-known phenomena like *code switching*, linguistic mockeries, *sound play*, and *language mixing* further complicate the issue.

In terms of my earlier discussion of transcripts trying to catch both the *what* and the *how* of talk-in-interaction, one can say that rendering the 'words spoken' in standard orthography involves an idealization of *speech* in terms of the standard *language* (cf. Duranti, 1997: 125). This obviously harms the purpose of rendering the *how* of actual speech. Therefore, many transcribers modify the standard orthography in order to catch some of the ways in which the actual speech practice *deviates* from the model implied in standard orthography, as Jefferson has done in the transcripts exemplified in excerpt 6.1 (cf. line 2: 'Missiz Schmidt'). Since readers are used to texts in standard orthography, however, such modifications seem to have a stronger impact on the reader's experience than the transcriber may have intended. The fact that such modifications seem to suggest stronger deviations than actually heard on the tape may picture the speakers as remarkably sloppy or stupid, and their overall speech as overly regional or 'ethnic' (Duranti, 1997: 137–44; Heritage & Atkinson, 1984: 12; Jefferson, 1983; 2004a).

In other words, the dilemmas created by the effort to combine the *what* and the *how* in a readable way force one to make an explicitly reasoned choice and to stick to it if one wants to avoid confusion. Let me discuss some possibilities:

- One solution would be to use standard orthography throughout, ignoring language variation as well as everyday 'sloppiness' or 'informality', even if possibly locally relevant for the interaction. In so doing, one would lose the possibility of noting and studying many interesting phenomena. Most conversation analysts would be of the opinion that this is too close to a secretarial conception of transcription.
- A second solution would be to use standard orthography most of the time, but use some modification to mark some specially significant 'deviations'. The problem with this is that it seems hard to decide when to choose one or the other option, when in fact the difference is very gradual. This method creates variations in the transcript which are not clearly related to variations in the talk.
- A third option is to use modifications continuously and as far as possible consistently. This seems to work best for the researcher's own purposes, that is the 'noting' and 'archive' functions discussed before, but may be difficult for uninitiated readers of CA transcripts.

This discussion[6] leads me to the overall suggestion that one should adapt one's transcription style to one's purpose and audience, that one should be clear about one's method, and that one should use it consistently.

Sounds as uttered

Apart from the vocal sounds that can be interpreted as words, all other sounds that might play a role in the interaction are to be noted as well. These include vocal sounds that can be rendered as 'tch', 'pt', 'eh' or 'uh', and 'mhm' (and many variants), inhalation and exhalation, and laughter. The general idea behind this practice is that these vocalizations can have interactional meaning, for instance as a claim to a turn of speaking.

EXCERPT 6.3

```
32  A:  Ye:s u[h huh
33  B:      [°Mm.°
34  B:  °M[m,°
```

From a 'language'-oriented perspective, however, this aspect of the Jefferson tradition has again been criticized as being overdone (Haegeman, 1996; O'Connell & Kowal, 1994). One argument for the inclusion of such elements is that they contribute to a 'picture' of the *rhythm* of the talk, especially when the 'transcription' is done in a manner that represents their construction out of 'syllable-like' parts, as can be done quite well with laughter (see, in particular, Jefferson, 1985b). This is what has been tried in the just quoted excerpt (6.3). Similar efforts to 'picture' visually the stream of vocal sounds influence other parts of the system.

Furthermore, words can be spoken in a laughing manner which can, of course, be very important interactionally (cf. Glenn, 2003; Haakana, 2001; Jefferson 1979; 1984a; 1985b; Jefferson et al., 1987). The same can be said about crying, which has been much less treated; a recent paper by Hepburn (2004) is a welcome exception. It can be remarked that just going by a transcript, laughter and crying may look rather similar, so adding a description (see below) may be useful.

There are, of course, sounds on the tape that are not sensibly 'transcribable' in this way, but these are mainly non-vocal sounds. These can be *described* rather than *transcribed*. Such descriptions are put within double brackets, to indicate their non-transcript status. The following excerpt (6.4), representing the start of an emergency call (CT = Call-Taker; C = Caller), has both.

EXCERPT 6.4, FROM ZIMMERMAN, 1992: 433 [MCE/20–10/196]

```
1  CT:  Mid-City police and fire
2        ((background noise and music on the line))
3  C:   (YA::H) Thiz iz thuh (      ) ((voice
4        is very slurred))
5        (1.5) ((loud background noise))
6  CT:  Hello:?
```

Inaudible or incomprehensible sounds or words

It is quite common that some vocal sounds are not easily transcribable because they are not comprehensible to the transcriptionist. In such cases, one can still try to guess what might have been said or to capture the sound as best as one can, and one can try to preserve the rhythm of the sound, including the number of 'beats' (syllables), the duration, and any intonational or stress patterns (see below). Such uncertain transcriptions are put within single brackets. It is also possible to note alternative hearings between which one cannot for the moment make a choice. Experience shows that one will quite often be able to 'hear' what was said when one returns to the data at a later date, or have someone else listen to the fragment. One can try to fit in one's mind various alternatives to the sound, until one of these seems to 'click', so to speak.

Spaces/silences

It is clear from many studies that pauses in speech can be very significant, although it may be unclear at first what their significance is. Pauses can occur when one party stops speaking and no one else takes the next turn, at least not immediately, in the 'rhythm' of the interaction so far (cf. Sacks et al., 1978). When the previous speaker continues speaking after such a 'break', for example by what has been called a 're-completor', it becomes a 'within-turn pause'. Or another may finally speak, 'to break the silence' as they say, possibly changing a topic which has run out; the break would then have become a 'between-turns pause'. One can also find occasions where someone has initiated an action or has given information and no uptake follows. When the projection for this uptake is clear, as with adjacency pair formats, such an 'absence' is noticeable and accountable (Schegloff, 1968). When it concerns a telling that *might* have been taken up, this is much less so (cf. e.g. Ten Have, 1991a). Still another possibility is that at a moment no one is speaking, a non-vocal action takes place, which is only discernible using a video recording. In any event, noting pauses has proven to be important, but what a pause 'means' may be difficult to decide.[7]

The issue, then, is not *whether* pauses are to be noted, but *how* this will be done. In the CA tradition a denotation given in numbers in parentheses has become the habitual method; (0.7) meaning one seventh of a second, for instance. Again, this practice has been criticized as being 'overdone' and suggesting a level of exactitude that one is not able to realize in actual practice (Haegeman, 1996; O'Connell & Kowal, 1994).

Gail Jefferson starts her paper on the length of silences in conversation with the following 'confessions':

> For most of the 18 years that I have been producing transcripts for the analysis of naturally occurring conversation, I have been timing silence in tenths of seconds. While I try to be accurate, I have not given particular attention to the phenomenon of silence *per se*, and have been content with rough timings. (So, for example, I started out using a stop-watch but in 1968 it broke and instead of replacing it I switched over to the method favoured by amateur photographers, simply mumbling 'no one thousand, one one thousand, two one thousand …'.) (1989: 166)

In the paper she describes how she became gradually aware of a 'possible metric which provides for a "standard maximum" silence of approximately one second'. She reports that in a later phase of her explorations, she 'started retiming and counting the silences in some face-to-face, multiparty conversations', and she adds:

> And given that there was now good reason to be as accurate as possible with the timings, I bought a digital stopwatch, now timing the silences both 'photographer' fashion and by clock. The timings are fairly consistent, within a tolerance of about a tenth of a second, but still rough. (182)

In their earlier mentioned paper on transcription practices, Psathas and Anderson (1990: 82, 86–90) also provide an extensive discussion of the timing of pauses. As they write:

> The systematic attention to and notation of silence, gap, or lapse as a timed and visually displayed unit is a standard practice in the Jeffersonian Transcription System. [...] The methodological maxim operative in the timing of these phenomena is that the transcriptionist strives to be internally consistent rather than to arrive at a standardized (clock time) demarcation [...]. The reason for this is that transcriptionists strive for a rendering that is as close as possible to the experience of those actually participating in the interaction. The transcriptionists' close and repeated listening to the interaction enables her/him to perceive the relative differences in the spaces (pauses, gaps, silence) that occur. (87)

The general idea seems to be that by closely attending to the pace of the talk, the transcriber can catch the local significance of pauses by an informal method of 'rhythm-sensitive timing'. This surfaces in the following quote, which comes after the one above:

> [...] a consistently used mnemonic and silently uttered 'metronomic beat', such as the phrase 'one one thousandth', which has five distinct beats, each equivalent to two tenths of a second, can serve as a 'self-standardized' measurement device. The transcriptionist can count this off whenever a space in the talk occurs and thereby achieve a consistently applicable estimate of the length of each silence. (87)[8]

On the basis of this 'relativist' method of timing, the authors warn:

> [...] readers are cautioned not to interpret these timings in an overly precise fashion; not to attempt to compare, across different analyst's transcripts, the occurrence of timings of different length. (87)

In my own practice, I have used both methods of timing. I must say that I feel more comfortable timing with a stopwatch. But even there, I use repeated timings, because one still has the problem of 'catching' the exact onset and finish 'points'. By closely monitoring one's timing activities, the closeness of the correspondence of one's 'clickings' with what one hears, one can observe which of the timings are better than others.

In recent times, a third method of timing pauses has become a real possibility. This is based on computer software (such as SoundEdit, CoolEdit, or WavePad) that can produce a visual display of digitized sounds. The idea is that one can just 'see' when the sound level is low, and use the horizontal time axis to 'measure' such periods. At the moment, I have neither the experience nor the technical competence to explicate and evaluate this method any further. Nor have I read any reports from conversation analysts who have used it.

In sum, there are three methods of timing pauses:

1 using an informal beat count as a proximate measure of 'rhythm-sensitive' pause length;
2 timing with a stopwatch, to approximate a clock-time pause length;
3 reading the acoustic pause length from a computer display.

As with other dilemmas in research, a practical solution will have to be found in the light of one's technical possibilities and analytic purposes. In any case, one should strive for a consistent and explicit method. A combination may offer the best results, because, in my opinion, both computer-based measurement and stopwatch timing should be seen as technical supports for the basic activity of hearing what is happening on the tape, rather than displacing it.

Overlapped speech and sounds

An essential feature of CA transcription is that it requires the transcriber to take careful note of phenomena of 'overlapping' speech. These phenomena are most significant in terms of speaker transition, competition for the floor, etc., in short the operation of the turn-taking system, as analysed in the classic paper by Sacks, et al. The basic idea of that paper (originally published in 1974, but used here in the 1978 version) is that turns–at–talk in ordinary conversation are constructed in the actual course of speaking, using locally recognizable 'units' (TCUs, for turn constructional units; cf. Schegloff, 1996a) as their 'building blocks'. During the production of any TCU, the current speaker will be treated as the 'owner' of the turn, but as soon as it is finished, another speaker might come in, unless special measures are taken to prevent this. This 'moment' is therefore called a 'transition relevance place' or TRP. Many CA studies have paid close attention to the management of these 'moments' or 'places' in the flow of talk, demonstrating the enormous interactional importance of a whole range of phenomena related to them (cf. Jefferson, 1973; 1986; 2004b; Ochs et al., 1996; Schegloff, 2000). It is essential, therefore, that one tries to capture the details of turn management as closely as possible in one's transcripts.

Excerpt 1.1, repeated below, is an excellent illustration of the usefulness of careful transcription of overlaps:

EXCERPT 1.1, FROM HERITAGE, 1984A: 236 [NB:VII:2]

```
E:    Oh honey that was a lovely luncheon I shoulda ca:lled you
      s:soo[:ner but I:]l:[lo:ved it.
M:         [((f)) Oh:::]  [(  )
E:    It w's just deli:ghtfu[:l. ]
M:                          [Well]=
M:    I w's gla[d        you] (came).]
E:             ['nd yer f:] friends] 're so da:rli:ng,=
M:    =Oh:::   [: it w'z ]
E:             [e-that Pla:t isn'she a do:[ :ll?,]
M:             [iYe]h isn't she pretty,
                 (.)
E:    Oh: she's a beautiful girl.=
M:    =Yeh I think she's a pretty gir[l.=
E:                                   [En' that Reinam'n::
                 (.)
E:    She SCA:RES me.
```

The special 'interweaving' of the assessments that characterizes this fragment would be completely lost if the lines were just typed one below the other, without marking the overlap starts and stops.

Or take a look at the next example:

EXCERPT 6.5, FROM JEFFERSON, 1989: 172 [FR: USI:2:R:2:SO] (FACE-TO-FACE)

```
[line numbers added]
1   Carol:  Victor
2   Vic:    Ye:h?
3   Carol:  Come here for a minute.
4                    (1.0)
5   Vic:    You come he[: r e.    ] please?,]
6   Carol:            [↑You can] come bla:ck=
7   Vic:    =I ↑have to go to the ba:th↓room.=
8   Carol:  =°Oh:.°
```

As Psathas and Anderson write:

> […] it is possible to display (1) where the overlap began; (2) with which other speaker the speech/sound was overlapped; (3) when the overlap ended (though this becomes difficult to do in transcription and is often not precisely noted); and (4) what the speech/sounds were within the overlapped segment, for both parties. (1990: 82)

In the earliest CA publications, the place where a 'second' overlapped a 'first' was marked with double slashes ('//'), but this device is no longer used, being replaced by the square bracket system already demonstrated above. The latter device allows for a much more mnemonic display of the overlap, especially when closing brackets are in fact used, as they are in excerpts 1.1 and 6.5 above.

In some cases, Jefferson 'stretches' the display of one of the overlapped parts by using extra spaces, in order to provide a clearer 'picture' of the fact that the two parts in actual speech took about the same time, although the transcription in itself is of unequal length, as in line 5 in excerpt 6.5, and in the detail from excerpt 1.1 quoted below:

EXCERPT 1.1, DETAIL

```
M: I w's gla[d    you] (came).]
E:          ['nd yer f:] friends] 're so da:rli:ng,=
```

This practice, like some of Jefferson's others, has been criticized for its inexactitude, but I like its suggestiveness.

Pace, stretches, stresses, volume, etc.

Under this rubric, Psathas and Anderson collect a number of conventions that further elaborate the *process* rather than the *content* of talk. This includes:

- 'latching', when one spate of talk directly follows another, with no gap between the two, indicated by an equals sign, as in lines 6 and 7 in excerpt 6.1;
- cut-off of a word in a markedly abrupt fashion, marked by a dash-at the end of the word, as in line 12, excerpt 5.3;
- stretching, of words and other sounds, indicated by full colons after the stretched syllable, letter or sound, with the number of colons suggesting the length of the stretch, as in lines 1, 3, 6, and others in excerpt 6.1;
- stress, the (part of a) word or other sound that is stressed being <u>underlined</u> or printed in *italics*, as can be seen in the excerpts in this and other chapters;
- volume, where markedly loud parts are printed in CAPITAL letters, while softly spoken words are enclosed by degree signs, as in line 10, or double degree signs for very soft, as in line 6, both in excerpt 6.1;
- intonation, marked by a special use of punctuation, with a question mark signalling rising intonation at the end, a period a downward, 'closing' intonation, and a comma a non-final intermediate one; in addition to this punctuation for intonation practice, some transcribers use arrows to indicate marked rising or falling of intonation; check excerpts 6.1 and 6.5 for examples.

Some of these conventions have been seen as problematic by some people. For all conventions, there is a problem of 'quantity': how much should an element be stretched or stressed in order to be noted as such, how steep should the rise in intonation be, how loud or soft the word marked as such, etc.? Here the remarks about the relativism of the enterprise, as made before concerning the timing of pauses, are again relevant. Intonation and stress, for instance, are rather subtle aspects of speech. Some transcribers mark intonation and stress only when they deviate from 'expected' variations, for instance when someone stresses a word that would not ordinarily be stressed in such a sentence; a 'natural' stress and intonation pattern would then not be marked in the transcript at all. This strategy is similar to the one noted earlier, to use standard orthography except for marked deviations. But in both of these cases, such practices introduce a 'normative' element in the transcription process that may be inevitable, but that others might like to minimize.

As an illustration of this problem, consider the following, not uncommon experiences. In a Spanish text, the name of the painter Goya does not have an accent, although the first syllable is ordinarily stressed and the second not. When someone in a Dutch conversation uses that name in a Spanish manner, should one transcribe it as 'Goya'? Or consider the case of a Dutch speaker who does not know the rules of Spanish pronunciation very well, and who stresses the second syllable, as in French, 'Goy↑a'. In any case, the decision on whether to transcribe one or another syllable as stressed is at least partly based on normative considerations. But if one fails to make such indications, some imaginable later utterances, such as corrections, 'Goy↑a? oh, you mean ↑Goya', might become unintelligible. In short, making useful transcriptions requires both care and compromise!

Formatting issues

In the general literature on transcription, a distinction is often made between different ways in which the transcript can be arranged *visually* on the page. Jane

Edwards (in Edwards & Lampert, 1993: 10–12) differentiates what she calls 'vertical', 'column', and 'partiture' systems. The Jefferson system is a 'vertical' one, in that the utterances by different speakers are printed one below the other in the order in which they were spoken. In the column system each speaker has his or her column, which suggests essential differences between the parties. The 'partiture format is highly efficient for capturing stretches of an interaction that involve many simultaneous utterances or actions', writes Edwards (Edwards & Lampert, 1993: 11). It is structured as in a musical score, with each speaker having his or her own line, which indeed facilitates the precise noting of overlaps.[9] One could say that the way overlaps are displayed in the CA system is a 'borrowed' element from a 'partiture' system into a 'vertical' one.

In fact, when I started making transcripts, I began using a partiture system. But I soon took up the Jeffersonian system, for two reasons. The first was that I did not want to create a huge and inessential difference between my transcripts and those of other CA researchers, for reasons of 'membership' as well as readability. And the second reason was that it proved to be less easy to refer to particular turns in a transcript when one uses a partiture system, because it allows for more than one turn on a line. In any case, what I am discussing here is the system that is used in CA, but this comparison raises some further issues in the formatting of transcripts that are also noted by Psathas and Anderson.

In a 'vertical' system like the one used in CA, you have to decide what kind of 'unit' you will put on a line, or, to formulate it differently, when to start a new line. The simplest solution would be to continue putting transcription text on a line until you reach the right margin, or the current speaker stops and another starts. This seems generally to be the way Jefferson works, as in excerpt 6.1.

There are good reasons to make lines in a transcript fairly short and change to a next line earlier than at the usual right margin. A major one is that the number of characters one can put on a line varies from one word processing format to another, depending on font type and size. One could, of course, use rather narrow margins for a transcript, and produce short lines in a 'mechanical' fashion, just on the basis of who speaks and how the margins are set. One could also argue, however, for a strategy in which one would try to have a line's content to display some kind of 'unit'. Psathas and Anderson (1990: 85–6) mention several possibilities:

- 'breath units', what 'the speaker could produce in one breath';
- 'phrasal or clausal units', 'distinct or partial phrases or clauses as semantic/ grammatical units';
- 'turn constructional turn completion units', 'turns or turn constructional components which may or may not become 'turns' as a result of the next speaker beginning or not beginning to talk'.

They conclude their consideration of this issue with the following remarks:

It should be clear that the transcriptionist's choices in breaking speech and action into line units with numerical indicators may be based on any number of analytic considerations. We should also note that the same data, when analyzed for different purposes, may be re-transcribed with different line-by-line divisions. Although there is no single 'best' linear representation, we urge the reader to consider the ways in which the choices regarding the line-by-line production of a transcript may affect the analysis. We would certainly caution readers of transcripts not to take the number of lines in a transcript to be an indicator of the temporal length of the transcript. (86)

A special issue in the 'line formatting' aspect of transcript is the role of pauses. Look again at excerpt 6.1, partially repeated below:

EXCERPT 6.1, DETAIL

```
 1   Maude:   I says well it's funny: Missi:z uh: ↑Schmidt ih you'd
 2            think she'd help<·hhh Well (.) Missiz Schmidt was the
 3            one she: (0.2) assumed respo:nsibility for the three
 4            specials.
 5            (0.6)
 6   Bea:     Oh↓*::. °°M-hm, °°=
 7   Maude:   =Maybe:lle ↑told me this.
 8   Bea:     Ah ↓hah,
 9            (1.2)
10   Bea:     °Uh-hah, ° ·hh Isn't ↑her name ju:t plain Smi:th?
11            (0.7)
12   Maude:   Schmidt.h
```

You will see that there is a (0.2) pause in line 3, after which talk by the same speaker, Maude, continues. On line 5, there is a (0.6) pause, which has been given its own line, so to speak. After that pause, Bea takes the next turn. The first pause, then, is formatted as an *intra-turn* pause, while the second is an *inter-turn* one. But now look at the (1.2) pause in line 9. It also has its own line, but after it, the previous speaker, Bea, continues. So here the two rules for starting at a new line (at turn change and on reaching the right margin) do not suffice. On some occasions of within-turn silence, then, Jefferson notes that silence on a new line, followed by subsequent speech by the same speaker on another new line, while in other cases, a similar silence is included on the same line as the preceding speech, with more speech being typed at the line after the silence.

One could think that this is an arbitrary matter, maybe based on visual, aesthetic preferences. But I agree with Psathas and Anderson (1990: 88–90) that the format in these cases carries an analytic suggestion. In a sense, then, a formatting choice in this matter reflects what a pause is considered to 'be' interactionally. In fact, in scanning some extended transcripts by Jefferson, the pauses that she formatted as being *intra-turn* seem generally to be small and occur either between a 'starter' (like an in-breath or a 'well') and the turn 'itself', or within a TCU which, at the place where the pause occurs, is evidently not finished. The point of all this is

that the transcript may and does incorporate some analysis, as it is being produced by the transcriptionist. The seemingly simple matter of how interaction is presented in a line-by-line format should be carefully considered when interpretations of interactional phenomena are based on the 'display conventions' rather than the 'actualities' of phenomena. (Psathas & Anderson, 1990: 89–90)

A transcript, then, is, as Psathas and Anderson (1990: 90) say, a 'post-hearing/seeing depiction', 'a *constructed* version of the actualities and particularities of the interaction'. They note seven properties of transcripts that should be taken into account, seven ways in which the experience of reading a transcript is bound to be different from the experience of the lived interaction that is being depicted. Most of these have been discussed in the preceding sections. Transcribing recorded talk is a necessary but rather imperfect, instrumental task within the CA enterprise. It is essential to work hard on it, and to recognize inevitable limitations.

Adding visual information

The CA conventions, as discussed above, evolved from the transcription of vocal sounds available in audio recordings of both telephone and face-to-face interaction. In later periods, researchers working on different kinds of materials have added conventions to depict the particular phenomena that they wanted to investigate. Max Atkinson's earlier-mentioned studies of political oratory, focusing on *applause*, for instance, necessitated a careful 'transcription' of applause in close connection to the speech to which it was a reaction (cf. Atkinson, 1984a; 1984b; 1985). In a similar fashion, researchers working with *video* materials, like Charles Goodwin (1979; 1981; 1986; 1987; 1994b; 1996, etc.; Goodwin & Goodwin, 1996), Marjorie Harness Goodwin (1995), Christian Heath (1986; 1988; Heath & Luff, 1996), and Christoph Meier (1997), to name but a few, have developed and used methods to add information on visual phenomena to a transcript of vocal actions. As noted before, this book deals mainly with the analysis of auditory materials, but I think a few notes and references concerning the depiction of visuals are in order (cf. Duranti, 1997: 144–54; Goodwin, 1981: 46–53; 2000b; Heath, 1986: ix–xiv, 1–24; 1997; Heath & Luff, 1993; 2000; Jordan & Henderson, 1995; Meier, 1997: 41–8).

The basic procedure used in CA studies based on video recordings has been to start with a detailed transcription of the vocal part of the interaction, and add descriptions or symbolic depictions of the visual activities, like gaze, gesture, posture, and others, to the 'timeline' provided by the transcript, either above or below each line. In order to clarify the 'location' of activities during vocal pauses, these may be indicated by 'dashes' ('-'), each for a tenth of a second.

> The researcher should at least indicate the onset and completion of particular movements [. . .]. It is also useful to indicate any critical junctures within the development of a particular movement. Movements are represented by a continuous line, although in fact a whole range of ad hoc signs and symbols are often used to represent particular aspects of movement. (Heath & Luff, 1993: 317)

In order to make it clear how this works for one aspect of visual conduct, let me quote from Charles Goodwin's explication of his system for the notation of gaze, on which his early work (1979; 1981) was focused:

> Gaze will be transcribed as follows: The gaze of the speaker will be marked above the utterance and that of the recipient(s) below it. A line indicates that the party being marked is

gazing toward the other. The precise place where gaze reaches the other is marked with a capital X tied to a specific place within the talk with a bracket. [. . .] The movement bringing one's party gaze to the other is marked with dots, whereas the movement withdrawing gaze is indicated with commas. (1981: 52)

This system is exemplified in the following:

EXCERPT 6.6, FROM C. GOODWIN, 1981: 52

```
A:     _____,,,,,,,,
       We went down to- (0.2) When we went back ...
                          [
B:               . . X _____
```

In addition to these transcriptions, some aspects of the original video can be made available in print by still pictures, either in the form of *drawings* made after the original video picture (as in Heath, 1986; 1988; McIllvenny, 1995) or so-called *frame grabs*, digitized frames taken from a video tape (as in Goodwin, 1994b; M.H. Goodwin, 1995; Meier, 1997; Suchman, 1992). The drawing technique has the advantage of preservation of the anonymity of the participants, while the digitized frame pictures allow for the addition of explicative symbols like arrows (who speaks to whom) and initials (as in Meier, 1997). When using electronic publishing, on CD-ROM or the World Wide Web (see Appendix C), even more sophisticated techniques are possible, including 'sound bites' and even 'video clips'. It seems clear that the possibilities of these technologies will be more fully used in the near future.

Translation

The methodological literature of CA hardly ever discusses problems of translation, but for anyone who has to present to an audience which is not familiar with the language used by the participants, translating such materials is a difficult task (see Duranti, 1997: 154–60). These difficulties are reflected in the various ways in which translations are presented, or not, in actual CA publications. I have seen publications in which:

- the materials are only presented in translation into the language of the publication;
- the materials are presented in translation into the language of the publication in the body of the text, with the original transcript given in an appendix (cf. Bergmann, 1992);
- the materials are presented in translation into the language of the publication in the body of the text, with the original transcript given immediately below it, as a separate block of text (cf. Houtkoop-Steenstra, 1991), or the other way around, first the original and then the translation (Ten Have, 1991b);
- the materials are presented in the original language, with a translation into the language of the publication immediately below it, line by line (cf. excerpt 5.3);

- the materials are presented in the original language, but with first a morpheme-by-morpheme 'gloss', and then a 'translation' into the language of the publication immediately below it, line by line (cf. excerpt 6.7 below).

In my view, only the last three options are acceptable, since I think that one should provide the readers with as much information on the actual, original interaction as possible. The difference between the last two options seems to be related to the 'distance' between the two languages involved. When the two are not too different, as in the cases of Dutch/German or Dutch/English, one can catch a lot of the original interaction in an almost word-for-word translation. In such a case, the translator has to balance the two interests of, on the one hand, rendering the original talk as faithfully as possible and, on the other, of producing a translation that seems 'natural' in the destination language. When the two language systems are very different, however, as in the pairs Finnish/English or Japanese/English, these dilemmas may be impossible to solve in an acceptable manner, because various means of expression natural in one system are simply absent in the other. In such case, the researcher has to provide both morpheme-by-morpheme glosses and a free translation. Below is an example of this method, with Finnish being the original language. The second lines provide not only 'words', but also grammatical information, which is explained in an appendix to the paper from which the example has been taken (Sorjonen, 1996: 326–7).

EXCERPT 6.7, FROM SORJONEN, 1996: 281–2

```
1   S:   Hy[vä juttu        ]
         good thing
         Goo:d              ]

              [
2   T:   [>·h ↑Arto ei  pääse ] tule-e Se on vähä
         [ 1nameM NEG be able to come-ILL it is a little
         [>·h ↑Arto can't make it. That's a bit of a
3        tyhmä-ä<.
         stupid-PAR
         nuisance.
```

This example amply illustrates the difficulties involved in translating orally produced materials, I think. And when the interests of the analysis are directed at specific *linguistic* phenomena, such as word order or particles, this three-line format might also be sensibly used in situations where the two languages are more similar than Finnish and English.

Practical issues

Making transcriptions is extremely time consuming. One should, therefore, carefully consider which parts of the available recordings should be transcribed and in what kind of detail. This, of course, will depend on the particular research interests one has. If you are interested in, say, the overall structure of telephone conversations, it makes sense to make complete transcriptions of a limited set of examples. But if you are after a particular kind of interactional feature that happens now and then in a large corpus of video tapes, you should rather transcribe only those relevant episodes.

Especially when working with video tapes, it makes good sense to start by making an inventory of the tape's 'content', a 'content log' (Goodwin, 1994a; Jordan & Henderson, 1995: 43; Suchman & Trigg, 1991). Listening to the tape, or viewing it, one makes summary descriptions of what happens, adding notes on especially interesting happenings, non-recorded contextual particulars, etc., using either the counter numbers or time stamps (on video) as an index (but see the section on Transana for supporting this inventory work). In this way, one gets an overview of what is available, which allows a relatively quick retrieval of episodes to consider for more detailed consideration and/or transcription.

Douglas W. Maynard (personal communication) suggests still another sensible strategy for large projects:

> If you've collected a large number of very long recordings in some setting, it may be extremely inefficient to do detailed transcriptions of the entire corpus. Instead, you may be interested in 'advice-giving', or 'diagnostic news delivery', or the 'medical exam' (in doctor–patient interaction, for instance), and only do the detailed transcripts of those aspects of the interaction while writing standard transcripts of the rest. This way you can read at least rough versions of the entire interview and know what happened before and after focal episodes, while having the details on just those episodes themselves.

My general suggestion for making transcripts is to do it in 'rounds': start by putting down *what* has probably been said in standard orthography, and add the various details concerning the *how*'s later, one type after the other. One can, of course, make a note of remarkable details in earlier rounds than those in which one concentrates on a certain type, but it proves a good practice to focus on particular kinds of phenomena one after the other, for instance 'intonation', 'pauses', etc.

Transcription is a process involving three 'parts': a playback machine, a transcriber, and a writing device. Originally the first was an audio or video recorder/ player and the last a typewriter. Later, more sophisticated playback machines became available with a foot pedal for quick rewind and replay of fragments to be transcribed. The typewriter became obsolete when word processors became the default writing tools. Nowadays, the two separate machines for playing the recording and writing the transcription can be integrated in one specialized transcription program installed on a computer. One such program is Transana, which I will characterize later in this chapter.

The evolution of playback machinery did not produce particular difficulties. It mostly just extended the possibilities and eased the overall process. The change from using a typewriter to word processing on a computer was more radical. There were various kinds of difficulties in adapting the typewriter-based transcription conventions to this new platform (cf. Jefferson, 2004a). One concerned the production of specific transcript symbols, while another had to do with aligning simultaneous speech. These are discussed below. But using a word processor also has advantages, of course, over using a typewriter, and some of these that are relevant to presenting transcriptions will also be noted.

In most cases, the signs and characters available on the QWERTY keyboard can be produced without any difficulty using a word processor. As noted, you can use either 'underlines' or 'italics' to indicate stress, which are available as standard facilities. Underlined letters or words tend to be more easily distinguishable than *italic* ones. The extra symbols, however, may be difficult, especially when you convert a text to another format, or even to another font (some suggestions are available at http://www.paultenhave.nl/Transcription.html).

When transcribing episodes in which one participant's talk overlaps that of another, indicated by the use of square brackets, it helps to align the portions of simultaneous speech as precisely as possible. This creates special difficulties with modern word processors, which tend to use 'proportional fonts' (also called 'variable-pitch fonts'). With such fonts, the horizontal space a letter is accorded on the line varies with its size, 'w' getting more than 'l' etc., and with the number of letters in relation to the length of the line. Consequently, the exact place that a point of overlap starts or finishes can vary when something is added or when the margins are changed, or when a different font is chosen. As a solution one can try using a 'fixed-pitch' or 'monospaced' font, but it may require a bit of experimenting with one's word processor fonts as well as one's printer. An alternative method is suggested by Goodwin (1994a), who puts a TAB before the bracket and adjusts the TAB stop using the 'Ruler Bar'.[10]

Another suggestion of his (cf. Goodwin, 1994a) is that it can be useful to use a word processor's table feature to type the transcripts. One can define columns of different width for different purposes such as 'line number', 'time', 'arrows', 'speaker', 'utterance', and 'notes'. A 'landscape' format may be helpful so that each row can be longer than usual. The 'notes' column may be used to add 'observations' on hard-to-transcribe details, such as tone of voice or – in the case of video tapes – visual aspects. Alternatively, or in an additional column, one might add 'analytic' comments, pointing out remarkable phenomena that deserve attention in a later phase etc. In presentations or publications, such non-transcript columns can be deleted and the table lines can be hidden (by changing the preferences for line display in the layout menu to 'none').

Software support: Transana

Over the last few years, various software programs have been developed to 'support' the qualitative analyses of various kinds of research data (cf. my discussion in Chapter 8, page 158, and check http://caqdas.soc.surrey.ac.uk/ for an overview). There are also programs to facilitate transcription activities. I will describe here some features of a program that combines these two functions and that seems very suitable for CA. It is called *Transana*, and was originally written by Chris Fassnacht to facilitate Conversation Analysis for his dissertation. He gave it to the University of Wisconsin, Madison, where it was adopted by the Wisconsin Center for Education Research. There, it is currently being expanded and maintained by David Woods. It is a *free* program that can be downloaded from the website: http://www.transana.org. I will describe just the main features, but the website or, even better, the downloaded program itself will provide a fuller picture. The program comes with an extended manual and a 'Tutorial'. The authors' summary characterization is:

> Transana is designed to facilitate the transcription and qualitative analysis of video and audio data. It provides a way to view video, create a transcript, and link places in the transcript to frames in the video. It provides tools for identifying and organizing analytically interesting portions of videos, as well as for attaching keywords to those video clips. It provides a mechanism for searching for portions of analytically interesting video by keyword and by combinations of keywords. It also features database and file manipulation tools that facilitate the organization and storage of large collections of digitized video.

The program can handle file formats like MPEG-1, MPEG-2, and AVI for video, and MP3 and Wave for audio. Viewing the video in one screen and/or hearing the sound, you can type a transcription in another screen. The program offers facilities to include the major Jeffersonian symbols: up and down arrows, degree signs, and 'high dots' (to signal inhalation). You can add time codes, which link a frame in the video to a spot in your transcript. This allows you to play a relevant part of the video from the transcript, and while the video is playing, the relevant part of the transcript is highlighted. From this, you can use various features to further document and organize your analysis. You can make different kinds of transcripts related to the same data file. You can select special fragments, group them in various ways, add keywords, etc. In short, the program allows one 'place' in your computer to file your data, their transcription, and carry out various analytic steps as discussed in Chapters 7 and 8. There is also a multi-user version, which allows multiple, geographically dispersed analysts to work on the same data at the same time.

Learning to transcribe

Looking at any Jefferson transcript may make one wary of ever trying to make transcripts oneself, but – as many have suggested – making transcripts is an essential part of the craft of CA. Some may be more talented at the job than others, but all can learn to make useful transcripts. Probably the best setting is one of 'friendly supervision'. If you are working in a group, you might select a 5- to 10-minute fragment, provide all participants with a copy on tape, and have each make a transcript individually, using the same set of conventions. Then, go over the transcripts collectively, comparing the transcripts, listening to the tape, trying various 'hearings' of parts on which there is disagreement, try to reach collective agreement, and preserve alternative solutions if no agreement is available. This exercise could be repeated until each participant has acquired a minimal level of competence and confidence. If one is working individually, one might try to find an experienced transcriber willing to go over one's transcript together with the tape, and discuss any problems.

Links to various Internet-based resources for transcription are collected at http://www.paultenhave.nl/Transcription.html

EXERCISE

Make a transcription of a 10-minute fragment of recorded verbal interaction, using the various suggestions of this chapter, including the last section. Keep notes on the process of making, discussing, and revising the transcript and write a report in which you confront your working experiences with the observations and suggestions of this chapter.

For the individual options, A and B, it would make sense if you could seek a volunteer who would be willing to check the transcription. For the collective ones, C and D, there are various ways of checking each others' transcripts. You can decide, for training purposes, that all members shall start out by transcribing the same fragment and compare the results; or you can form into pairs doing the same fragment in order to compare afterwards and try to reach an agreement; or each can do his or her own fragment and have it checked by another. The point is that you should be confronted with different versions and discuss those differences in order to reach an agreement, and learn from it about typical difficulties and compromises.

RECOMMENDED READING

Duranti (1997: 122–61); Ten Have (2002); Hepburn (2004); Jefferson (1985b; 1989; 1996; and esp. 2004a); Psathas and Anderson (1990).

Notes

1. This conception of transcription as translating 'speech' into 'language' was inspired by a presentation by Jan Blommaert at the 4th IWIA Symposium on 'Oral Communication in Organizations', University of Antwerp, 17 October 1997; see also Duranti (1997: 122–61).
2. Cf. Jefferson (1985b) for her progressively refined rendering of laughter and its gains and similar rewards in other respects in Jefferson (2004a). For more extended discussion of transcription practices, comparing approaches from CA, social psychology and linguistics, see Section 3: Transcription Procedures, in Roger and Bull (1989), and for CA especially Psathas and Anderson (1990).
3. Transcription conventions are summarized in Appendix A. Gail Jefferson has published her own description with an introduction in a recent volume with studies from the first generation (Lerner, 2004: 13–31); an earlier one can be found in an appendix to the paper from which this excerpt was taken (cf. Jefferson, 1989: 193–6). That paper contains a large number of instructive examples of Jefferson transcripts.
4. My discussion owes much to the one provided by Psathas and Anderson, but my preferences and suggestions differ from theirs on a number of points, to be noted as I go along.
5. See my discussion in Chapter 4, pages 45–7, and Silverman (1998: chaps 5, 7) and Schegloff (2007b) for general discussions of Membership Categorization and the MCA/CA relationship.
6. I have only provided a brief and selective summary of what might be said on these issues; cf. Duranti (1997: 122–61), Edwards and Lampert (1993), Haegeman (1996: 87–110),

Jefferson (1983; 2004a). It should be stressed that some criticisms of the Jeffersonian practices refer to the argument that one wants to facilitate computer searches in large collections of data. As this does not seem to be a sensible practice for CA, it is not a relevant argument concerning transcription within the CA tradition.

7. You might want to check excerpt 6.1 and think about the local significance of the various pauses there.

8. I was puzzled at first by the notion that 'one one-thousandth' would have 'five distinct beats', but apparently the 'th' at the end should be pronounced as a full 'beat'.

9. The best known example of such a system is called HIAT (*Halbinterpretative Arbeitstranskriptionen*, which means 'semi-interpretive working transcriptions') and has been developed by Konrad Ehlich and Jochen Rehbein in Germany; see Ehlich's contribution to the Edwards and Lampert (1993) volume.

10. Consult your word processor's 'Help' for how to use TAB settings and the Ruler Bar.

Part 3

Analysing Data

7

Analytic Strategies

Contents

Although collecting recordings and making transcripts are essential parts of 'doing conversation analysis', they are, in a sense, still preparatory activities. The basic task, conversation analysis, still lies ahead. But how to begin? Most CA publications, like those discussed or mentioned in Chapter 2, offer exemplars of analyses as finished products. These may contain useful suggestions as to how to start an analysis and how to proceed, but they were not designed to do so. The present chapter will try to do just this: it will present ways in which a beginning CA researcher might try to come to grips analytically with transcribed conversational data. I will discuss some options, available in the literature, and construct a synthesis that might be helpful as a general guideline for the beginning researcher. The analytic process will be described and exemplified here as one of an individual researcher struggling with his or her data. In actual practice it is often a good strategy to share one's data and insights with others in a group. This will be discussed in a final section on the 'data session'. While the present chapter will focus on analytic exploration of single cases, the following one will deal with elaboration, extending an analysis using a larger collection of data in a comparative fashion.

It may be useful, in this context, to reiterate some earlier observations on CA's general purpose, or, in other words, to re-specify the 'animal' CA is after. On the surface, CA's analytic object consists of 'patterns of interaction' or' 'sequential structures'. The basic interest, however, is in 'the social organisation underlying the production and intelligibility of ordinary, everyday social actions and activities (Heath & Luff, 1993: 306). Alternative formulations include the 'competences' or 'procedures' that participants in interactions use, but the general idea is that these are somehow shared among members and a normative part of membership (cf. Garfinkel & Sacks, 1970: 342). I suggested earlier, in Chapter 3, that CA involves both an 'inductive' search for patterns of interaction, and an explication of the emic logic that provides for their significance.

How to begin

So, when one has collected some recordings and transcribed some parts of them, one can start the real job of CA, the analysis: finding patterns and explicating their logic. This means that one can begin by building a data-based argument about some aspect of talk-in-interaction. But which aspect? And where to start and how to do it? As in any qualitative enquiry, there is not *one best way*. One might start an analysis from a pre-given 'question', probably inspired by the literature, some theoretical thinking, practical interests, or common-sense presuppositions. But such a strategy is generally looked upon with some suspicion in CA (cf. Chapter 3). As Psathas writes:

> The variety of interactional phenomena available for study are not selected on the basis of some preformulated theorizing, which may specify matters of greater or lesser significance. Rather the first stages of research have been characterized as unmotivated looking. Data may be obtained from any available source, the only requirements being that these should be naturally occurring. (1995: 45)

While earlier he wrote:

> This [unmotivated looking] is, of course, a contradiction or paradox since looking is motivated or there would be no looking being done in the first place. It is a term which is intended to imply that the investigator is 'open' to discovering phenomena rather than searching for instances of already identified and described phenomena or for some theoretically preformulated conceptualization of what the phenomena should look like. (1990a: 24–5, n. 3)

And he adds some quotes from Sacks' *Lectures*, including:

> Treating some actual conversation in an unmotivated way, i.e., giving some consideration to whatever can be found in any particular conversation you happen to have your hands on, subjecting to investigation in any direction that can be produced off of it, can have strong payoffs. Recurrently what stands as a solution to some problem emerges from unmotivated examination of some piece of data, where, had you started out with a specific interest in that problem, it wouldn't have been supposed in the first instance that this piece of data would

be a resource with which to consider, and come up with a solution for, that particular
problem. (Sacks, 1984a: 27)

In one of his papers, Emanuel Schegloff (1996b) has provided a very useful explication of the idea (ideal?) of 'unmotivated looking', which specifically deals with
subsequent steps in the analytic process. After a summary discussion of a number
of CA findings, he writes:

> Virtually all of these results emerge from an 'unmotivated' examination of naturally occur-
> ring interactional materials – that is, an examination not prompted by prespecified analytic
> goals [. . .], but by 'noticings' of initially unremarkable features of talk or of other conduct.
> The trajectory of such analyses may begin with a noticing of the action being done and be
> pursued by specifying what about the talk or other conduct – in its context – serves as the
> practice for accomplishing that action. Or it may begin [. . .] with the noticing of some
> feature of the talk and be pursued by asking what – if anything – such a practice of talking
> has as its outcome. (1996b: 172)

Then he mentions 'three distinct elements' that ideally should be present in an
empirical account of 'the action that some utterance implements':

1   'a formulation of what action or actions are being accomplished';
2   'a grounding of this formulation in the "reality" of the participants';
3   an explication of how a particular practice, i.e. an utterance or conduct, can yield
    a particular, recognizable action.

Requirement 1 has to be extensively exemplified with data displays and analyses.
Requirement 2 involves the demonstration that the participants in the data have
indeed understood the utterance as doing that kind of action, most often by
inspecting subsequent talk. Requirement 3 indicates that such demonstrations of
particular understanding are not, in themselves, sufficient. One should 'provide
analytically the grounds for the possibility of such an understanding' (Schegloff,
1996b: 173), whether that was actually discernible in subsequent utterances
or not.

   These are rather strong requirements which show that a seemingly 'loose' idea
like 'unmotivated looking' should not be taken to open the door to a 'sloppy' kind
of analysis. An 'open mind' at the start does not preclude a rigorous analysis later
in the project.

   So, the generally preferred strategy is to *start* from the data at hand, and not
from any preconceived ideas about what the data 'are' or 'represent'. However, as
I suggested before, the conceptual apparatus that has been built up over the last
40 years or so provides a present-day researcher with a general perspective on conversational data which it would be silly to ignore completely. Indeed, Schegloff's
more recent analyses (as in 1992a; 1996a; 1996b) are evidently based on his and
others' cumulative insights and findings. Therefore, I take a 'moderate' position on this
issue by recommending a tentative, open-minded approach to the data at hand, using
just a few basic concepts from the CA tradition to structure one's 'looking'. But even
then, the fundamental 'material' with which one is working is one's understanding of
what the participants are *doing* in and through their talk-in-interaction, and for this

hearing and/or looking at the recording, with the transcripts at hand, is still the essential way to proceed (and to check later in the analytic process).

My proposals in this matter are partly inspired by some earlier suggestions by Schegloff. In a 'Didactic Seminar' given at the American Sociological Association Meetings in San Francisco, August 1989, he proposed a preparatory analytic routine in three steps:[1]

1   Check the episode carefully in terms of *turn-taking*: the construction of turns, pauses, overlaps, etc.; make notes of any remarkable phenomena, especially on any 'disturbances' in the fluent working of the turn-taking system.
2   Then look for *sequences* in the episode under review, especially adjacency pairs and their sequels.
3   And finally, note any phenomena of *repair*, such as repair initiators, actual repairs, etc.

Schegloff presented these suggestions in terms of 'roughing the surface' before one actually starts the analysis. Therefore, I suggest that a beginning CA researcher should first collect a set of transcribed interactional episodes, and then *systematically* work through these data in a series of 'rounds' of prespecified analytic attention, guided by a list of broad CA concepts like those in this list. This will be the basic idea of the general strategy that I will present later in the chapter, but before that, I will survey one other proposal.

Questions to ask and areas to consider

In their introductory chapter on CA, Anita Pomerantz and B.J. Fehr (1997: 71–4) offer their readers some 'tools to help you develop your conversation analytic skills', which consist of 'questions to ask and areas to think about' in inspecting tapes and transcripts. They formulate five tools to be applied subsequently.

1.   Select a sequence.

Here, also, the idea is to start with a 'noticing', which is not premeditated in any way. Then, they suggest, you should search for both the start and the end of the sequence of which the noticed talk or action is a part:

> For the start of the sequence, locate the turn in which one of the participants initiated an action and/or topic that was taken up and responded to by coparticipants. For the end of the sequence, follow through the interaction until you locate the place in which the participants were no longer specifically responding to the prior action and/or topic. [. . .] When looking at (or for) sequence openings and closing, treat them as product of negotiation. (Pomerantz & Fehr, 1997: 71)

While this sounds simple, it may not be so easy to 'locate' sequence beginnings and endings in particular cases. One issue is that in many cases a 'thread' does not start with a marked 'initiative', but rather with something being 'hinted' at. The utterance in which this hint is taken up would then be the 'official' start of the sequence. In the analysis of the full sequence, however, the utterance that in fact provided for its possibility should also be considered. At the other end, sequences may 'trail off', rather than being clearly concluded. Then, one could use the marked start of a next sequence as, in fact, ending the previous one. Quite often, however, the two seem to be relevant at the same time, in the sense that participants alternate between the two, or that one still talks in terms of the previous one, while another has already started a new sequence. These remarks should not discourage efforts to try to find sequences, but rather pass a warning that you might encounter hard-to-decide, and therefore interestingly deviant, cases (cf. pages 37–8).

2. Characterize the actions in the sequence.

Here the idea is to describe a sequence's actions on a turn-by-turn basis. This involves trying to answer the question 'What is this participant doing in this turn' for each consecutive turn. By doing this systematically for all the turns that make up the sequence, one produces an 'actional' description of the sequence, so to speak, which should be completed by a consideration of the relationship between the actions, for instance as initiatives and responses of some sort. Again, this may not always be an easy task, as a turn's action(s) may be complex and ambiguous. One should treat these characterizations as provisional, and therefore as open to revision when the analysis progresses.

3. Consider how the speakers' packaging of actions, including their selection of reference terms, provides for certain understandings of the actions performed and the matters talked about. Consider the options for the recipient that are set up by that packaging.

The notion of 'packaging' refers to the *form* chosen to produce the action, from the alternatives that might have been available, as in the many ways in which a 'greeting' may be done or the variety of correct but different ways in which one can refer to a person:

> For a given action, consider how the speaker formed it up and delivered it. Consider the understandings that are tied to the packaging that the speaker used in relation to alternatives that might have been used but were not on this occasion. Also, consider the options that the packaging the speaker used provided for the recipient. Alternative ways of packaging an action may set up different options for the recipients. (Pomerantz & Fehr, 1997: 72–3)

The interesting thing about this is that there are always different ways in which 'something' can be done, and that the 'selection' from the set of possibilities carries meaning. Therefore, one should always consider an actual expression as meaningfully chosen from the set of relevant alternatives for it.

4. Consider how the timing and taking of turns provide for certain understandings of the actions and the matters talked about.

This involves a detailed turn-by-turn consideration of the turn-taking process:

> For each turn in the sequence, describe how the speaker obtained the turn, the timing of the initiation of the turn, the termination of the turn, and whether the speaker selected a next speaker. (Pomerantz & Fehr, 1997: 73)

This refers to the essential aspect of 'getting the floor' in a conversation. A fuller discussion of the issues involved in considering 'turn-taking' will be given later in the chapter.

5. Consider how the ways the actions were accomplished implicate certain identities, roles and/or relationships for the interactants.

This final area of consideration refers to the 'rights, obligations, and expectations' that are constituted in the talk. It seems a bit surprising that the authors formulate this area in terms of such 'traditional' concepts as 'identities, roles and/or relationships', which carry a relatively 'fixed' status. I take it, however, that they would agree that 'identities, roles and/or relationships' are being (re)negotiated at every moment during the talk.[2] I think one might try to differentiate, in the analysis, firstly the 'rights, obligations, and expectations' that are demonstratively oriented to in the interaction itself, and, secondly, how these local orientations relate to certain more permanent 'identities, roles and/or relationships'. Examples of the first might be 'story-teller/recipient', 'questioner/answerer', etc., while the second would include things like 'mother/child', 'doctor/patient', etc. (for these issues, consult the remarks on membership categorization analysis in Chapter 4 at pages 45–7).

In the conclusion of their chapter, Pomerantz and Fehr write:

> In our guidelines, we included five areas to consider in developing analyses. We selected these five because we feel they are fundamental. One area we omitted is topical organization. Our decision to omit it rests upon the complexity that is involved in studying it. (1997: 87)

To my mind these are interesting and useful proposals which I will take up again in my own 'synthesis', to be elaborated below. For the moment, let me note that in this strategy, as in the one described as 'unmotivated looking', the starting point is some 'noticing' in the transcript that something 'interesting' seems to be happening at some moment. From that moment on, the purpose of the strategy is to elaborate and contextualize that rather intuitive moment.

Except for the issues of 'identities, roles and/or relationships', that last-mentioned 'area' in the proposal by Pomerantz and Fehr, the strategies discussed so far have suggested a concentration on the talk 'itself', rather than its 'context'. In other words, these proposals have referred to 'pure CA', rather than 'applied CA', as distinguished in Chapter 9.[3]

A general strategy for data exploration

The suggestions and proposals that I have discussed so far in this chapter are not to be seen as *required* ways of doing CA. In fact, its authors explicitly say that there are many ways in which one can approach data in a CA project. So my to-be-proposed synthesis is not better than the ones discussed above, but rather one I happen to prefer for present purposes and which I will use to elaborate and illustrate a number of the issues involved. For the moment, I will present the first part of my proposal, which concerns the analytic exploration of a piece of data, however that may be selected. In the next chapter, I will return to the issues of data selection, both for the starting point of the analysis and for the further elaboration of it.

My proposed general analytic strategy, as far as the analytic exploration of single instances is concerned, consists of the following general suggestions, which presuppose the availability of a recording of naturally occurring verbal interaction, and a detailed transcript, as discussed in the previous chapters:

- Starting with an arbitrarily or purposively selected part of the transcribed data, work through the transcript in terms of a restricted set of analytically distinguished but interlocking 'organizations'. For this purpose I propose the following four: *turn-taking organization*; *sequence organization*; *repair organization*; and *the organization of turn-design*. This 'work-through' involves a turn-by-turn consideration of the data in terms of practices relevant to these essential organizations, such as taking a turn in a specific way, initiating a sequence, forgoing taking up an issue, etc. In other words, the task is to specify practice/action couplings as these are available in the data, where the actions are as far as possible formulated in terms of the four organizations.
- In actual research, this may be done in a variety of practical formats, as *remarks* written on a printed transcript, as 'analytic descriptions', or as *codes and observations* added in a separate column to the transcript, or by using a specialized computer program like Transana (cf. Chapter 6, page 112–13).
- On the basis of this process, try to formulate some *general* observations, statements, or rules that tentatively summarize what has been seen. When a particular interest or phenomenon has emerged, focus on it, but keep it in context in terms of these four organizations.

These are, of course, very general suggestions. Therefore, I will try to put some detailed, empirical flesh on these abstract and general bones below. For the moment, I only want to articulate the similarities and differences in relation to the strategies previously discussed. The proposal picks up the major ideas of the 'unmotivated looking' strategy, but with two modifications. The first is the suggestion of working through the data systematically, and the second is that the noticing process is framed within the four organizations, which, to my mind, summarize CA's basic analytical knowledge, as it has been built up over the years. The requirements and suggestions from Schegloff that I have discussed before, including grounding in the 'reality' of the participants and explication of the practice/action coupling, are included in my proposal.

Compared with the proposal by Pomerantz and Fehr, I think that my synthesis covers most of their 'areas and questions'. The order in which one or another 'area' should be covered could be a point of discussion. Where they suggest starting with a sequence, for instance, I propose working through the turn-taking first. My reason is that I feel that speaking-at-all precedes building relations between spoken utterances.

Furthermore, as I discussed in the section on their proposal, I prefer to restrict provisionally the consideration of the 'identities, roles and/or relationships' involved in the interaction to those that are formally describable in terms of local issues of turn-taking, sequencing, etc. In other words, 'rights, obligations, and expectations' are taken up in terms of the four organizations only, at least provisionally. A similar restriction is proposed regarding various other contextual or structural properties like gender, age, social class, ethnicity, institutional tasks, etc. As I suggested, knowledge of such properties may be needed to *understand* the actions that utterances perform, but I would rather *bracket* such institutional or structural properties for a first round of formal analysis.

Therefore, I have not included any references to permanent identities or institutional settings in the proposal. I prefer to start with an analysis in terms of the formal properties of the organization of talk-in-interaction, *before* tackling issues of how practices/actions relate to 'context'. In other words, I would prefer to start the analytic process by 'bracketing' any 'fixed' knowledge about institutional roles and restraints. But I would *not* invite analysts to ignore contextual features as far as these are used as an aid in understanding the local action performed in the utterances and other conduct.[4] In short, I would like to propose building up a sense of *genre*, including issues of identities, relationships, tasks, etc., from the formal data analysis, rather than presupposing these issues as being globally, and therefore locally, relevant (cf. Schegloff, 1991).

A data fragment

In order to be able to demonstrate some aspects of my proposal, I will first give a data fragment that can be used to exemplify some of the phenomena I will be talking about. It is taken from a GP consultation, recorded in the Netherlands,[5] in which a mother (M) consults with her 9-year-old daughter (L), because the latter has been 'tired' and 'giddy' for a while. We enter the consultation when the physician (D) has just given a preliminary assessment of the case, a blood shortage, and in the second line (72), he announces a blood test. Before that, however, he apparently fills in the patient's record card and talks a bit with her. She is not very talkative, however, and later her mother adds a few comments.

EXCERPT 7.1

```
71   D:   >'k wee- niet of het wat ↑is=
71   D:   I don't know whether it's something=
72   D:   =maar we kunnen ('t) even (↓ prikken).<
72   D:   =but we can just prick.
73        (1.4)
74   D:   ·hh ↓draaierig,
74   D:   ·hh giddy,
75        (7.8)
76   D:   ·hh want dat is ↑ niet leuk hè?
76   D:   ·hh 'cause that's no fun, is it?
```

77   (0.6)
78   D: als je zo loopt te t<u>o</u>bben.
78   D: when you are having to struggle like that.
79   M: huhm
80   (2.5)
81   D: welke ↑ kl<u>a</u>s zit je Liesbeth?
81   D: which form are you in Liesbeth?
82   (0.8)
83   L: in de ↑ v<u>ie</u>rde.=
83   L: in the fourth.=
84   D: =in de v<u>ie</u>rde gaat g<u>oe</u>d?
84   D: =in the fourth going alright?
85   (0.8)
86   L: ja=
86   L: yes=
87   D: =j<u>a</u>?
87   D: =yes?
88   D: m- je >kan nou=
88   D: b- you can(not) now=
89   D: =je bent nou nat- te m<u>oe</u> om te ↑ w<u>e</u>rken of niet een beetje.<
89   D: =you are now nat- too tired to work or not a bit.
90   (.)
91   D: soms.
91   D: sometimes.
92   L: ↑nee hoor.
92   L: no.[6]
93   D: nee?
93   D: no?
94   (2.6)
95   D: alleen als je ↑th<u>ui</u>skomt.
95   D: only when you come home.
96   (.)
97   L: (°nhee°)
97   L: n(h)o
98   M: 's↑m<u>o</u>rgens
98   M: in the morning
99   (0.7)
100 M: >°kan ze ook echt niet=
100 M: she really cannot=
101 M: =oh ik ben nog zo m<u>oe</u> zegt ze dan=
101 M: =oh I'm still so tired she says then=
102 M: =ja: je moet toch uit b<u>e</u>d komen<
102 M: =yes you still have to get up
103   (.)
104 M: maar °hh
104 M: but·hh
105   (2.5)
106 M: °(nou is ze een) ↑ochtend (slapertje)=
106 M: but she is a morning sleeper=
107 M: =want 'avonds moet ik (ze) dringen om naar ↑b<u>e</u>d te gaan°=

```
107  M:   =because in the evening I have to press her to go to bed=
108  M:   =(°°en smorgens dan°°)
108  M:   =and in the morning then
109       ((8.2: writing))
110  D:   ·hhh hhh
111       ((4.7: writing))
```

Four types of interactional organization

In this section, I will explain in somewhat more detail the four analytically distinguished but interlocking organizations that I propose to use in the exploratory analysis of data segments like the one just given. These are, to repeat: *turn-taking organization*; *sequence organization*; *repair organization*; and *the organization of turn-design*.

Turn-taking organization

The idea of 'turn-taking' as an organized activity is one of the core ideas of the CA enterprise. As Sacks has observed, the basic fact about 'conversation' is that, overwhelmingly, there is one and only one person speaking at a time, while speaker change recurs with minimal gap and minimal overlap. This 'fact' is seen as a continuous achievement of the parties to the conversation, which they accomplish on a turn-by-turn basis, or, more precisely, at any 'transition relevance place' (TRP), at the end of any 'turn constructional unit' (TCU). The latter can be equated to the 'turn-constructional component' of conversation's turn-taking system, as defined in the classic paper on turn-taking by Sacks et al.:[7]

> There are various unit-types with which a speaker may set out to construct a turn. Unit-types of English include sentential, clausal, phrasal, and lexical constructions. Instances of the unit-types so usable allow a projection of the unit-type under way, and what, roughly, it will take for an instance of that unit-type to be completed. [. . .] The first possible completion of a first such unit constitutes an initial transition-relevance place. Transfer of speakership is coordinated by reference to such transition-relevance places, which any unit-type instance will reach. (1978: 12)

In the paper it is argued that there are several ways in which speaker change can be organized: a next speaker can be selected by the previous one, a speaker can self-select, or the present speaker can continue speaking. These three options are, according to the authors, hierarchically organized: other-selection goes before self-selection, which goes before continuation. This 'system' of conversational turn-taking has a number of interesting properties, including that it is 'locally managed', as well as 'interactionally managed' or 'party administered'. This involves that the system works 'again and again' at each next possible completion point, after the production of each TCU, and that this management is an interactional one, involving all the parties in the interaction. Sacks et al. remark:

For conversationalists, that turn size and turn order are locally managed (i.e. turn-by-turn), party-administered (i.e. by them), and interactionally controlled (i.e. any feature being multilaterally shaped), means that these facets of conversation, and those that derive from them, can be brought under the jurisdiction of perhaps the most general principle particularizing conversational interaction, that of 'recipient design.' With 'recipient design' we intend to collect a multitude of respects in which talk by a party in a conversation is constructed or designed in ways which display an orientation and sensitivity to the particular other(s) who are the coparticipants. In our work, we have found recipient design to operate with regard to word selection, topic selection, the admissibility and ordering of sequences, the options and obligations for starting and terminating conversations, and so on. (1978: 42–3)

In other words, turn-taking is one aspect of conversation in which a locally sensitive fine tuning takes place, which not only is actively adapted to the particular recipients involved, but in so doing co-constitutes the parties as participants in 'this conversation'.

It is essential, I think, for an adequate understanding of the CA enterprise, to see that what basically defines the 'units' of the turn-taking system, the TCUs, is not some objectively describable set of structural, such as grammatical, prosodic, or whatever, properties, but its *action potential for participants*:

What can we say TCUs have in common, aside from intonation (if that) and possible completion? The key may be that they are productions whose status as complete turns testifies to their *adequacy as units for the participants*, units which are addressable with the generic issue for practical actors (Schegloff and Sacks, 1973: 299): 'why that now?' Overwhelmingly this issue is grounded for practical actors as parties to interaction by some version of the *action(s)* the unit is doing. (Schegloff, 1996a: 111–12)

In other words, it's the ability to 'do' something, be it proposing, requesting, accepting, showing surprise, or whatever, that makes a sound or string of sounds into a TCU, an ability that it may share with a nod, a gesture, or a smile. This 'actional' perspective does not exclude, of course, that syntactic, intonational, and other properties of utterances might be interestingly examined to see how they can be used to contribute to discernible action completion for participants (cf. Ford & Thompson, 1996).[8]

Demonstration 1

I will now try to demonstrate a perspective on turn-taking organization by discussing a few turn-taking phenomena that are discernible in the transcript (excerpt 7.1) given above. As to the 'one-at-a-time, no-gap, no overlap' properties, we can see that there is no overlapping speech in this particular segment, but that there are gaps, and some are even quite long, over 1 second (cf. Jefferson, 1989), as in lines 73 (1.4), 75 (7.8), 80 (2.5), 94 (2.6), 105 (2.5), 109 (8.2), and 111 (4.7). The first two are 'owned' by D, who is writing in the record, so his talk, as in line 74, can be seen as a kind of 'secondary activity' in relation to his 'main involvement', writing (cf. Goffman, 1963). His tone of speaking, in 74, has an 'absent' quality; audible on the tape, but not transcribable. The last two very long pauses seem also due to the writing activity, which is audible on the tape. One can observe that, in this episode, the doctor addresses the girl but is not very successful in getting her to talk at any length. He does not react at all, however, to the later 'fill-ins' by the mother (98–108), probably having returned to his writing after a bit of 'conversation' with the daughter. The other longish pauses can be related to this situation: the (2.5) one in 80 follows a sequence in which the daughter has not reacted verbally; the (2.6) in 94 is 'owned' by the doctor, who was not successful in getting her confirmation for his suppositions (in 88–9); the (2.5) pause in 105, finally, is 'owned' by the mother, and may be related to the fact that no reaction from D is forthcoming.

Another aspect of turn-taking, which is relevant in a three-party situation, like this one, is *speaker selection*. I have touched on this, saying, firstly, that D addresses L, who only reacts minimally if at all (76–97), and, secondly, that M's explanations (98–108) are ignored by him. In both phases, it is quite clear who is being addressed, from the content, the address forms, and the 'epistemological situation' (who can be supposed to have or not have which kinds of information), but it will probably also have been 'enacted' by the speaker's body: turning to, or at least looking at the addressee.

In short, these summary observations should suffice to show that considering a spate of interaction in terms of turn-taking already gives you a penetrating understanding of what is going on in it, and forces you to consider other aspects of the interaction, to which we now turn.

Sequence organization[9]

A second core idea of CA is that utterances in interactional talk are *sequentially organized*. The idea of 'sequence' refers to the common experience that 'one thing can lead to another'. This may be one reason why people sometimes refuse a simple act, such as returning a greeting, because they do not want to be involved in what might follow from that (cf. Sacks, 1992a: 49–51).

For conversations, this means that any utterance in interaction is considered to have been produced for the place in the progression of the talk where it occurs (i.e. the 'slot' it 'fills'), especially just after the preceding one, while at the same time it creates a context for its own 'next utterance'. The concept of *adjacency pair* (AP), as discussed in Chapter 2 (page 20), is the major instrument for the analysis of sequential organization, but a full sequence quite often includes more than just two pair-parts. Taking a 'core sequence' as a point of reference, additional sequences can be seen as expanding it in various ways (see below; and more extensively Schegloff, 2007a). It is an essential part of the adjacency pair format that the relationship between the two parts is a *normative* one. After a first pair-part, the next utterance is, at first, heard as a relevant response to the first, as a fitting second pair-part. When that is not possible, when there is no response, or when it does not 'fit', that is an accountable matter, a 'noticeable absence' (cf. the discussion in Chapter 2, including the explication of 'conditional relevance'). Various kinds of expansions, such as a third position acknowledgement, however, while possible, are not normatively required to the same extent. As was made clear in the extended definition of adjacency pairs, quoted in Chapter 2, the second pair-part is expected in the immediately *next* position. There are cases, however, where this does not occur, without this non-occurrence being 'noticeable'. One example is that a new sequence can be 'inserted' in the one that was just started, for instance by a request for clarification or specification (cf. Schegloff, 1972: 76–9; 2007a: 97–114). So a first question (Q1) can be followed by another question (Q2) by the would-be answerer, which is then first answered by the speaker who produced Q1 (A2), before the questioned answers the first answer (A1); thus you get the order Q1, Q2, A2, A1. This is just one type of *sequence expansion*, which serves to illustrate the point that nothing in the AP structure works 'automatically'; whether a sequence format is followed through, restricted, expanded, or broken off, that is up to the parties to negotiate on a turn-by-turn basis (cf. Jefferson & Schenkein, 1978).

Some AP-formatted utterance pairs function as a preparation for a next pair, as a *pre-sequence*, so you can have pairs that have implications for what can follow. They can be designed to check whether a certain condition for a possible next action exists, and they are conventionally heard to be doing just that (Sacks, 1992a: 685–92; Schegloff, 1980). A variety of *pre*'s have been described in the CA literature, including pre-invitations, pre-requests, and pre-announcements. A special kind of pre-sequences are those that may lead to a temporary 'lifting' of the ordinary turn-taking system, in the sense that one party gets the right to produce a multi-turn unit like a story or a joke and thus becomes the 'primary speaker', while the other(s) become recipients of that 'discourse unit' (Houtkoop & Mazeland, 1985). Such tellings are often prepared by a *preface*, which offers a kind of preview about what will be told, enquires into its 'tellability' (i.e. 'do you know X?', 'have you heard about Y?'), and thereby instructs the recipients in what kinds of response is expected (laughter, alignment, etc.) and when (at the punch-line etc.). Such longer units can have their own internal sequential structures, of course, which permit the recipients to time their reactions, in response sequences (cf. Sacks, 1974; 1978).

While a 'pre' is evidently designed to do the preparatory work it does, explore whether the conditions for a particular *core sequence* are met, conversationalists can also be seen doing such explorations in a much less obvious way. Gail Jefferson has analysed such tricks, as when people give a *trouble-premonitory* response to an inquiry (1980), or when they offer a *gloss* that may be 'unpacked' if the recipient shows any interest in such an expansion (1985a). So even the start of a sequence may be a negotiable matter, whether openly or covertly.

A different kind of expansion can take place after the core sequence is possibly complete, a *post expansion*. I already mentioned one type of it, a third-position acknowledgement or assessment, which often functions as 'closing sequence thirds' (Schegloff, 2007a: 118). But more extensive expansions are also possible, as in repairs or other ways in which the topic of the core sequence is taken up or reworked (Schegloff, 2007a: 148–68).

So, in terms of their placement vis-à-vis the core sequence, Schegloff (2007a: 26) distinguishes three kinds of expansions:

		← Pre-expansion
A	First pair-part	
		← Insert expansion
B	Second pair-part	
		← Post-expansion

Another kind of sequence-like structure consists of repetitive *cycles* of similar sequences, such as question–answer sequences in an interrogation or interview. In a discussion of questions and answers in two-party conversations, Sacks has written:

> A person who has asked a question can talk again, has, as we may put it, 'a reserved right to talk again,' after the one to whom he has addressed the question speaks. *And*, in using the reserved right he can ask a question. I call this rule the 'chaining rule,' [. . .]. (1972: 343)

So this would allow for an endless repetition of question–answer sequences. Similarly 'endless' series may consist of arguments and counter-arguments, reproaches, and defences, etc.

Sequences, then, are *patterns* of subsequent actions, where the 'subsequentiality' is not an arbitrary occurrence, but the realization of locally constituted projections, rights, and obligations. These remarks should suffice, for the moment, to suggest ways in which a sequential analysis of interactional data might proceed.[10] Let us now take another look at our data fragment from the Dutch GP consultation.

Demonstration 2

We enter the consultation at a point where the physician, D, concludes the previous sequence, and announces a later action (71–2). After a (1.4) pause, we get a one-word utterance, '·hh ↓draaierig,' ('*hh giddy,*), in 74. As I see it, this is not addressed to anyone in particular, although it might have been taken as a 'formulation' of one of the symptoms that has been voiced earlier by the mother. In that case, it might have been affirmed, as a positive 'decision' on it.[11] In any case, it is not taken up (at least not vocally), so we have a kind of 'no sequence' case here.

After the pause, D provides a kind of 'emphatic' assessment of the child's condition in two parts (76–8). It is designed as an alignment with her, and therefore invites her confirmation; this is enforced by the tag 'hè?' She does not, however, react at all (at least not vocally). The mother does, in a vague way (79). As noted before, there follows a longish pause, which may be related to this lack of uptake. Then D has another go with a rather stereotypical '*which form are you in Liesbeth?*' (81). This question gets an answer, although it does not come too quickly. Rather than being 'just' an informative question, it works as a 'pre'. D acts in accordance with the 'chaining rule', discussed above, by speaking again, first repeating the answer just given, and then attaching an equally stereotypical next question to it: '*going alright?*' (84). This gets the 'projected' affirmative answer from the child, which is, again, repeated. I have called the two questions 'stereotypical' because they seem to belong to a restricted standard repertoire for any adult wishing to 'have a conversation' with a child of that age; no negative evaluation is intended.

Still following the 'chaining rule', D has repeated the girl's yes-answer, but with a 'try-marked' (Sacks & Schegloff, 1979) intonation contour, 'ja?' (*yes?*; 87). He does not provide space for any elaboration of her answer, however, and continues with what turns out to become a 'formulation' of what can be considered to be an 'upshot' of some of the descriptions that have been provided earlier by the mother. Although the turn (some aspects of its construction will be considered later) clearly projects a positive decision from the girl, she reacts with '*no* plus particle':'↑nee hoor.' (cf. discussion in Demonstration 4). D again produces a try-marked repeat of the answer (omitting the particle) and subsequently offers another 'restriction' on the formulation: '*only when you come home*' (95). The girl, however, persists in not endorsing it, although with a rather soft and timid '(°nhee°)' (97).

Then the mother offers an unsolicited 'addition' to previous descriptions, containing homely observations and reported speech from both her daughter and herself (98–102). D does not react vocally, however. After a pause, she adds a kind of 'context' for these descriptions, in the sense of an overall typification of her daughter's sleeping habits,[12] but this trails off (108) while the physician is writing.

Talk-in-interaction is mostly 'other-directed', either inviting the other to respond, or responding itself. In the fragment we have been discussing, such appeals were not too successful: it takes two to sequence. But even the very limited answers that L gave were used by D to build a series of connected sequences, the first (81–3) becoming a pre-sequence to the next (84–7), which in turn acts like a pre-sequence for the core sequence of this part (88–93). Next we will consider a type of organization that sometimes complicates the sequential picture, leading to special insertion sequences.

Repair organization

In Chapter 2, we encountered instances of *repair*, organized ways of dealing with various kinds of *trouble* in the interaction's progress, such as problems of (mis)hearing or understanding. What we saw in those instances was that repair has to be initiated, for instance by a complaint like 'I can't hear you', and that, once initiated, it creates an urgency which can lead to a postponement, or even abandonment, of a projected next action. In a series of later papers, especially by Schegloff, phenomena of repair have been analysed in depth as sequentially structured phenomena (the classic source is Schegloff et al., 1977; later studies include Schegloff, 1979b; 1987b; 1992a; 2000; see also Jefferson, 1974; 1987, on the more specific phenomena of 'error correction', and Macbeth, 2004, on 'repair' and 'correction' as organizations to be differentiated).

At its simplest, a repair sequence starts with a *repairable*, an utterance that can be reconstituted as the *trouble source*. It should be clear that any utterance can be turned into a repairable. The initiative can be taken by the speaker of the repairable, which is called a 'self-initiated repair', or others can take such an initiative, 'other-initiated repair'. And the repair itself can be done by the original speaker, 'self-repair', or by others, 'other repair'. One can observe that speakers sometimes cut off the current utterance to restart it, correcting an obvious mistake, or using a different expression (cf. Jefferson, 1974, for examples and analyses). A speaker can also use the transition relevance place (TRP), just after an utterance is completed, to initiate self-repair. Another type of repair sequence emerges when a turn's recipient reacts to it in a way that demonstrates some kind of misunderstanding, after which the original speaker, recognizing the trouble from the uptake, initiates repair on his or her previous turn, in 'third position', so to speak (Schegloff, 1992a). These would all be cases of self-initiated self-repairs.

When another participant initiates repair, this is most often done in the next turn, by a *next turn repair initiator* (NTRI for short). This is quite often done with a short item like 'huh?', 'what?', etc. This gives the original speaker an opportunity to self-repair the trouble source, by offering a clearly articulated repeat, or by using a different expression, possibly preceded by 'I mean' or something like that. Alternatively, another speaker may also offer a candidate understanding of a target utterance, possibly in a format like 'you mean X?', which the original speaker can then accept, reject, or rephrase.

You may remember from my discussion of Sacks' first lecture that he observed that an item like 'I can't hear you' can be used any time, any place. It is, as he called it: 'an "occasionally usable" device. That is to say, there doesn't have to be a particular sort of thing preceding it' (Sacks, 1992a: 6). The other side of this coin is that when it is *not* used, when no repair is initiated in 'next turn', that itself is an event, a 'not doing repair'. In other words, because 'next turn' is the natural place for other-initiated repair, any next turn that is not used for that purpose thereby 'is not doing repair'. Therefore, Schegloff (1982) has argued that one significant aspect of 'continuers' like 'uh huh' is that they signify that the recipient of a previous turn does *not* use this place for initiating repair (or any other marked action). This would not absolutely exclude a repair initiation on the previous turn-taking place later, but such an initiative would require more 'work'. As an additional observation, one can say that when 'next turn' is used to do the action projected by the previous one, this is even a stronger way of 'not doing repair'. In short, although manifest repair may be more or less rare in a particular stretch of talk, as a possibility repair is omni-relevant.

These notes should suffice for a recognition and provisional analysis of repair phenomena; the literature cited should be consulted for more elaborate insights into their organization.

Demonstration 3

It should be clear that repair phenomena, while frequently occurring, are not a 'regular' part of talk-in-interaction. Repair is typically 'occasioned' by problems of understanding. Looking at the fragment of the Dutch consultation discussed earlier, we seen no apparent repair phenomena or anything else resembling 'problems of understanding'. The interactants do seem to have problems, with which they deal in various ways, but these seem to be problems of 'misalignment' rather than misunderstanding. In fact, I scanned the complete transcript from which the fragment was taken, but there was no instance of repair to be used here for a demonstration. Therefore, I have selected a clear instance of repair from another Dutch consultation, quoted below:

EXCERPT 7.2

```
7   D:   vert<u>e</u>l het es
7   D:   what's up
8   P:   ·hh nou dokter ik heb de laatste twee weken m<u>aag</u>pijn (.) en als ik
         <u>ee</u>t
```

8	P:	·hh well doctor I've had stomach ache for the last two weeks (.) and when I eat
9	P:	h dan is het net of er hier wat begint te bew<u>eg</u>en hierin
9	*P:*	*h then it's like as if something starts to move in here*
10	D:	hmmhm
11	P:	ook als ik dr<u>i</u>nk
11	*P:*	*also when I drink*
12	D:	met<u>ee</u>n
12	*D:*	*at once*
13	P:	e:h [ja meteen als ik gege- 'f ten minste als ik dus me' eten binnen heb
13	*P:*	*uh [yes at once when I('ve) eat- o' at least when I've m' food inside*
14	D:	[(of daarna)
14	*D:*	*[or afterwards*
15	P:	of als ik gedronken heb (.) en danne: ·hh ja dan naderhand heb ik m<u>aa</u>gzuur
15	*P:*	*or when I've drunk (.) and then uh ·hh then afterwards I have gastric acid*
16		(2.1)
17	D:	h<u>a</u>rtwater
17	*D:*	*heartburn*
18		(2.0)
19	P:	watt<u>i</u>sta'
19	*P:*	*what's that*
20	D:	hh
21	P:	huhh
22	D:	<u>o</u>prispingen
22	*D:*	*belches*
23	P:	ja: da- dat noem ik dan m<u>aa</u>gzuur
23	*P:*	*yes tha- that's what I call gastric acid*
24	D:	ja het zuur denk ik dan pr[<u>oe</u>f je [ook ech[t zuu[r
24	*D:*	*yes acid I think in that case you really taste acid*
25	P:	[·hh [d'r [komt[water
25	*P:*	*·hh water comes up*
26	D:	ja
26	*D:*	*yes*
27	P:	en dan naderhand dan br<u>a</u>ndt het
27	*P:*	*and then afterwards then it burns*
28	D:	ja
28	*D:*	*yes*
29	P:	en dan wordt het z<u>uu</u>r
29	*P:*	*and then it becomes acid*
30	D:	hmm<u>hm</u>

We enter the consultation as the physician asks the patient to tell her story (7). She explains her problem: stomach ache and a funny feeling in her stomach when she has eaten or drunk something (8–11). He asks about the timing of the feelings in relation to the eating or drinking (12), which she then explains (13, 15). She then uses the expression 'maagzuur' (*gastric acid*, 15). There is a (2.1) pause, after which he offers an alternate description 'hartwater' (*heartburn*, 17). After another long pause (2.0, line 18), she utters an NTRI, 'wattista' (*what's that*, 19), in a surprised/amused tone. After a bit of laughter, D offers another alternate expression: 'oprispingen' (*belches*, 22). This leads to an extended exchange of descriptions (23–9). P confirms D's 'oprispingen' and adds that this is what she calls *gastric acid* (23). D, in turn, confirms her description, and adds a further detail, tasting (24). P, starting in overlap, offers an even more extended characterization in three phases (25, 27, 29), each of which is confirmed by D (26, 28, 30). Now a sufficient understanding is apparently achieved, as D continues with a question concerning possible causes (not quoted here).

So the physician, in this case, offers a more restricted term, *heartburn*, as an alternative to a relatively vague one, *gastric acid*, in the patient's complaint description. The issue, for him, is apparently whether she just feels the acid in her stomach area, or whether she tastes it in her mouth. She, however, does not seem to know the term *heartburn*, so she requests an explanation. This leads to an exchange of descriptions which solves the issue. Both parties actively cooperate in achieving a solution, demonstrating their shared interest in a correct description.

In the technical terms of repair organization, the primary trouble source seems to be *gastric acid*. D's alternative, *heartburn*, is then a case of other-initiated other-repair. This becomes a trouble source on its own, however, as P uses a shortened NTRI, *what's that*. D repairs his *heartburn* with *belches*, but now that the issue of correct and specific characterization has been raised, the parties cooperate in an exchange of more extended description until the issue is apparently solved. Repair, then, offers participants an important secondary device for achieving intersubjective understanding.

The organization of turn-design[13]

The fourth type of 'organization' that I want to propose in an exploratory analytic shopping list does not have an elaborate, structured approach in the CA tradition as have the previous three. There are a number of more or less separate sets of ideas and insights that can throw light on the procedures underlying the construction of utterances and their components, whether 'TCUs', starters, or completers. I will just summarize a few of these, without any hope of being comprehensive.

Consider the concept of *recipient design*, which was summarized in the quote from Sacks et al. (1978) in the section on turn-taking above (at page 129). The general idea is that a speaker builds an utterance in such a way that it fits its recipient. This may be an issue of constructing the utterance for it to be understandable for this particular recipient, given the knowledge that the speaker presupposes the recipient to have. Consider how you might refer to a person, for instance, when talking to someone else. In a five-and-a-half-page essay, Sacks and Schegloff (1979) have discussed two 'preferences' with regard to the organization of 'reference to persons', one for 'minimization' and one for 'recipient design'. There are many correct ways in which one can refer to a person, but one of the most efficient ways is to use a 'recognitional', such as a first name. It may require quite an elaborate analysis of the mutually supposed knowledge of the speaker, the recipient, and the situation to use a first name effectively, without a need for a repair. In an earlier paper, Schegloff (1972) analysed reference to places, or 'locational formulations', for which similar analyses may be required. It should be noted, however, that this involves not only the two parties to the interaction, the speaker and the recipient, but also understanding the current activity. In a context of direction giving, for instance, more precise locational indications may be required (cf. Psathas, 1991) than for constructing the setting for the telling of a funny anecdote.

A different conceptual tradition within CA that is related to issues of turn-design goes under the somewhat confusing name of *preference organization*. The general idea is: (1) that, when alternative actions are open possibilities, one may be 'preferred', that is expected and chosen if possible; and (2) that the difference between 'preferred' and 'dispreferred' alternatives is demonstrated in the *turn shape* chosen for doing one or the other. In other words, turns can be designed to *show* they are doing the preferred, or the dispreferred, alternative action. For instance, an invitation projects an acceptance as a preferred response. An accepting utterance will display this status by being quick and direct, no specific 'account' being given. A rejection, however, will tend to be delayed, preceded by a 'formal' acceptance, more often inferable than directly formulated, and quite often accounted for by giving a reason for it. To quote from a classic study of 'preferred/dispreferred turn shapes':

> Two types of shapes are of interest [here]: One type is a design that maximizes the occurrence of the actions being performed with them, utilizes minimization of gap between its initiation and prior turn's completion, and contains components that are explicitly stated instances of the action being performed. The other type minimizes the occurrence of the actions performed with them, in part utilizing the organization of delays and nonexplicitly stated action components, such as actions other than a conditionally relevant next. The respective turn shapes will be called *preferred-action turn shape* and *dispreferred-action turn shape*. (Pomerantz, 1984: 64)

In short, turns can be 'packaged' or 'formulated' in ways that show their relative 'preference' status. It should be noted that there are two aspects of 'preference' that have been discussed in the CA literature; only one, referring to 'turn shapes', is discussed here. The other has to do with structural regularities as to which kinds of alternatives are generally preferred or dispreferred. Schegloff (1988b: 453–5) calls the latter 'sequence-structure-based', and the earlier mentioned one 'practice-based' (cf. Heritage, 1984a: 265–80, and Levinson, 1983: 332–45, for overviews which stress the structure-based approach; also Sacks, 1987; Schegloff et al., 1977; and Lerner, 1996, for various applications and elaborations).

So, any conversational action can be performed in many *different* ways; how a turn is designed is a meaningful *choice*. That choice will be informed by a speaker's knowledge of the situation in general and the participants in particular. In designing a turn's format, the speaker fits the utterance to the evolving momentary situation as well, for instance by using previously used expressions and compatible pronouns, and the attention given by the hearers at the moment the utterance is being produced (cf. Goodwin, 1979). Hearers, on their part, will understand the utterance in a similar fashion as 'designed' for its occasion, as chosen from a set of alternatives, etc. Some utterance choices can be seen as falling in two classes, such as 'positive' and 'negative', while others seem to be 'scalable' or 'gradable' on a continuum, for instance in enthusiasm. These classes or scale positions may differ in terms of 'preference', as discussed above, in terms of 'formality', in terms of grades of positive or negative evaluation (Pomerantz, 1978; 1986), or as speaking 'for oneself' ('I') or 'for the organization ('we'). This list is obviously incomplete, but I think the lesson is clear that formatting choices deserve serious attention.

Demonstration 4

For my demonstration of these issues of turn–design, I propose to return to our first example (excerpt 7.1), of the mother consulting with her daughter, and discuss two sequences selected from that segment. Here's the first one:

EXCERPT 7.1, DETAIL A

```
76   D:   ·hh want dat is ↑niet leuk hè?
76   D:   ·hh 'cause that's no fun, is it?
77        (0.6)
78   D:   als je zo loopt te tobben.
78   D:   when you are having to struggle like that.
79   M:   huhm
80        (2.5)
```

D has chosen rather emphatic and informal ways of packaging his actions here. 'Leuk' (76) is a standard positive assessment of almost anything, especially among young people. The expression 'tobben' (78), on the other hand, seems to be too strong for the occasion, since it is ordinarily used for more serious kinds of troubles and worries. Taken together, these word choices contribute to what seems a rather patronizing way of talking.

As a second example, let us take a later sequence, starting with the child's answer to the question as to which form she is in:

EXCERPT 7.1, DETAIL B

```
84   D:   =in de vierde gaat goed?
84   D:   =in the fourth going alright?
85        (0.8)
86   L:   ja=
86   L:   yes=
87   D:   =ja?
87   D:   =yes?
88   D:   m- je >kan nou=
88   D:   b- you can(not) now=
89   D:   =je bent nou nat- te moe om te ↑werken of niet een beetje.<
89   D:   =you are now nat- too tired to work or not a bit.
90        (.)
```

```
91  D:  soms.
91  D:  sometimes.
92  L:  ↑nee hoor.
92  L:  no.⁶
93  D:  nee?
93  D:  no?
94      (2.6)
```

As I have suggested before, D seems to have carefully arranged a situation in which he can return to a discussion of the ways in which she might experience her symptoms. The way in which the utterance is constructed, which 'accomplishes' this return to medical matters, displays the difficulties he is experiencing while doing it: 'm- je >kan nou=je bent nou nat- te moe om te ↑werken of niet een beetje.<' (b- you can(not) now=you are now nat- too tired to work or not a bit.' (88–9). He starts with a cut-off 'm-', which I take to project the conjunction 'maar' (but). This projects a contrast with 'being in fourth form'. It is followed by an unfinished 'je >kan nou', which, in the present context, I take to project a negative assessment of the ability to do her schoolwork well (rendered in English as b- you can(not) now, 88). Then there is a grammatically complete clause, although one word is cut off: 'je bent nou nat- te moe om te ↑werken' (you are now nat- too tired to work), in which 'nat-' can be understood to project 'natuurlijk' (naturally, in the sense of 'of course', 89). This clause, while being answerable in itself, is followed by two 'post-completors', 'of niet' (or not) and 'een beetje' (a bit), which offer first a negative and then a mitigated alternative to the strong too tired to work in the main clause. After a mini-pause, still another mitigated alternative is offered: 'soms.' (sometimes., 91). The girl answers '↑nee hoor.' (no + particle, 92). I hear this as a negation of the main clause, with therefore the three mitigated alternatives included. If she had chosen one of these, she would have indicated this by saying something like 'yes, sometimes'. She uses 'nee' (no) with the particle 'hoor' to package her action. Dutch particles like 'hoor' are very hard if not impossible to translate. 'Hoor' is only used in an interactional context and seems to have a 'mitigating', reassuring, or soothing effect. In the present case, the 'mitigation' may concern the fact that she is contradicting the physician, or it may be heard as suggesting that the situation is not as bad as the mother has presented it.[14]

It seems clear, in any case, that both parties work hard here, to be careful in what they are saying. The physician breaks off a first attempt before he formulates a personalized candidate assessment for the girl to endorse, in line with the descriptions offered earlier by the mother, but before she gets an opening to respond, he adds two alternatives, and after a mini-pause even a third. It may very well be that the girl has shown some reluctance to endorse the main clause, or even shakes her head, but I cannot know that because I have to rely on an audio recording only. The girl's adding of the particle 'hoor' to her no can be seen as displaying attention to the relationship-sensitive aspects of her contradiction.

These two short demonstrations should suffice to support the claim that it is worthwhile to pay close attention to the ways in which turns-at-talk are constructed and designed.

Discussion

These 'demonstrations' have illustrated how a first 'go' at some pieces of data might be organized as a systematic analytical exploration. The result would be an analytically informed description of the interaction on display in the data. When such a description has raised a specific interest, or when the situation is rather complex, it might be developed into a full-blown case study. Quite often, one would feel the need to support some of the claims in such a study with additional data, for example to demonstrate similar usages elsewhere, or contrastive examples that might be used to put the focus observations in perspective. Alternatively, one might take the case at hand as a 'first' in a collection of related phenomena. In order to build such a collection in a sensible way, you would have to decide on a category which your first case exemplifies. Such a decision can, of course, be revised or specified later, as you consider more and more cases. 'Analytic elaborations' will be the topic of the next chapter. Before I bring this chapter to a close, however, by inviting you to consider another 'exercise' and some 'recommended reading', I want to discuss a particular format of *collective* data exploration that seems to be a rather unique feature of CA practice: the so-called data session.

Data sessions

As noted before (pages 32-4), data exploration involves two related but distinguishable processes, 'understanding' and 'analysis'. In the previous sections of this chapter, I offered suggestions for organizing these operations as these would be done by an individual researcher confronting a piece of data. In actual CA practice, however, collective explorations in 'data sessions' play an important part, both in principle and in practice. The principle is that both in the 'understanding' and in the 'analysis', the issue is not one of individual 'interpretations', but rather of sharable and shared understandings which can and should be analysed in procedural terms. Individual intuitions do play a part in the analytic process, but these should be disciplined in various ways, by inspecting the data for any demonstration of local, practical analyses or formulations, but also by explication of one's findings and insights for others to inspect critically. The data session can be seen both as a kind of playground to inspire mutually one's understanding of the data, and as an environment that requires a rather specific 'discipline'.

A 'data session' is an informal get-together of researchers in order to discuss some 'data' – recordings and transcripts. The group may consist of a more or less permanent team of people working together on a project or in related projects, or an ad hoc meeting of independent researchers. The basic procedure is that one member brings in the data, for the session as a whole or for a substantial part of it. This often involves playing (a part of) a tape recording and distributing a transcript, or sometimes only giving a transcript. The session starts with a period of seeing/hearing and/or reading the data, sometimes preceded by the provision of some background information by the 'owner' of the data. Then the participants are invited to proffer some observations on the data, to select an episode which they find 'interesting' for whatever reason, and to formulate their understanding, or puzzlement, regarding that episode. Then anyone can come in to react to these remarks, offering alternatives, raising doubts, or whatever. What is most important in these discussions is that the participants are, on the one hand, *free* to bring in anything they like, but, on the other hand, *required* to ground their observations in the data at hand, although they may also support them with reference to their own data-based findings or those published in the literature. One often gets, then, a kind of mixture, or coming together, of substantial observations, methodological discussions, and also theoretical points.

Spontaneous reactions to interaction displays often have a more or less subjective, impressionistic, and individualistic character. People have a kind of 'natural trust' in their primary reactions to other people. In a collective data-based and data-responsive discussion, these first and naively trusted impressions can be subjected to constructive criticism in order to check them against what is available in the data. Furthermore, the group can 'force' the individual observer to go beyond individualistic assessments of actions in order to start reasoning in terms of the ultimate goal of CA, which is to explicate the resources used to accomplish particular (inter)actions, to explicate the procedural infrastructure of interaction. These sessions are especially useful when the group is mixed in terms of background and expertise, as long as there is a basic agreement on method and purpose. It is very useful and beneficial for all if some participants have a linguistic background, for instance, and others a social science orientation.

Data sessions are an excellent setting for *learning* the craft of CA, as when novices, after having mastered some of the basic methodological and theoretical ideas, can participate in data sessions with more experienced CA researchers. I would probably never have become a CA practitioner if I had not had the opportunity to participate in data sessions with Manny Schegloff and Gail Jefferson. And, on the other hand, having later to explicate my impressions and ideas to colleagues with different backgrounds, both novices and experts, helped me to be more clear about those ideas, methodologically, theoretically, and substantively.

My discussion of data sessions has, so far, been based on my own experience. In fact, the only real description I have been able to find in the literature is included in a very practically instructive paper by Brigitte Jordan and Austin Henderson (1995: 43–6). Group sessions, they write, are an important part of what they call 'interaction analysis', as practised in the Institute for Research on Learning and Xerox PARC, both in Palo Alto, California. At these labs 'multi-disciplinary collaborative work groups [...] are assembled for particular projects', but they also have arranged

> the Interaction Analysis Laboratory (IAL), an ongoing permanent forum in which researchers from different projects present tapes. The IAL meets for 2 or 3 hours each week. Researchers ('owners') bring tapes, often with transcripts or content listings, from their respective projects and, after a brief introduction to the setting of the recorded activities and any special interests the researcher may have, the group works together to analyse the tape. (Jordan & Henderson, 1995: 44)

The general process reported is that the tape runs and is stopped whenever someone wants to make a remark on the activities recorded. Observations and hypotheses 'must be of a kind for which the tape in question (or some related tape) could provide confirming or disconfirming evidence'. In order to avoid endless speculation it is sometimes agreed to stop the tape for no more than 5 minutes:

> Collaborative viewing is particularly powerful for neutralizing preconceived notions on the part of researchers and discourages the tendency to see in the interaction what one is conditioned to see or even wants to see. (44)

The authors cite several examples of cases in which trained observers were convinced that they had seen something happening, or not happening, while repeated group viewing proved them wrong. They further stress that 'ungrounded speculation about what individuals on the tape might be thinking or intending is discouraged', but that it is often possible to discuss 'mental events' on the basis of what is visible in the actual situated practices and reactions. The discussions are audio recorded and used later by the 'owner' of the tape as a resource for more extensive analysis, or more focused data collection.

In short, when the data are challenging, the company mixed, and the atmosphere serious but relaxed, a data session is one of the most rewarding experiences in the CA enterprise.

EXERCISE

Select an interesting data excerpt, say half a page to a page of transcript, which can be seen as a 'natural unit', or a few 'natural units', in its setting. Consult the tape with the transcript and make a detailed analytic description of the excerpt, using the proposed strategy as a general guideline. Write a report containing the preliminary findings, suggestions for the issues that you would like to pursue in later work, and methodological reflections on the process of discovery and your experiences with the analytic strategy.

For the focused options, B and D, you should select (an) excerpt(s) in which 'questioning' is done, of course. In the individual cases, A and B, you might still seek a volunteer to give comments on your analytic report.

When you are working in a group, options C and D, my suggestion would be to start by organizing one or more data sessions along the lines provided in the relevant section above. Experiment a bit with different formats. Evaluate these at the end of the (last) session(s). Then take a number of transcribed data excerpts and let two or three members work on the same excerpt, another duo or trio on another one, etc. Let each individual start working on the chosen excerpt alone, with the recording at hand, and produce a detailed analytic description of the excerpt. Then the members of the duo or trio should meet to discuss their reports, see what they have analysed similarly or differently, and try to reach agreement. Finally, write a report giving the major findings and a reflection on the process of discovery and the various experiences with the strategy.

RECOMMENDED READING

On analytic strategies and CA methodology: Pomerantz and Fehr (1997).

Some exemplary studies which focus on one case: Goodwin (1987); Hopper (1995); Sacks (1974); Schegloff (1978); Whalen et al. (1988).

On turn-taking: Sacks (2004); Sacks et al. (1978); Schegloff (2000).
On turn organization: Schegloff (1996a).
On sequence organization: Sacks (1992a; 1992b; Sacks discusses sequence organization in a number of lectures, for instance in the fall of 1967, vol. I: 624–92); Schegloff (1980; and esp. 2007a); Note: the studies reviewed in Chapter 2 are also very relevant for this topic.
On repair: Schegloff (1979b; 2005); Schegloff et al. (1977).
On turn-designs: Pomerantz (1984; 1986); Sacks and Schegloff (1979); Schegloff (1972; this paper is also relevant to the topic of sequence organization).

Notes

1. The formulation of these 'steps' is mine, based on my recollection of Schegloff's proposals.
2. In fact, this is how I read the two 'demonstrations' that they provide in the chapter, to which the reader is referred for more elaborate discussions of this strategy.
3. I have postponed a discussion of John Heritage's (1997) proposal concerning the analysis of institutional talk to Chapter 9.
4. Therefore, I have, in the transcripts included in this book, kept the institutional identifications, rather than changing these to A, B, etc.
5. Therefore, the transcript is bilingual, with the Dutch original being followed line by line with a gloss in English. For the general argument you can read only the gloss; for details you need to consult the Dutch. I am sorry for the inconvenience.
6. Dutch particles like 'hoor' are very hard, if not impossible, to translate; cf. the short discussion in Demonstration 4.
7. For convenience, I have chosen to use a variant version of the paper, published in a collection edited by Schenkein in 1978, to be referred to as Sacks et al. (1978). See Sacks (2004) for an early formulation.
8. There is now an extensive literature dealing with various aspects of turn-taking, including complications like overlapping talk and multi-unit turns, some of which will be mentioned in the recommended reading section of this chapter.
9. Schegloff's book on sequence organization (2007a) offers a rich and extensive resource for the consideration of this theme which I recommend to any serious practitioner of CA.
10. For institutional settings, a variety of specialized sequential structures have been described, but these will be discussed in Chapter 9.
11. The concept of a 'formulation' is used here in the sense introduced in Garfinkel and Sacks (1970) and elaborated in Heritage and Watson (1979; 1980) referring to the phenomenon that the character, *upshot*, or *gist* of a conversational activity may be made explicit in a later utterance, which is then called the 'formulation' of that activity; when it refers to things done or said by another party, it invites that party to decide on its correctness, elaborate its meaning, or whatever. In that sense it is a 'first pair-part' of an AP.
12. Cf. Locker (1981) for the use of 'person types' in lay explanations of symptoms etc.
13. The expression 'turn-design' has been chosen to collect a number of aspects of how participants construct, design, formulate, or package their turns.
14. These observations were partially inspired by an email message from Robert S. Kirsner of UCLA; cf., for example, Kirsner and Deen (1990).

8

Elaborating the Analysis

Contents

In the previous chapter, the focus was on the analysis of single data excerpts. In most CA studies, however, multiple fragments are considered, even extended collections. This chapter offers suggestions for extending analyses of single cases in various ways. The essential operation in such an elaboration is to compare instances, which involves a selection of instances to compare. After another illustrative 'demonstration' a general strategy for data elaboration is offered. A final section is concerned with another kind of extension of an analysis: by taking visual aspects into account.

On comparison in CA

When I was discussing Harvey Sacks' first lecture, in Chapter 2, I remarked that 'it is important to note that at CA's very beginning, Sacks' strategy was to *compare* instances of sequences which were similar in terms of their institutional setting (the psychiatric emergency service), their structural location (a call's opening), and the basic procedures (paired actions), but different in the ways in which these were used' (page 15). And later, I offered some more elaborate remarks on Sacks' use of data in the following terms:

> How did Sacks use his data in his first lecture? The first three instances he quoted were his primary objects of analysis, which he discussed in a comparative fashion. I will call this his 'focal' observations. But he also referred to general regularities and possibilities that are not supported by concrete instances. He talked about how things 'regularly' happen (or rarely, or always, etc.), as regarding callers being reluctant to give their names. I would call these 'specific background observations', that is references to instances which the analyst knows of, could provide, but does not do so explicitly. Later in the lecture, Sacks also referred to some cases which he did cite, for instance to demonstrate that repair initiators like 'I can't hear you' are being used throughout conversations. This I would call 'supportive observations'. He also seemed to refer now and then to knowledge that any competent member is assumed to have on the basis of his or her own experience, for instance concerning non-acquainted persons exchanging names at the start of a call. I would call these 'general background observations'. Finally, he used some 'ethnographic' information, things he learnt from being in the field and talking with professionals, such as the importance of getting clients' names. (page 24)

On the 'focal observations', I observed:

> The interesting thing about the choice of the three focal instances is that (1) and (2) are depicted as routine or regular, that is where the devices chosen are 'working' properly, while (3) is a deviant case in which these routines break down. It is the contrast between the routine and the deviant that does the trick here. It is used to open up the field for analysis. By comparing instances with each other, and with general experiences and expectations, their formatted properties, sequential placement, and local functionality can be related and explicated. (page 24)

In a similar fashion, I used some general expectations and observed regularities as general background in my explorations of the GP episodes in the previous chapter. Exploratory analyses and subsequent elaboration cannot be strictly separated.

As to the next case discussed in Chapter 2, I wrote:

> In Schegloff's analysis of openings, a similar strategy is used, in the sense that his 500-item corpus provides a strong basis for the formulation of his 'first rule', while the one exception to this rule occasions a deeper consideration of the *logic* of opening sequences, which has a much wider relevance than the cases under consideration. (page 24)

This is, of course, the famous strategy of 'deviant case analysis', which will be discussed later in the chapter.

As we can see in these classic instances, a basic issue is the selection of cases to *compare*, or, to use a different kind of formulation, the relevance of comparisons. In Sacks' reasoning in his first lecture, the puzzle provided by the special case was solved by looking at standard cases, routine openings, and identifications in such an environment. In Schegloff's 'Sequencing' paper, the special case presented itself as an exception to the 'first rule' of telephone conversations. So in both analyses, the argument is built on the confrontation of a standard or routine problem/ solution pair with an exceptional or deviant instance. As these cases involve variation within a class, I will call these *within-type comparisons*.

A different kind of comparison, which underlies many later CA studies, is the one between what is often called 'mundane', 'informal', or 'ordinary' conversations, typically among peers, and those that are called 'formal' or 'institutional' ones, for example between an 'agent', such as a physician or social worker, and a 'client'. This might be called an *across-type comparison*. As will be discussed at greater length in Chapter 9, such a comparison is based on, or at least suggests, a fundamental, principled, and a priori difference between these two types of talk-in-interaction. Some conversation analysts maintain that this is an open issue, to be decided empirically. It is important, therefore, to be very clear about the theoretical or empirical grounds on which cases to compare are selected as representing 'standard' versus 'deviant' cases in a category, or as belonging *in principle* to one or another type.

In terms of the overall strategy for analytic elaboration, there is, on the one hand, an issue of corpus construction and, on the other, one of *case selection* within the corpus. For an across-type comparison, one might select a two-class corpus, as when one might compare 'story-telling' in an informal setting and in the setting of a medical consultation, or police officer's questioning of a suspect or a citizen reporting a burglary. As I suggested above, such comparisons tend to be based on a 'pre-analytic' endorsement of the importance of a setting, specific identities, or other conditions.

Within-type comparisons would probably be based on the selection of instances within a pre-selected corpus. As I suggested in Chapter 2, the first two studies discussed there were focused on practices having a specific 'structural location', as in telephone openings. For many other topics, however, there is no such predefined location. For those topics, such as 'repair', a clear and manageable 'definition' of the phenomenon to be investigated is needed, but arriving at such a definition is the product of, rather than the starting point for, the comparison.

In short, a basic operation in many CA studies is to compare cases in order to arrive at clear types. In a sense, then, any comparison, even one with predefined 'conditional' classes, can and should be considered to be tentative.

Data selection in analytic elaboration

Analytic elaboration in CA means that, when one instance has been analysed, resulting in an 'analytically inspired description' of the interaction represented in it, others that are interestingly similar or different in procedural terms should also be considered, to elaborate the primary observations. I have already touched a number of times on the question of *how to select cases* for such an elaboration (cf. section on sampling issues in Chapter 5). Most of the analytic strategies that I have discussed in the previous chapter seem to take a rather 'loose' stance towards the selection of instances to be analysed. Although I agree that *starting* with an intuitively selected, 'noticed', instance can be very useful and inspiring, I think that in *subsequent* phases of analytic work, it may be better to use a more systematic data selection procedure. In this section, I will therefore discuss two sets of ideas concerning the selection of cases, called 'theoretical sampling' and 'comprehensive data treatment', respectively.

Theoretical sampling

'Theoretical sampling' is a term coined by Barney Glaser and Anselm Strauss (1967: 45–77) in their classic treatment of qualitative analysis, *The discovery of grounded theory*. In this book, and in later publications (cf. Strauss, 1987; Strauss & Corbin, 1990), an inductive approach to qualitative analysis is advocated that is oriented to the construction of a 'theory' that is to 'emerge from the data', especially through the comparison of instances, the so-called *constant comparative method*:[1]

> Theoretical sampling is the process of data collection for generating theory whereby the analyst jointly collects, codes, and analyzes his data and decides what data to collect next and where to find them, in order to develop his theory as it emerges. (Glaser & Strauss, 1967: 45)

So the idea is to select further data instances for their theory-elaborating potentiality or *theoretical relevance*. For some purposes, it may be useful to select cases for maximum *similarity*, while for others building a corpus to maximize *diversity* may be more sensible. Working with similar data may help to bring out essential properties and show any fundamental differences within the category, while maximum diversity may stimulate the consideration of both essential uniformities and the character of any diversity. For 'pure CA', one might in general prefer similar phenomena (patterns, action-types, sequence-types, etc.) taken from a wide variety of contexts (institution, medium, number of participants, etc.), unless one does have an *analytical* (or practical) reason to opt for a specific set of cases. For 'applied CA', a more restrictive policy will often be advisable, as the scope of one's findings will often be intentionally limited to a specific setting or interaction type.

An essential notion within the approach advocated by Glaser and Strauss is the idea of *saturation*:

> *Saturation* means that no additional data are being found whereby the sociologist can develop properties of the category. As he sees similar instances over and over again, the researcher becomes empirically confident that a category is saturated. He goes out of his way to look for groups that stretch diversity of data as far as possible, just to make certain that saturation is based on the widest possible range of data on the category. (1967: 61)

In other words, it only makes sense to take more and more instances into consideration *if* they provide additional information, stimulate new ideas, or serve a purpose in proving generality. But after some time, taking more data into account does not add anything and can be stopped. It is hard to know when this moment has arrived, of course, so most of the time you have to make a somewhat arbitrary decision.

A lot of case selection in CA resembles this style of work, except for the ultimate analytic purpose, of course.

Comprehensive data treatment

The second strategy to be characterized here has been used and explicated by researchers much closer to, if not members of, the CA community. In essence, this strategy consists of *first* building a *data corpus*, and *then* working through these data in a systematic fashion. Such a corpus should be constructed using only the most general criteria, including, of course, practical availability. So for 'pure CA' a corpus consisting of a varied set of 'conversations' might be used, but if one has a special interest in a specific institutional kind of talk, or if one wants to go on to 'applied CA', a set of 'institutional' interactions of the relevant kind would be sensible (see, again, Chapter 5, section on sampling issues). In submitting such a corpus to a *comprehensive data treatment*, one can prevent the complaint, which CA findings sometimes receive, that these are based on a subjectively selected, and probably biased, 'sample' of cases that happen to fit the analytic argument.

The concept of 'comprehensive data treatment' was introduced by Hugh Mehan (1979) in a study of classroom discourse. He writes:

> The policy [. . .] demands that all cases of data be incorporated in the analysis. This policy is adopted because people in situations are making sense all the time. Since this is the case, anomalies cannot be left unanalysed, for participants are acting in some purposeful way even at these 'anomalous' times. In order to assemble a complete description of social interaction, the researcher must account for the organization of participants' sense making at all times. (Mehan, 1979: 21)

The analysis may start on a small, arbitrary selection from the data, which is used to generate 'a provisional analytic scheme'. This scheme is then compared with other data and modified if necessary. This process is continued until the researcher has a scheme that covers all the data in the corpus. This strategy is, as Mehan himself says, 'analogous to analytic induction' and incorporates and systematizes 'deviant case analysis' (both mentioned in Chapter 3 and more fully discussed later in this chapter). Douglas W. Maynard (1984: 19–20) has used the same strategy in his study of 'plea bargaining', referring, on the one hand, to Mehan's work and, on the other, to Schegloff's (1968) study of telephone openings (discussed in Chapter 2).

This strategy seems especially useful if one tries to formulate a rule-set in order to account for an underlying order in a relatively structured core situation, as Mehan did with classroom discourse, Maynard with negotiations regarding plea bargaining, and, indeed, Schegloff with telephone call openings. In studying less frequently occurring or less clearly structured phenomena, the comprehensive data treatment strategy may involve a less efficient way of working. However, the principle of making oneself answerable to a wide range of cases that were not selected with a specific idea in mind seems to be very valuable.

Whether one should treat all the data in the corpus in a similarly in-depth fashion as used in the primary exploration depends on the topic chosen and its distribution across the corpus. Taking the exploration given as an example in the previous chapter as a starting point, one could, for instance, collect a set of GP consultations and focus on questions that can be considered to 'check' on, or ask for specification of, previously given complaint descriptions. This would mean that one should scan all instances of 'patient questioning' in the corpus in order to check whether any element from earlier complaint descriptions is later taken up in such questions. These latter instances would then constitute one's basic collection of relevant cases, but the instances in which complaint descriptions are not subjected to later questioning should be kept at hand as a collection of 'negative cases'. This would involve, then, a rather complete overall exploration of the corpus, for one would need to determine whether a complaint description was being questioned or not. But, after a superficial check, one would no longer have to consider, for instance, long explanations by the doctor. One might also, of course, choose to focus on a much more limited topic, say 'pre-sequences speci-fying conditions for symptoms to be discussed' in consultations. In that case, a much more focused and selective data treatment would be in order, limited to the episodes in which questions are used in this way.

Whatever the data selection made, the ultimate purpose is to use multiple instances to ground analytic observations regarding the organization of interac-tion. In the next few sections, I will discuss some phases of what I consider to be the basic operation of analytic elaboration, generalization, including the distinc-tion of types and the analysis of 'deviant cases'.

Generalization

In previous chapters, I have repeatedly stressed that a major aspect of CA is its use of *general* concepts to analyse *particular* instances, and the complementary use of particular instances to generate general formulations of 'devices', 'organizations', or 'systematics'. What concerns us in this chapter in general, and this section in particular, is how this generality can be achieved.

The framework that I will develop in this section is centred on the twin concepts of 'analytic induction' and 'deviant case analysis' that have already been touched upon in Chapter 3. But firstly, I want to reflect upon the notions of *generality* and *generalization* themselves. While many if not most kinds of scientific research strive for some kind of generality, there are different kinds of 'general results'. Some sciences produce *laws*, or at least law-like statements, of the format 'When X then Y', or variants of this such as 'When X, your chances of getting Y are Z times as high, at least under conditions P and Q.' At a different level, many social scientists strive for *empirical generalizations* in quantitative form, such as state-ments that describe 'populations' in terms of a limited number of 'variables' and the statistical relations among them. This involves a complex set of methodologi-cal transformations, including the operationalization of those variables in order to measure individual instances in their terms, and the generalization of results based on a representative sample of a population. This corresponds to 'quantitative research' as characterized by Charles Ragin (1994; cf. Chapter 3). He has used two other types to distinguish the diversity of social research. One of these, 'compara-tive research', as he uses the expression, is still different from CA, since it is focused on patterns of differences and similarities of cases, interpreted as 'conditions' and 'consequences'. As I said in Chapter 3, CA fits best in Ragin's typification of 'qual-itative research on the commonalities that exist across a relatively small number of cases' (see also Ten Have, 2004a: 1–13).

Even within the context of qualitative research, however, the ways in which CA deals with 'generality' and 'generalization' are special in certain ways. A quote from

Harvey Sacks' *Lectures* provides a good starting point for an explication of these issues:

> The gross aim of the work I am doing is to see how finely the details of actual, naturally occurring conversation can be subjected to analysis that will yield the technology of conversation.
>
> The idea is to take singular sequences of conversation and tear them apart in such a way as to find rules, techniques, procedures, methods, maxims (a collection of terms that more or less relate to each other and that I use somewhat interchangeably) that can be used to generate the orderly features we find in the conversations we examine. The point is, then, to come back to the singular things we observe in a singular sequence, with some rules that handle those singular features, and also, necessarily, handle lots of other events. (Sacks, 1984b: 411)[2]

I read this as saying two things:

1 The ultimate 'results' of CA are a set of formulated 'rules' or 'principles', which participants are demonstrably oriented to in their natural interactions.
2 The way to arrive at such results is to analyse singular instances, formulate rules, and 'test' these with comparable other instances.

This means that CA is not after 'laws' or 'empirical generalizations', as these concepts are used in standard social science, and neither is it interested in 'relations between variables', 'representative samples', or 'patterns of conditions and consequences'. CA's purpose is *not primarily* to describe empirical patterns of (inter)actions, but rather to get a *theoretical* grasp of interactions' underlying 'rules' and 'principles', or, to repeat an earlier quoted expression, 'the *procedural infrastructure of interaction*' (Schegloff, 1992a: 1338).

As to CA's overall analytic strategy, I have already noted its resemblance to 'analytic induction' (cf. Chapter 3), which, in turn, is in some ways similar to the concept of 'analytic generalization' as defined by Robert Yin (1994) in his book *Case study research*. He contrasts this to 'statistical generalization', 'that is generalizing from a sample to a population or universe'. In 'analytic generalization' each case is related to a 'theory', and any next case, therefore, can be seen as a 'replication' of the previously used theory/case relationship, as is done in an experimental science. He further distinguished 'literal' and 'theoretical' replications: in the first instance, the relationship would be 'similar' (as in testing a hypothesis in terms of verification/falsification); in the second, there would be different relationships, but for theoretically interesting reasons (as in 'deviant case analysis').[3]

The two aspects of Sacks' remarks, as I have read them, are related, in the sense that the analytic strategy fits the analytic 'animal' CA is after. As I remarked in Chapter 3, using Jeff Coulter's (1991) terms, CA tries to explicate the *endogenous logic* of interaction, or, to paraphrase an earlier paper of his (1983), CA's sequential analysis focuses on a priori structures, rather than on contingent ones. The purpose of 'generalization', therefore, is to see whether and how some a priori rule or principle is oriented to by participants in various instances of natural interaction.

Most published treatments of CA methodology (Heritage, 1984a: 244; 1988: 131; 1995: 399; Hutchby & Wooffitt, 1998: 95–8; Peräkylä, 1997: 210–12; Wooffitt, 2005: 61–3; Wootton, 1989: 250) stress the importance of *deviant case analysis* – the detailed analysis of any case that seems to depart from a previously formulated rule or pattern – as an essential part of 'analytic induction' (cf. Chapters 2 and 3). In a paper confronting ethnomethodology and CA, Steven Clayman and Douglas Maynard (1995) discuss deviant case analysis as a continuation, of sorts, of Garfinkel's 'breaching experiments'.[4] The most obvious difference, of course, is that deviant case analysis starts from 'natural' rather than 'experimental' data, but the idea that departures of some sort may be analysed to elucidate standard patterns is similar. Furthermore, for deviant case analysis the 'deviance' is from a pattern that *the analyst* has tried to establish, not necessarily from members' expectations:

> Conversation analysts typically deal with deviant cases in one of three ways, only the first of which is directly related to Garfinkel's approach. First, some deviant cases are shown, upon analysis, to result from interactants' orientation to the same considerations that produce the 'regular' cases. [. . .]
> A second way of handling a deviant case is to replace the initial analysis with a more general formulation that encompasses both the 'regular' cases and the 'departure'. [. . .]
> If these approaches fail, a third option is to produce a separate analysis of the deviant case, one which treats it as bringing about, in effect, an alternate sequential 'reality'. (Clayman & Maynard, 1995: 7–9)

The first type, then, can be used to *reinforce* the earlier analysis directly, by showing the participants' orientation to both the normative basis of the pattern and the excusability or local rationality of the deviation from it. Clayman and Maynard mention cases in which using an utterance recognizable as a 'first pair-part' establishes a 'conditional relevance' for a fitting 'second pair-part', which, if not forthcoming, may lead to excuses, reproaches, accounts, etc., or may be made locally acceptable by starting an insertion sequence. The second type concerns cases that cannot be integrated into the earlier formulation, and therefore forces the analyst to change his or her earlier formulations. This type is explicated by reference to what apparently is the 'standard example' of deviant case analysis, Schegloff's (1968) analysis of telephone openings (cf. Chapter 2). The third option is for the analyst to seek for particular local reasons that may be invoked to account for the deviance. Clayman and Maynard refer to Gail Jefferson and John Lee's (1981) analysis of a 'troubles telling' which may be transformed into a 'service encounter', by reacting to a troubles story with advice, leading to some sort of 'format negotiation'.[5]

Demonstration

Let us now return to some empirical 'demonstrations' in order to put some empirical flesh on these abstract bones. I have already suggested some ways in which the analytic explorations given in Chapter 7 might be used in an analytic elaboration of some of the observations presented there. Let us take the 'pre-sequence' analysis presented in the demonstrations in Chapter 7. Here is the relevant excerpt again:

EXCERPT 8.1, CF. 7.1, DETAIL

```
81   D:   welke ↑klas zit je Liesbeth?
81   D:   which form are you in Liesbeth?
82        (0.8)
83   L:   in de ↑vierde.=
83   L:   in the fourth.=
84   D:   =in de vierde gaat goed?
84   D:   in the fourth going alright?
85        (0.8)
86   L:   ja=
86   L:   yes=
87   D:   =ja?
87   D:   =yes?
88   D:   m- je >kan nou=
88   D:   b- you can(not) now=
89   D:   =je bent nou nat- te moe om te ↑werken of niet een beetje.<
89   D:   =you are now nat- too tired to work or not a bit.
90        (.)
91   D:   soms.
91   D:   sometimes.
92   L:   ↑nee hoor.
92   L:   no.[6]
93   D:   nee?
93   D:   no?
94        (2.6)
95   D:   alleen als je ↑thuiskomt.
95   D:   only when you come home.
96        (.)
97   L:   (°nhee°)
97   L:   n(h)o
```

In line 81, D asks a question which, as I said, is a rather stereotypical question for an adult to ask of a child (*which form are you in Liesbeth?*). When a child is confronted with such a question, he or she does not know whether it is an ordinary question, 'just to make talk', or whether it is a pre-question for which the adult has a specific sequel in mind. It is, in any case, hard to refuse to provide such innocent information. Here, I suggested, it is also used 'for a purpose', to return to medical issues and ask for a confirmation or specification of the complaint description provided earlier by the mother.

How could one try to elaborate such an analysis? One needs at least one or more instances that are similar to it, in one or another way, in the sense that those other instances can be analysed in a similar fashion, or can be seen as exemplifying the same or some related concepts. I happen to remember a case that seems to be similar in a certain way. It is from another consultation, by another physician with an adult patient who suffers from colds and muscle aches. Here is the relevant excerpt:

EXCERPT 8.2

```
43   D:   en waar werk je
43   D:   and where do you work
44   P:   in eh in een bàr?
44   P:   in uh in a bar?
45   (.)
46   D:   en dat doe je nog? of niet
46   D:   and you are still doing that? or not
47   P:   jaa
47   P:   yes
48   D:   en dat dat gaat nog wel je kan nog je werk=
48   D:   and that that's still going you can still (do) your work=
49   P:   =ma- ik ben nou twee dagen vrij dus eh
49   P:   =bu- I have two days off now so uh
50   D:   o:h
51   P:   ten minste gister en vandaag 'hh ma- ben gister expres een
51   P:   at least yesterday and today 'hh bu- stayed yesterday expressly a
```

[lines omitted in which P elaborates on his actions and ideas about the complaints]

```
69   D:   en die verkoudheid? (.) [is dat
69   D:   and that cold? (.) [is that
70   P:                          [ja ik ben nog steeds verkouden maar ik
70   P:                          [yes I still have a cold but I
71   P:   bedoel dat is nou al
71   P:   mean that is now already
72   D:   (hmhm) (.) in welke bar werk je? in welke bar werk je?
72   D:   (hmhm) (.) which bar do you work in? which bar do you work in?
73   P:   Paradiso op de Markt
73   P:   Paradiso on the market
74   D:   ohh (.) ·h als je eventjes dit uitdoet (.) en dan het overhemd
74   D:   ohh (.) ·h if you could take this off (.) and then the shirt
75   D:   e::h (.) omhoog (.) dus dat is dan een drukke: eh toestand hè?
75   D:   uh (.) up (.) so that is then a busy uh situation right?
76   P:   jaa (.) we zijn eigenlijk nooit ziek hè     [(   )
76   P:   yes (.) we are in fact never sick you know [(   )
77   D:                                              [je (mag t'r) nooit ziek zÿn
77   D:                                              [you are not allowed to be
                                                    sick there
78   P:   nee
78   P:   no
79   D:   (hheh)
80        ((7: shuffling sounds))
81   D:   zucht eens diep
81   D:   sigh deeply
```

In line 43 we find the utterance that I propose to analyse as a 'pre-question', *and where do you work*, while in 46, *and you are still doing that? or not*, and 48, *and that that's still going you can still (do) your work*, you get the sequels for which the 'pre' provided the starting point. As it happens, P just had two days off, so D's question as to whether he could still do his work does not exactly fit P's situation. He uses his account, however, to provide the kind of information D was after, that he had stayed in bed, and he adds some more information that proves to be important later in the consultation. During the physical examination, D comes back to the work issue with a subsequent work-related question: *which bar do you work in? which bar do you work in?* (72). This seems to be even less 'medical' and more 'social' than the earlier one, but it does serve as a kind of 'pre' again, as it is followed by a proposed assessment of the workload from D, *so that is then a busy uh situation right?* (75), which is answered by the medically oriented *we are in fact never sick you know* (76), to which D responds with *you are not allowed to be sick there* (77), which P confirms (78). In the end, after a diagnosis and at the suggestion of P, they agree that the complaints might be caused by P's working conditions, the air-conditioning in the bar.

The point, for the moment, is that a question concerning one's routine every-day activities, for children *'which form are you in?'*, for adults *'what kind of work do you do?'*, which in a setting of sociable talk among relative strangers may lead to various types of more detailed sociable talk, may lead, in a medical setting, to explications concerning the relation between the complaints and those activities. Here is another example, from an encounter with an adult woman who consults another GP for a strained muscle in her leg:

EXCERPT 8.3[6]

```
127   D:   en wat eh-=
127   D:   and what uh-=
128   D:   =U ↑werkt gewoon op 't ogenblik?
128   D:   =you are working at the moment?
129        ()
130   P:   nou <ik heb (die) AOZet< dus dokter=
130   P:   well <I have (the) AOZ<[7] so doctor=
131   P:   =ik werk twee ochtenden als be↑aarden↓helpster
131   P:   =I work two mornings as a home help for the elderly
132   P:   [˙hhh
133        [(0.5)
134   P:   maar ↓dat↓ heb helemaal geen ↓punt↑
134   P:   but that's not a point at all
135        (0.5)
136   P:   dach[t ik
136   P:   I thought
137   D:       [gaat dat-=
137   D:       [that goes=
138   D:   =gaat ↑allemaal ↓best.
138   D:   =goes alright.
139        (.)
```

```
140   P:   ↑ja↓:
140   P:   Yes
141        (0.8)
142   P:   i-as ik zit ben'k veel beroerder dan dat as ik loop↑
142   P:   I- as I'm sitting I'm worse off than when I walk.
143        (0.9)
144   D:   na:↑ maar ik bedoel met 't bedden opmaken.
144   D:   (na) but I mean with making beds.
145   D:   want dat moet u ook doen en zo=
145   D:   because you have to do that also and like=
146   D:   =merkt u- merkt u dan niks?=
146   D:   =you don't notice anything then?=
147   P:   =nee
147   P:   =no
148        (.)
149   P:   ↓ja↑ dat is wel een beetje ↑moeilijker
149   P:   yes it is indeed a bit harder
150   P:   maar eh
150   P:   but uh
151   P:   [·hh
152        [(.)
153   P:   ↓nou 't is maar ↓een↓ bed
153   P:   well it's just one bed
154        (0.6)
```

The question about work is a bit different, here. A first try, *and what uh* (127), is cut off and replaced by *you are working at the moment?* (128). The first might have become *and what kind of work do you do?*, but this would presuppose that she has a paid job, while the second version asks whether she does have such a job. This can be seen as a case of self-initiated self-repair by D, leading to a more focused 'category-designed' utterance.

When the type of work is established (131), the ability to do the work is first discussed in general terms, by the patient (134 etc.), and then related to a specific activity by the doctor (144 etc.). In other words, the medical relevance of 'work' is at first brought forward by the patient, initially because she wants to keep working, and later in a more specific, diagnostic sense.

To sum up the preliminary 'results' of this small elaborative exercise, we can now formulate a candidate general *device* for initiating talk between people who do not know each other very well: 'Ask for the other's workaday activities. For children and young adults, this would concern their education, for most adults their paid job.' Within a medical setting, this *general* device can be applied to *specific* professional purposes, and seen to be so used by the recipients.

This summary analysis could be further elaborated using the concepts developed by Harvey Sacks in his work on membership categorization. As I noted before (Chapters 4 and 6), some writers advocate the combination of membership categorization analysis (MCA) with the sequentially oriented conversation analysis. Furthermore, the sensitivity to category-specific expectations that D exhibits in his self-repair may be related to the particular locally and temporary specific 'culture', this recording being made in the 1970s when the participation of married Dutch women in the labour force was rather weak compared with other periods and countries.

We have been looking, then, at three questioning episodes in medical settings. After the first (excerpt 7.1, repeated as excerpt 8.1), I selected the second and the third from the same institutional environment, but also because they seemed to contain a similar *sequential* structure: a pre-sequence enquiring about everyday activities, followed by one or more sequences devoted to queries about the current ability to carry out those activities. Questions *ask* their recipient to provide specific items of information, but they also *require* background information. The pre-sequences about institutionalized everyday activities seemed designed to make certain kinds of background information available, or at least to make it inter-actionally 'present', as a starting point for further medical questioning. But these pre-questions themselves required background knowledge of a more general kind, and at that point the issue of membership categorization came in.

Now, these reflections can be further elaborated by considering a larger set of examples. Since this is not a chapter about 'medical questioning' as such, I will keep both illustrative examples and their analysis to a minimum, but I do want to demonstrate how the co-selection of examples might work in a specific project. While the previous two instances were relevant as demonstrations of *similarity*, the next two provide a *contrast*. Here, then, are two more examples of questioning sequences from a medical setting, in fact from the same consultation that was the source of excerpt 8.1:

EXCERPT 8.4

```
49   M:   en °nou voor half acht is ze d'r ?nooit°=
49   M:   and well before half past seven she's never there
50   D:   =ergens↑ pijn heb je niet hè?
50   D:   you don't have pain somewhere have you?
51        (1.1)
52   D:   ↑hm
53   L:   huh
```

EXCERPT 8.5

```
113       ((6.2: writing))
114  D:   ·hh verder is er ↑niks met je::
114  D:   for the rest there's nothing wrong with you
115       (0.7)
116  D:   Liesbeth.
117       (0.5)
118  D:   verder heb je nergens ↑klachten van,
118  D:   for the rest you have no complaints,
119  D:   nergens ↑pijn,
119  D:   no pain anywhere,
120  D:   ja zo nu en dan wat in je ↑hoofd,
120  D:   yes now and then in your head,
```

```
121        (1.0)
122  D:   maar
122  D:   But-
```

Apart from the fact that a similar question is asked twice, it is remarkable that both questions, *you don't have pain somewhere have you?* (50) and *for the rest there's nothing wrong with you* (114), are *not* directly related to the preceding utterances. The first follows after an extensive description by the mother of her daughter waking up late, while the second is preceded by a long pause during which D is writing. Questions asking for 'any symptom', 'any pain anywhere', etc., can be asked any time, although they tend to be asked as *last-in-a-series*, as an 'any other business' question. Such questions do not require any preparation, such as pre-sequences, apparently, and they are offered as a 'last chance': they suggest that this is the last opportunity to report on the topic. And indeed, after the exchanges represented in excerpt 8.4, D starts to give a preliminary diagnosis, while after the ones in excerpt 8.5, there is some further talk directly linked to the topic, followed by D's invitation to follow him for a blood test.

Comparing the first set of questionings (excerpts 8.1, 8.2, and 8.3) with this last one (8.4 and 8.5), we may tentatively distinguish two broad types: (1) sequences in which specific medically oriented questions are preceded by quite general non-medical pre-questions; and (2) medically oriented questions which are not prepared in any way, and which are formatted in a way that seems 'closing implicative', as 'last in a series'. In a full-blown project, both types could be elaborated much further, and other types could be added to these two, especially questions that are neither prepared nor unconnected, but rather carefully 'tied' to some preceding item produced by the other party. Using larger data sets, one might also investigate when and where such types are used, varying phases of encounters, topics, settings, etc., and what kinds of effects such types have, what kinds of strategic uses are discernible, etc.

For the moment, this limited 'demonstration' should be seen as indicating some ways in which instances can be compared in order to develop an analytic topic in a data-based fashion. The instances were selected in a rather unsystematic manner from a few encounters I happened to have at hand. This selection could serve as a first phase of a process of *theoretical sampling*, taking as a guideline 'similarity' and 'difference' in terms of the evolving analytic topic. An alternative could be firstly to construct a corpus, in this case of GP consultations, and then examine all instances of a rough category such as 'questioning sequences' in the manner of *comprehensive data treatment*. Or, one could firstly develop a topic, like I have demonstrated above, followed by the comprehensive data treatment of the relevant instances in a corpus.

I will now continue the general discussion of analytic elaboration with some special issues, including the use of 'quantitative' analyses and the analysis of visual information on video.

On countability: quantitative CA?

In the preceding demonstration, I have been using a number of concepts to talk about various phenomena, such as 'questions' and 'pre-questions'. I proposed that these phenomena had some essential properties in common with others 'collected' under these rubrics. In so doing, I treated (some) conversational phenomena as being analytically 'collectable' or 'classifiable'. This property of being 'collectable' is, of course, routinely assigned to research objects in many if not most sciences, grounding the various operations that lead to 'results', including 'coding' and 'counting'. The question of whether such operations can be used in CA depends, then, on whether conversational phenomena can be sensibly 'collected' on analytical grounds. My general impression is that most conversation analysts would answer this question affirmatively, but also would add some notes of caution, while non-CA ethnomethodologists would tend to be even more cautious.

As I mentioned before, it is basic to the CA enterprise that order-producing devices are, in principle, 'repeatable', as definable procedures can be 'used again'. CA aims to analyse devices and competencies at a quite general level, available to 'any member', practices that are relatively 'context free', although capable of a delicate 'context sensitivity' (Sacks et al., 1978). Seen from this perspective, it is quite rational that many CA studies are not limited to an extensive discussion of one or a few fragments of talk, but take on the systematic examination of larger collections of instances. When one reads these kinds of studies, one is struck by the very frequent(!) use of various kinds of quantifying expressions, such as 'routinely', 'regularly', 'frequently', 'a substantial number', 'often', 'generally', 'recurrent', 'comparatively rare', 'commonly', 'massively recurrent', or 'absent'. In this way, the discussion of specific instances is given a wider relevance as an exemplary treatment of something that is typical or atypical in some sense. Usually, however, the quantitative information is kept relatively vague: the primary focus is still on the quoted fragments themselves.

Explicit debates of issues of codability and classifiability are rare, however, in the CA literature, and when they occur, it is mostly in discussing less common (within CA) strategies of analytic elaboration, especially statistical or more general aspects of quantitative analysis, and the use of 'qualitative data analysis' programs (or QDA programs, for short).[8] The relation between such elaborations and single case analyses is made very clear by Schegloff, when he writes:

> [. . .] in studying large amounts of data, we are studying *multiples* or *aggregates* of *single instances*. Quantitative analysis is, in this sense, not an alternative to single case analysis, but rather is built on its back. (1993: 102)

In other words, the basic idea is that analysis of aggregates requires a preliminary analysis of single instances, and we have seen that such is not a routine matter. It involves understanding, based on one's membership knowledge, efforts to ground this understanding in the demonstrable reality of the participants, and an explication of the procedures used to bring off the action. Even a small elaboration, like the one 'demonstrated' in the previous section, would require quite an extensive report if done according to 'the rules'. In the usual forms of quantitative analysis, such an elaborate case-by-case accountability is not reinforced, because researchers routinely take recourse to procedures of 'standardization', which are, indeed, accountable in a global rather than a case-by-case manner. This is often done by explicating some manner of 'operationalization' of coding operations.

In contrast to the 'informal' type of CA 'quantification', noted above, there exist a number of studies which, while claiming some sort of relationship to CA, have put their focus on quantification itself, in the sense of presenting their major findings in terms of percentages and tables. The best known examples of this kind of applied CA are a series of studies by Candace West and Don Zimmerman on gender-based differences in interactional behaviour, especially interruption (starting with Zimmerman & West, 1975, already mentioned in Chapter 4). The same approach has been taken by West in her later studies of medical consultations, focusing on interruptions and the distribution of various kinds of questions among participants (West, 1984). In a similar vein, Richard Frankel (1984) has reported research on physicians' use of 'the third turn option', after a patient has answered a question.

What is remarkable about these studies is that, while they do discuss some excerpts qualitatively, they tend to base their counts of instances on specified relatively 'objective' criteria. For example, West provides an 'operational definition' of an interruption, referring to her earlier work with Zimmerman:

> An interruption is an initiation of simultaneous speech which intrudes deeply into the internal structure of a current speaker's utterance; operationally, it is found more than a syllable away from a possibly complete unit-type's boundaries (Zimmerman & West, 1975: 113–15). (West, 1984: 55)

And Frankel uses a similar kind of definition of two types of 'third turn' objects:

> For purposes of analysis, all third turns containing one or more contrast-class terms, e.g. good–bad, right–wrong, true–false, etc. were coded as Evaluation sequences. Similarly, all third turns containing one or more neutral terms were coded as Acknowledgement sequences. (1984: 157)

Although these definitions presuppose some analytic capabilities – to be able to discern unit-type boundaries, for instance – they tend towards the kind of coding instructions one finds in conventional quantitative research. Such an approach implies that the analysis of these kinds of research objects can be specified in such a way that it can be responsibly delegated to a 'clerk' or a 'machine'.

Schegloff (1993) has organized his extensive 'Reflections on quantification in the study of conversation' in terms of three topics, based on the 'simplest statistic' of a proportion that is something happens 'x out of every y times':

> First, quantitative analysis requires an analytically defensible notion of the denominator. I call it 'environments of possible occurrence' or, more explicitly, 'environments of possible *relevant* occurrence.' [. . .] Second, quantitative analysis requires an analytically defensible notion of the numerator, the set of types of occurrences whose presence should count as events and, given an adequate conception of environments of relevant possible occurrence, whose nonoccurrence should count as absences. That requires [. . .] an understanding of what sorts of occurrences or practices are alternatives to one another for the *participants*. Third, quantitative analysis requires an analytically defensible notion of the domain or universe being characterized [. . . i.e.] a warranted conception of analytically coherent universes that it is relevant for a statistic to refer to, because they are relevant organizational domains of activity for the participants in interaction. (103)

In his discussion of the first requirement, concerning the 'denominator', Schegloff concentrates on 'responsive' activities like laughter, items such as 'uh huh', as well as full talk. Whether such an activity is relevantly present or absent cannot be stated without a full analysis of the interaction involved. And, it could be added, it may be that the fitness of a situation for a certain type of response is, in part, constituted by that particular response. In other words, the character of an activity and its environment (a numerator and its denominator) are often 'reflexively related' (cf. Heritage, 1995: 402–3).

When considering the problem of the numerator, we encounter some issues that are 'mirrors' of the ones just discussed. What a simple object like 'uh huh' is doing will depend on its environment. At a point when an introduction to a story is under way, it may work as a 'continuer' (Schegloff, 1982), but just after a joke's punch-line, it seems to be a rather negative act of *not* laughing. Absences, *not* doing something when it would be appropriate, when a 'slot' has been created for that particular 'filler', are indeed very interesting 'occurrences', but parties may take action to avoid specific slots from being created in the first place. And when clear absences can be observed, the interesting thing is quite often not the non-occurrence per se, but how it is oriented to by the participants (for instance, by a reproach, an apology, or whatever; see the earlier discussion of deviant case analysis). All of this requires single case analyses.

The third issue concerns the 'domain' of the data and the analytic claims. For Schegloff, the important thing is that various kinds of talk-in-interaction are organized differently: 'the adequacy of findings therefore derives not only from the correctness of their substantive claims but from the bounding of the domain for which they are asserted' (1993: 110). He mentions as examples 'ordinary conversation, interviews, meetings, and courtroom proceedings'. Focusing on 'interviews' as an example, he makes it clear that particular distributional findings based on interview talk should not be generalized to 'discourse', or talk-in-interaction in general. And he continues to argue for even finer distinctions, such as a variety of types of interviews. What matters ultimately is what is being done in an interview, or rather the 'questioning' of one by another. One should, therefore, 'situate' any findings in a particular domain,

> a domain bounded and informed by our understanding of how those producing the talk-in-interaction understand the context they are in, the context that they *constitute* by employing its *practices* in the production and appreciation of their conduct. (114)

As Schegloff remarks, 'quantification is no substitute for analysis' (114), and his reflections lead him to the conclusion that, 'with some exceptions', quantification is, for the study of talk-in-interaction, 'premature'. One would need to have a rather extensive analytic knowledge of a phenomenon, and it would need to be well defined and relatively simple, occurring in well-structured environments, and limited to a relevantly bounded domain, before one could consider a sensible quantification. But then, one would need to specify what the 'distinctive pay-offs' of quantitative analysis might be, for example in the context of systematic comparisons:

It *may* turn out that there is nothing both distinctive and defensible to be gained from quantitative studies of talk-in-interaction. Should that happen, we *could* face a curious irony [...]. In contrast to much of the subject matter of the social sciences – which has been taken to be fundamentally *in*determinate at the level of the individual occurrences and orderly only at the aggregate statistical level – conduct in talk-in-interaction *could* then appear to be demonstrably orderly *at the level of the singular occurrence only* and, in effect, *not* orderly in any distinctive, relevant, or precisely determinate way in the aggregate. (117)

While the general tone of Schegloff's 'reflections', then, is one of extreme cautiousness, John Heritage (1995: 404), who is also calling for cautiousness, seems to be a bit more positive in this regard. He does suggest a few possibilities for a sensible use of statistics in CA:

1   'as a means of isolating "interesting phenomena"';
2   'as a means of consolidating intuitions which are well defined, but where the existence of a practice is difficult to secure without a large number of cases';
3   in 'cases in which independent findings about a conversational practice can have indirect statistical support'; and
4   finally, 'in almost all cases where a claim is made that the use or outcome of a particular interactional practice is tied to particular social or psychological categories, such as gender, status, etc., statistical support will be necessary'.[9]

In a future-oriented essay, called 'CA at century's end: practices of talk-in-interaction, their distributions and their outcomes', Heritage continues these expectations in the following terms:

Some [...] new research questions will arise because of the current success of CA in generating empirically grounded findings that will support quantitative analysis. The accumulation of these findings makes it increasingly likely that questions about the *distribution* of interactional practices can be asked with some likelihood of success. Granted that particular interactional practices are available to be deployed, who deploys them, when and where? Such questions can be meaningfully raised for data where environments are broadly standardized, and participants have choices among actions which are analytically well understood (Schegloff 1993). (Heritage, 1999: 70-1)

He discusses a number of examples, including some of his own work such as a study of audience reactions to various rhetorical figures (Heritage & Greatbatch, 1986) and one investigating changes in journalists' questioning practices during presidential press conferences (later published as Clayman & Heritage, 2002b), as well as studies by others. He mentions Anna Guthrie's (1997) study of academic advising sessions, which examined students' use of different acknowledgement tokens in a variety of analytically definable points in advisors' utterances, and a study by Elisabeth Boyd (1998) of interactional processes involved in surgery authorizations for an insurance company, in which particular kinds of openings could be demonstrated to be related to particular decisional outcomes.

So while both Schegloff and Heritage urge conversation analysts to be cautious in using quantification, the latter is much more optimistic regarding present and future possibilities. If you consider using quantification in a CA context, careful study of Schegloff's (1993) paper is to be recommended, as well as consulting some of the examples mentioned by Heritage, and some published after his essays, such as Anssi Peräkylä (2006) and Tanya Stivers (2002; 2005), which are very sensitive to the problems of quantification.

The case for case-by-case analysis

To sum up my arguments in this chapter, for a serious analysis in the tradition of CA, there is no escape from a careful and sensitive *case-by-case* analysis. Each case should be considered in detail, in order to make an accountable decision that it is indeed a case of the phenomenon one is looking for, as a *specimen* of, say, a 'questioning initiative' or a 'pre-sequence', in its context, and for the participants. Analysing cases, one after the other, could lead one to make distinctions of types within the overall class, as I have in distinguishing 'prepared questions' from those that have an 'anything else?' character. These types might be related to various aspects of the situation in which the specimens were produced, such as sequential environments or functioning as available from their uptake. Any rule or pattern or device that is tentatively formulated should then be confronted with more cases, and if one encounters any deviant cases, these should be accorded special analytic attention.

These are formidable requirements, but they should be taken seriously, even by a beginning researcher. CA is a cumulative enterprise, and all contributions are welcome, even small ones. In order to be able to make such contributions, it might be a better learning strategy to study relatively *few* cases intensely than to throw oneself into the analysis of *large* collections. Such a careful learning strategy should be complemented by extensive reading of the CA literature, both in a general fashion and focused on your particular topic or theme. This should contribute to what Glaser and Strauss (1967: 46) have called *theoretical sensitivity*, the ability to see things with an analytic eye – and CA has a rather special eye, of course. But remember my earlier warnings, towards the end of Chapter 3, against any 'mechanistic', thoughtless application of established CA concepts. Any coding should be seen as 'accountable' and should be done in a 'responsible' manner.

The CA literature offers many examples of good collection studies in which each case is carefully considered on its own, as well as a specimen for its category or type (see the recommended reading list).

An illustration

As a final *illustration* of working with a collection of cases, I will give a rough sketch of the structure of one of these by Schegloff (1996b), called 'Confirming allusions: towards an empirical account of action'. It starts with some theoretical and methodological sections, which are extremely useful and clear, and therefore highly recommended. (I discussed some of these ideas in the first section of the previous chapter.)

The paper's empirical argument starts with two 'initial noticings and a puzzle'. The noticings concerned two moments in a long conversation in which one speaker repeats a previous utterance by the other and thereby seems to demonstrate some sort of agreement:

> The initial puzzle was, Is something special going on here? What are these repeats doing? Put more precisely, what (if anything) are these repeats being distinctively used to do when employed as the means for agreeing or confirming? (1996b: 175)

Schegloff notes that there are other, more common ways in which an agreement can be done, so the question becomes focused on what this particular type of agreement is doing, besides agreeing. In order to investigate this issue, Schegloff has collected a large number of cases of repeats, which he has then narrowed down by eliminating cases that were relevantly different from the two with which he started. He describes seven different features that he has used in this 'purification':

> From a quite broad collection of repeated utterances, we have progressively focused our attention to those that are repeated, *virtually identically*, in *next turn*, by *recipients of the first saying*, with the repeat embodying a *second* or *third* position in its sequence. We are looking at repeats that are doing agreement. The repeats either are all of what is in the turn or *are the first thing* in the turn. [. . .] The (final) feature is that the speaker of the initial saying, in saying it, is offering a candidate observation, interpretation, or understanding of the *recipient's* circumstances, current or past. (180)

It is this last feature that gives the repeats the character of a confirmation, as a more specific type of agreement.

Having in the process offered a kind of definition of the phenomenon, Schegloff now presents a 'candidate solution' to the earlier 'puzzle'. He suggests that the repeat not only confirms the *sense* of the first saying, but also 'that that sense *had* been "alluded to," *had* been conveyed without being said. The repeat confirms the allusion, and confirms it *as* an allusion' (181). This 'solution' is explicated using one of the primary cases, and another one in which the latter part of this reading is made explicit by the participants.

Schegloff's next step is to 'explore the practice in diverse contexts', for which he uses a number of instances from the purified 'core collection'. Firstly he examines three that seem to confirm the earlier reading, then he discusses a 'less transparent instance', and finally some in which the practice is avoided or does not occur (although it might have). It should be noted that each of these instances is analysed in detail, although the discussion is framed in terms of the larger argument.

Having 'established' the practice, so to speak, Schegloff now offers a sketch of 'the fit between the practice and the action' (199), contrasting repeating one's own previous utterance with repeating another's formulation of what one has said (implied) before. In this sketch, three other cases are analysed. It is by *not* repeating one's own previous implicit saying, *but* the other's explication, that the previous inexplicitness is confirmed.

While most of the instances analysed so far have been taken from situations that might be called 'conversational', from talk between intimates, in a next section, called 'Provenance', Schegloff demonstrates that the practice can be encountered in a wide variety of settings that would be seen as rather different in common-sense terms, such as a case conference in a university hospital, an editorial conference at a newspaper's office, a court session, and a farmers' market. Schegloff remarks:

> These episodes from work settings, ranging from the informality of an open market to the formality of a court of law in session, underscore the robustness of the practice of confirming allusions across social and interactional contexts and across compositional features of the participants. Here, at least, the interactional phenomenon does not appear to vary across 'contexts' as conventionally understood. It appears then that not everything must. (208)

In his 'Concluding considerations', Schegloff remarks that, before this analysis, he had 'not the slightest idea that there *was* such a function, such an action, such a practice' (210) as the one he discovered as being part of 'the culture's repertoire'. There is, apparently, no established word for it, it is not explicitly recognized as such, but still it can be demonstrated, as Schegloff has done, that it is being used, not very frequently, but across a wide range of circumstances. Take this as an encouragement: it is still possible to make discoveries; there's gold in the dust waiting for you.

A general strategy for data elaboration

In the previous chapter, I formulated a general strategy for data exploration as a possible synthesis of the proposals for an analytic strategy for CA. That strategy was focused on single case analyses, so now it is time to formulate a more encompassing strategy that covers collection studies as well.

As a first phase, I propose the following:

- Try to use a substantial *corpus* of data which, while relevant for the purpose at hand, has not been pre-selected with any particular notion, expectation or hypothesis in mind. Except for projects which are targeted at phenomena that have a principled structural 'place' within the temporal development of an encounter, try to work with complete, start-to-finish recordings of the events to be investigated.
- In general, try to make complete and detailed *transcriptions* of the recordings. Again, whether this is sensible will depend on the character, frequency, and distribution of the phenomena of interest. Making detailed transcriptions first, and working with simplified versions for specific purposes, is quite often recommended because it makes these details available for unforeseen and unforeseeable analytic benefits, while working up simple transcripts later might bias the transcriptions.

Then, the idea is to start with a single case analysis, for which I repeat the suggestions given in the previous chapter:

- Starting with an arbitrarily or purposively selected part of the transcribed data, work through the transcript in terms of a restricted set of analytically distinguished but interlocking 'organizations'. For this purpose I propose the following four: *turn-taking organization*; *sequence organization*; *repair organization*; and *the organization of turn-design.* This 'work-through' involves a turn-by-turn consideration of the data in terms of practices relevant to these essential organizations, such as taking a turn in a specific way, initiating a sequence, forgoing taking up an issue, etc. In other words, the task is to specify practice/action couplings as these are available in the data, where the actions are as far as possible formulated in terms of the four organizations.

- In actual research, this may be done in a variety of practical formats, as *remarks* written on a printed transcript, as 'analytic descriptions', or as *codes* and *observations* added in a separate column to the transcript, or by using specialized computer software such as Transana (see the relevant section in Chapter 6, pages 112–13).
- On the basis of this process, try to formulate some *general* observations, statements, or rules that tentatively summarize what has been seen. When a particular interest or phenomenon has emerged, focus on it, but keep it in context in terms of these four organizations.

And, after that, extend the analysis, using more instances, for which I give the following summary suggestions:

- After this analytic summary, select *another* piece of data, and work through that piece of data again in terms of the four organizations. Mark the observations you make in terms of their fit with the tentative summary. When this is done, revise the summary as required to make it fit with both the old and the new data. Repeat this with subsequent parts of the data until you have processed the complete corpus.
- Now you can *rework* the summary as it has been revised again and again in terms of its generality of data coverage. You may need to distinguish types, alternative solutions, etc. Try to construct a formulation that covers the general findings, the variation of types, and the deviant cases. Explore the structural bases for the variations and the deviations in terms of the functionality of the basic model.

Take this 'model' as a set of suggestions, to be adapted to your local purposes and possibilities.

Notes on the analysis of visual data

In the previous sections of this chapter, I have discussed ways to extend an analysis of a single case by looking at other cases, to 'broaden' the analysis, so to speak. In this section I will present some notes on another kind of elaboration, one going beyond an audio-based analysis to include visual aspects available through video recording.

As noted before, CA emerged as an approach to the analysis of *audio*-recorded interactions. As far as these were recordings of telephone conversations, this was not problematic, but for face-to-face interactions such an analysis was (and is) essentially incomplete, although not without value. It was only later that many researchers in CA turned to the analysis of video recordings. But even then the visual aspect of the interaction is often not targeted in a systematic way. This is not just accidental neglect, I think, but a reflection of the inherent difficulty of a visually oriented interaction analysis. Just think of the various visually available features of the participants' activity in an interaction: facial expressions, gaze direction, gestures, the orientation of various body parts, and various manual activities, like writing or typing. Furthermore, these possibly relevant features may change from moment to moment. I used earlier the metaphor of an interactional stream, which seems particularly apt to characterize visual aspects of interaction. As members of a writing culture, we have the ability to parse talk into separate units which we call words, sentences, and larger discursive units, such as 'a story'. But there do not seem to be equivalent 'units' in facial expressions, gazing, or even gesturing. These are rather continuously changing. Furthermore, there does not seem to be an established semantics or descriptive apparatus of such visual signs. In short, it is even harder to develop a systematic analysis of visual aspects of face-to-face interaction that proved to be the case for talk-in-interaction per se.

Because of these conditions, interaction analysis focused on visual features is even more contextual than that analysis of vocally realized actions. And the most tangible ones, gaze and gesture, have been most fruitfully subjected to analysis. As noted in Chapter 6 on transcription, the established practice among visually oriented CA has been to take vocalizations as a descriptive baseline to which characterizations of visuals can be selectively added. This is also characteristic of analysis: the analysis of talk tends to come first, and consideration of visually available details comes afterwards.

As noted throughout the CA literature, talk is considered as (inter)action, and, of course, the same stance can be taken towards body movements. As Christian Heath writes:

> As with utterances and talk, human movement performs social action and activity. A movement, whether a gesture or postural shift, a nod, or a look, may be used to accomplish particular tasks in face-to-face interaction. Movement performs 'locally' and gains its significance through its coordination within the moment-by-moment progression of action or activity, be it vocal, visual, or a combination of both. Moreover, there is no reason a priori to assume that doing things visually rather than through speech will be limited to particular types of action or activity, or certain forms of nonvocal behaviour. Rather, as with utterances and talk, it may be fruitful, at least in principle, to consider how the immense variety of movement found in face-to-face interaction may perform social actions and activities. (1986: 10)

Stressing the differences, as I have done above, should not blind us to the similarities between talk-as-action and visually available activities. Both similarities and differences make it extra worthwhile and challenging to investigate how vocal and visual activities go together, at times at odds with each other or mutually informing.

Because of these conditions, especially the less 'established' and varied form of visual analysis, it does not seem to make sense to propose a detailed 'recipe' for visual analysis, like the ones I proposed for talk. Each researcher will have to find his or her way towards a contextually relevant analysis. What repays the effort, however, is to study the analyses produced by one of the most prolific researchers in this area, namely Charles Goodwin, who was the first to explore systematically visual aspects of face-to-face interactions from a CA point of view. Let me, as a starting point for exploring that work, just point to some of his insights and findings.

On numerous occasions Charles Goodwin has shown intricate connections between the ways in which people speak and visually available features of their conduct. For example, 'A speaker can request the gaze of a recipient by producing a phrasal break, such as a restart or a pause, in his utterance. After such a phrasal break non-gazing recipients regularly bring their gaze to the speaker, (1979: 106; see also 1980; 1981: 55–94; 2000b). He links this finding to Schegloff's notion of a summons–answer sequence (1968; cf. Chapter 2, pages 16–17), suggesting that the break works as a summons, with the recipient's gaze as the sought answer. The point of these as well as a lot of other observations is that in face-to-face interaction the activity stream is not limited to just the talking, but at the same time involves a range of bodily enactments. In a paper on story-telling, for instance, Goodwin offers the following description of the teller of a little story:

> For the telling a distinctive body posture is adopted. Ann clasps her hands together, places both elbows on the table, and leans forward while gazing toward her addressed recipient, Beth. With this posture the speaker displays full orientation toward her addressed recipient, complete engagement in the telling of her story, and lack of involvement in any activities other than conversation. The posture appears to mark the production of a focused, extended turn at talk, that is, to constitute a visual display that a telling is in progress.
>
> Support for this possibility is provided by the sequential placement of the teller's position and by its contrast with the position of the speaker's body before and after this turn. (1984: 228)

In these ways, Ann displays her engagement in the telling, while the others present display their involvement in listening as well as in other activities such as eating.

In later work, partly in collaboration with Marjorie Goodwin, he has extended the scope of his work in different ways. He has enlarged both his conceptual perspective beyond CA's core set of sequential analysis and extended the range of investigated settings beyond informal conversation. While still taking talk-in-interaction as his core interest, the inclusion of visual information has apparently stimulated Goodwin to use more semiotic concepts like 'participation framework' and 'graphic fields', which go beyond the established notions of the CA tradition. In one of his later, theoretically oriented papers, he writes, for instance:

> the construction of action through talk within situated interaction is accomplished through the temporary unfolding juxtaposition of quite different kinds of semiotic resources, and that moreover, through this process, the human body is made visible as the site for a range of structurally different kinds of displays implicated in the constitution of the actions of the moment. (2000b: 1492)

Among the settings investigated in his later work we find children's playing on the street using Marjorie Goodwin's data, an airport operations room as part of a project initiated by Lucy Suchman, scientific fieldwork in archaeology and on a ship, and informal interaction with a man suffering from severe aphasia due to a stroke (cf. Chapter 10). In these ways, Charles Goodwin can be seen to use a video-enhanced CA to develop a general anthropology of human action and communication.

The second major figure in video-based CA, Christian Heath, has travelled a partly different path. In a first phase of his career he did an intensive study of doctor–patient interaction, using video as well as ethnographic observation, on which he reported in many papers and a book (1986). Later he went on to initiate a huge series of studies, using video and ethnography, of workplace interactions, again published as a series of papers and a book (Heath & Luff, 2000). A persistent focus of these studies was the local organization of work in 'technologically dense' working environments. Much of this later work was done in collaboration in teams with co-workers such as Jon Hindmarsh and Paul Luff. I will discuss some aspects of these studies in later chapters of this book. I will again present some short vignettes of findings and analytic suggestions to give an impression of the approach taken.

In short, it can be suggested that a video-based analysis of interaction might consist of two (related and to-be-related) parts:

1 sequential analysis of the talk, starting from a base sequence, with pre-sequences and/or post-sequences (cf. Schegloff, 2007a) or alternative sequential formats, such as stories;
2 visual analysis focused on 'alignment displays' (or 'involvement displays') such as gaze and body posture, plus gestures, and – when relevant – the coordination of multiple activities and involvements.

The challenge would be to show that and how these 'levels' are related in the interaction.

Up until now, I have presented CA as a project of individual workers, or teams, responsive, and responsible, to the data and the CA community. In the next chapters, I will widen my focus in diverse ways: firstly, in terms of various forms of the 'application' of CA, embedding CA within 'wider' disciplinary or practical concerns; and, secondly, in terms of making findings 'public', in various ways.

EXERCISE

Elaborate your previously analysed excerpt(s) using *new* data and taking some of the suggestions of this chapter into account. Write a report on these elaborations, and add some methodological reflections in terms of the arguments of this and the previous chapter.

The idea is, of course, to continue on the track started with the previous exercise. For the collective options, you might start again with one or more data sessions, and then continue working with the same sub-group as in the previous exercise, working collectively on the elaboration of a theme or candidate phenomenon

RECOMMENDED READING

There are not too many publications that deal with elaborating analysis, as discussed in this chapter. Therefore, I mention some publications that have been recommended already, and that you might want to read with this chapter, if you have not chosen these at an earlier occasion. I also mention the papers by Schegloff and Heritage on 'quantification' and I give a list of 'exemplary' collection studies, followed by some on visual analysis:

On CA methodology: see Heritage (1995); Psathas (1990b), already mentioned for Chapter 1; and Peräkylä (1997; 2004a), for Chapter 3; also Clayman and Maynard (1995).
On CA and quantification: Heritage (1999); Schegloff (1993).
    For exemplary studies using 'collections': see Button (1990); Heritage (1984b); Jefferson (1985a; 1990), mentioned as recommended for Chapter 2; and Pomerantz (1984); Sacks et al. (1978); Schegloff et al. (1977), for Chapter 7. Also Maynard (1997); Schegloff (1992a; 1996b).
On analysis of visual aspects of interaction, most of the publications by Charles Goodwin and Christian Heath are very instructive. For general introductions see Goodwin (2000b) and Heath (1997; 2004).

Notes

1. Glaser and Strauss's conception of research purposes in general, and 'theory' in particular, is rather different, of course, from the one underlying CA, but I do think their strategy of data treatment offers some nice suggestions for CA (cf. my discussion in Ten Have, 2004a: 135–50). The following quotes and paraphrases should be read with those differences in mind.
2. Cf. Sacks (1992b: 339) for a variant version.
3. Since Yin's conception of 'theory' is rather different from the one used in my consideration of CA, I have adapted his terminology to my present purposes.
4. As reported in Garfinkel (1967: chaps 2–3), and discussed in Heritage (1984a: chap. 4) and Ten Have (2004a: 38–41).
5. My formulations in this paragraph are partly based on Peräkylä's (1997) discussions of these options.
6. Transcription by Chriss Driessen and Heidie van Mierlo.
7. This refers to a local health insurance company.
8. On 'quantification' in CA, see Ten Have (1990), Heritage (1995: 402–6; 1999) and Schegloff (1993).
9. Heritage (1995: 404–6); this last option would be a case of 'applied CA', cf. Chapter 9.

Part 4

Applied CA

9

Applied CA: Institutional Interaction

Contents

In the preceding chapters, I have discussed various methodological and practical aspects of CA as a separate research discipline, focused on the procedural study of talk-in-interaction. I have used the expression 'pure CA' for such an enterprise 'in itself' and 'for itself'. This can be contrasted with 'applied CA', which involves CA-like practices which are carried out within a framework guided by different, let us say 'wider', concerns. These may include, on the one hand, those of various 'neighbouring' scientific disciplines like sociology, anthropology, (social) psychology, and (socio)linguistics, and, on the other hand, those of people who have a practical, moral, and/or political interest in the practices studied, in terms of the situations, organizations, and/or institutions that are co-constituted by those practices. In the present chapter, and the next one, I will sketch some of the problems and possibilities of 'applied CA', but I will not provide extensive instructions for 'doing applied CA' since that would extend the limits of this book much too far. The general tone of my remarks will be one of cautiousness. In the present chapter, I will focus my discussion on what is generally called 'institutional interaction', and more specifically on interviews and similar kinds of encounters involving, on the one hand, one or more institutional agents or professionals, and, on the other, one or more clients or in any case laypersons. In the next chapter, the focus broadens to a wider range of issues, including the application of CA for practical purposes, in some peculiar circumstances, and in the service of some more conventional disciplinary interests.

CA – 'pure' and 'applied'

CA was originally developed as a 'pure' science, motivated by the wish to discover basic and general aspects of sociality. Later, it was also 'applied', in the sense that interactions with an institutional purpose were studied in order to discover how those interactions were organized *as* institutional interactions. The expression 'applied CA' can also be used to denote the implicit or even explicit use of CA-inspired studies to support efforts to make social life 'better' in some way, to provide data-based analytic suggestions for, or critiques of, the ways in which social life can be organized (see Chapter 4).

I have kept my focus on 'pure CA' in the previous chapters for a number of reasons, the primary one being that for an introduction to the practices of CA, it seemed better to restrict our attention to *basic* operations of research. The contrast pure/applied might be thought to be based on whether one studies 'ordinary conversation' or 'institutional interaction'. I would like to stress, however, as I have done before, that 'pure CA' can be used to study *any* kind of talk-in-interaction, whatever its context or purpose. This has been clear from the very beginning of CA, as the studies discussed in Chapter 2 exemplified. Similarly, I have, in my earlier illustrative explorations in Chapters 7 and 8, used excerpts from a medical consultation to explicate some possibilities of CA per se, whatever its setting. In so doing, I have *not* ignored the obvious fact that there were patients and physicians talking with each other, but I have not given that fact a prominent place in my analysis.

It is important, of course, for a discussion of 'applied CA' to reflect on the character of 'ordinary conversation' versus 'institutional interaction', and on the variations between various kinds of 'institutional interaction' as well. I will summarize a proposal by John Heritage (1997; 2004) for *using* CA for the study of institutions. In a subsequent discussion and a brief 'demonstration', I will in particular focus on a theme that plays a central role in these considerations, namely 'questioning'. And finally I will discuss some aspects of various other 'applications' of CA.

'Conversation' versus 'institutional interaction'

One of the first, and most influential, discussions of the character of 'conversation', as compared with other forms of talk-in-interaction, can be found towards the end of the famous *turn-taking* paper by Sacks et al.[1] As I wrote earlier:

> This 'system' of conversational turn-taking has a number of interesting properties, including that it is 'locally managed', as well as 'interactionally managed' or 'party-administered'. This means that the system works 'again and again' at each next possible completion point, after the production of each TCU, and that this management is an interactional one, involving all the parties in the interaction'. (page 128)

In the paper, the authors argue that this particular system is but one in a *range* of turn-taking systems, although they suggest it is the 'basic' one (Sacks et al., 1978: 47).

Under the heading 'The place of conversation among the speech-exchange systems', the authors open up a large field for 'a sort of comparative investigation of the speech-exchange systems available to members of the same society, conceived of in terms of differential turn-taking systems', at least those that preserve the *one party talks at a time* feature. They claim to have 'barely been looking into' those other systems, but they do offer some interesting overall observations, suggesting that they might be 'linearly arrayed':

> The linear array is one in which one polar type (which conversation instances) involves 'one turn at a time allocation'; that is, the use of local allocational means, and the other pole (which debates instance) involves 'preallocation of all turns,' and medial types (which meetings instance) involve various mixes of preallocational and local allocational means. (46)

Finally, they remark:

> While we have referred to conversation as 'one polar extreme' on the linear array, and 'ceremony' as possibly the other pole, we should not be understood thereby to be proposing the independent, or equal status of conversation and ceremony as polar types. For it appears likely that conversation should be considered the basic form of speech-exchange system, with other systems on the array representing a variety of transformations on conversation's turn-taking system to achieve other types of turn-taking systems. In this light, debate or ceremony would not be an independent polar type, but rather the most extreme transformation of conversation, most extreme in fully fixing the most important, and perhaps nearly all, of the parameters that conversation allows to vary. (47)

By so forcefully arguing for the 'original' status of informal conversation and by showing how some of its most important features could be analysed in a systematic and empirical fashion, this paper can be seen as an 'invitation', so to speak, to start a *comparative* investigation of speech-exchange systems. This has been taken up now and then, although largely with a broader focus than just turn-taking, and including the setting-specific use of sequencing, as in questioning (cf. Atkinson & Drew, 1979: 34–81; Greatbatch, 1988; McHoul, 1978; Peräkylä, 1995: 37–102). The general idea is that for some institutional systems, there is a pre-established system of *turn allocation*, and quite often turn-*type* allocation:

> In debates, for example, the ordering of all turns is preallocated, by formula, by reference to 'pro' and 'con' positions. In contrast to both debates and conversation, meetings that have a chairperson partially preallocate turns, and provide for the allocation of unallocated turns via the use of the preallocated turns. Thus, the chairperson has rights to talk first, and to talk after each other speaker, and can use each such turn to allocate next speakership. (Sacks et al., 1978: 45)

From the late 1970s onwards, a large number of CA-inspired investigators have taken up the challenge to study a variety of institution-based interactional forms, implicitly or explicitly comparing these with those found in 'ordinary conversation'. Quite often, the underlying idea was that institutional forms could be seen as being more *restricted* than those found in conversation, in the sense of having one or more kinds of actions, forms, or sequences that could be observed in conversation excluded from the specific institution's repertoire, or from a particular type of party's expected or tolerated range of available options. The 'asymmetrical' distribution of questions and answers, which I will discuss at greater length later in this chapter, is but one example of such a 'restriction' (cf. Atkinson, 1982; Atkinson & Drew, 1979; Drew & Heritage, 1992a; Drew & Sorjonen, 1997; Heritage, 1984a; and for a broad overview, Arminen, 2005).

Within the debates that accompany these studies, there are two broad issues which I will summarize in their most general terms as follows:

1   The first issue has to do with the overall moral or political responsibility for the 'restrictions' observable in institutional interaction. A number of people tend to blame the institutional arrangements, or the agents embodying them, for these restrictions, characterizing them as limiting clients' freedom of expression. This seems to be typical for people 'using CA' for critical purposes, rather than for those who are oriented to CA as a discipline in itself. The 'critical' tendency can be observed especially in the writing of feminist studies of doctor–patient interaction, as in studies by Davis (1988), Fisher (1986), or Todd (1989), but it is not restricted to it, as can be seen in a study by Mishler (1984). CA researchers, on the other hand, tend to refrain from such judgements or suggest that such properties of institutional interaction formats are 'functional' in one way or another.

2   The second issue concerns the generality of such institutional properties. Many CA researchers working on institutional data tend to view these as ways in which institutional participants 'talk the institution into being', to use an expression by John Heritage (1984a: 290). Institutional talk *as* institutional action is seen to be constitutive *of* institutional settings and identities. A contrastive point is made by some ethnomethodologists, including David Francis, Stephen Hester, and Michael Lynch, who object to this view, calling it 'foundational', and saying that focusing on interaction within institutional settings as the application of general 'conversational' devices tends to ignore the specifics of local professional 'work' (see the overview of ethnomethodological critiques in Chapter 4, pages 47–50, and on this particular issue Hester & Francis, 2001).

For my present purposes, I will mostly take an agnostic position as regards these various claims and suggestions. I think it is useful to look at both the constitutive and the restrictive aspects of institutional interaction, while I agree that describing the local competence needed for work *in situ* is a primary requirement (cf. Ten Have, 1990; 1991b; 1995b). The crucial point in all this seems to be where one locates the 'centre of gravity' for understanding interactional phenomena: in the local interaction and its procedural infrastructure itself, in the general institutional arrangements, or in the institutionalized power of one category of participants over another (cf. Schegloff, 1991; 1992b; 1997; Wilson, 1991).

As emphasized by Paul Drew and John Heritage, in their overview of analyses of institutional interaction, CA studies activities as interactional products and takes a dynamic view of context, both the local context of consecutive utterances and the larger context of institutional frameworks (1992a: 16–19).[2] They seem to endorse the 'second' position, summarized above, and note:

A clear implication is that comparative analysis that treats institutional interaction in contrast to normal and/or normative procedures of interaction in ordinary conversation will present at least one important avenue of theoretical and empirical advance. (19)

Such a comparative approach is not as simple and straightforward as one might wish, however, since:

CA researchers cannot take 'context' for granted nor may they treat it as determined in advance and independent of the participants' own activities. Instead, 'context' and identity have to be treated as inherently locally produced, incrementally developed and, by extension, as transformable at any moment. (21)

Against this background, CA studies of institutional interactions will not produce hard and fast distinctions between the institutional and the non-institutional realms. Rather, not much more than a set of 'family resemblances among cases of institutional talk' (21) is to be expected.

Drew and Heritage (1992a: 21–5) elaborate three themes that have emerged from such efforts: (1) institutional talk is goal oriented in institutionally relevant ways; (2) it often involves 'special and particular constraints' on 'allowable contributions to the business at hand'; and (3) it may be 'associated with inferential frameworks and procedures that are peculiar to specific institutional contexts' (22). In other words, participants in such interactions assume and demonstrate their overall 'instrumental' orientation, leading to specific withholdings, and also, as Drew and Heritage note, positive preferences or allowances, while at the same time providing specific interpretive frames to account for such 'departures' from conversational practice.[3]

Turn-taking, questioning, and 'control'

I will now discuss one particular aspect of institutional interaction, which has probably been most consistently in focus in CA studies in this field: agents questioning clients. Let us return to the idea that there is, in many situations, a pre-established system of *turn allocation*, and quite often turn-*type* allocation.

Drew and Heritage summarize the findings of a number of studies of relatively 'formal' kinds of institutional interaction, including courtroom interaction, formal teaching, news interviews, and mediation, as follows:

All of these studies focus on turn-taking systems which, in their different ways, are organized through the preallocation [...] of questions and answers – most often to the institutional and lay persons respectively. (1992a: 39)

One frequently noted upshot of such a pre-allocation is that because the questioner has a pre-given *right* to a questioning turn, he or she can easily build a rather long, multi-TCU turn, until a recognizable 'question' is finally produced. The questioned, on the other hand, runs the *risk* of being interrupted as soon as a minimally adequate 'answering' component has been uttered. This demonstrates that turn allocation and turn-type allocation are intimately related, but other aspects of interactional organization also need to be taken into account.

It is an empirical fact that many if not most interactions between institutional agents and the laypersons with whom they talk have, at least for an important part of the encounter, the overall organizational character of a questioning. The analytically important point, however, is whether this empirically obvious division of interactional labour is an effect of an *institutional* pre-allocation of questioning rights and answering duties, or whether it is implied in general *sequential* properties of activity organization, irrespective of the institutional embeddedness of such an activity. This issue is discussed by Schegloff (1991) in his 'Reflections on talk and social structure' under the heading of 'Social structure or conversational structure?' The 'balance' between a 'focus on social structure' and a 'focus on conversational structure in studying talk-in-interaction' could be 'complementary', but 'they can also be alternatives in a more competitive sense':

> Each makes its own claims in organizing observation and analysis of the data, and one can preempt the other. In particular, the more familiar concerns with social structure can preempt new findings about conversational phenomena. (57)

It was such a fear of pre-emptive glossing of interactional phenomena in institutional terms that motivated my earlier 'pure' treatment of doctor–patient interactions. The distributional fact that doctors ask patients more questions than patients ask doctors can be discussed in institutional terms, as an aspect of 'professional dominance' for instance, but it can also be analysed in terms of the overall sequential organization of the encounter. Such an encounter ordinarily starts from a request for assistance, for a professional diagnosis and/or treatment, which requires additional information before it can be given. This information can be acquired in various ways, including questioning. In other words, the sequential structure of such encounters tends to consist of a request/service pair, with *a series of insertion sequences* between the two parts of the pair. This structure is evident not only in medical consultations (Ten Have, 1989; 2006), but also in other kinds of service encounters, such as calls for police assistance (Wilson, 1991; Zimmerman & Boden, 1991), and even in non-institutional situations when one party asks a complicated service of another (cf. Schegloff, 1991: 59). It is a fact, of course, that service requests and their disposal in interaction tend to occur mostly in specialized institutional settings. So it is the institutional specialization of *activities*, rather than the conventional institutional *format* like questioning, that is the crucial point here (cf. Wilson, 1991: 37–9). The questioning of patients by doctors, or of callers by complaint takers, would be, then, an issue *not* of *turn-type pre-allocation*, but rather of a sequential–organizational *effect* of an institutional *activity allocation*.

In other institutional situations, *turn-type pre-allocation* does play a role, however, in having professionals question laypersons, as in job interviews (Button, 1987a; 1992; Komter, 1991), news interviews (Clayman, 1988; 1992; Clayman & Heritage, 2002a; Greatbatch, 1988; 1992; Heritage, 1985; Heritage & Greatbatch, 1991), or various kinds of research interviews (Houtkoop-Steenstra, 1995; 1996; 2000; Mazeland, 1992; Mazeland & Ten Have, 1996; Stax, 2004; Suchman & Jordan, 1990). As I will try to show in a 'demonstration' later in the chapter, such 'institutional questionings' seem to differ in important respects from the 'interrogative series' inserted in request/service pairs, as discussed previously.

Before I turn to this 'demonstration', however, I will summarize and discuss an analytic strategy proposed by John Heritage for using CA to study institutional practices.

Using CA to study institutional practices

In a very useful chapter, John Heritage (1997; 2004) has reworked ideas like the ones included in the introduction to Drew and Heritage (1992a), discussed previously, in a systematic proposal for the study of institutional interaction within the framework of *institutional* research. Before he elaborates his proposal, Heritage produces a general introduction to CA and discusses some basic issues, namely 'sequence' and 'context'. In designing their turns-at-talk, participants orient to the preceding talk, which, thereby, is an important aspect of the 'context' of that talk. At the same time, such turns 'normally project (empirically) and require (normatively) that some "next action" should be done by a subsequent participant'. This (re)creates a context for the next speaker. Finally, by producing a 'next action', participants demonstrate an understanding of the previous action, building mutual understandings or *intersubjectivity* (Heritage, 1997: 162–3; 2004: 223–4).

Turning to institutional interaction, Heritage argues that the same ideas are still operative, that 'context' is still basically something incrementally built up or recreated during and *in* the interaction. Building on the earlier work with Paul Drew (Drew & Heritage, 1992a, as discussed above), he proposes that we can look at three main features of institutional talk:

1   Institutional interaction normally involves the participants in specific goal orientations which are tied to their institution relevant identities: doctor and patient, teacher and pupil, and so on.
2   Institutional interaction involves special constraints on what will be treated as allowable contributions to the business at hand.
3   Institutional talk is associated with inferential frameworks and procedures that are particular to specific institutional contexts. (Heritage, 1997: 163–4; 2004: 224-5)

These features, he writes, 'create a unique "fingerprint" for each kind of institutional interaction' (1997: 164; 2004: 225; referring to Heritage & Greatbatch, 1991: 95–6), the 'specific tasks, identities, constraints on conduct and relevant inferential procedures' that are used by the participants:

Implicit in this way of thinking is the idea that institutional interaction generally involves a reduction in the range of interactional practices deployed by the participants and in the sites they are deployed at, and a specialization and respecification of the practices that remain (Drew and Heritage, 1992a). [...] The institution of mundane conversation [...] exists, and is experienced as, prior to institutional interaction both in the life of the individual and in the life of society. (Heritage, 1997: 164; 2004: 225)

It is against this background that he proposes 'six basic places to probe the "institutionality" of interaction'. These are:

1   Turn-taking organization.
2   Overall structural organization of the interaction.

3   Sequence organization.
4   Turn design.
5   Lexical choice.
6   Epistemological and other forms of asymmetry.
    (Heritage, 1997: 164; 2004: 225)

It is not the purpose of this section to provide an extensive summary of Heritage's proposal, so I limit my discussion to a short explication and some remarks; anyone considering studying institutional data in order to research interactional management in such institutions is encouraged to read his text itself.

Heritage's first point, *turn-taking organization*, is based on ideas from the turn-taking paper discussed above (Sacks et al., 1978). What Heritage proposes is to study the *specific* turn-taking system of various kinds of institutional interaction displaying shared normative orientations towards the taking of turns. He mentions 'special turn-taking organizations' in court sessions (cf. Atkinson & Drew, 1979), news interviews (cf. Clayman & Heritage, 2002a; Greatbatch, 1988; Heritage & Greatbatch, 1991), and classrooms (cf. McHoul, 1978; Mehan, 1979), settings that have a more or less 'formal' character, with large numbers of potential participants and an 'overhearing audience', but he suggests that other kinds of settings may have their own particular system, for instance specific therapeutic regimes (cf. Peräkylä, 1995) or mediation hearings (Garcia, 1991).

Heritage's second point is concerned with the *overall structural organization of the interaction*.[4] He proposes that after the previous step, 'the next thing to do is to build an overall "map" of the interaction, in terms of its typical "phases" or "sections"' (1997: 166; 2004: 227). Having made such a 'map' from one particular example, he writes:

> [...] we can see that each of them involves the pursuit of a specific sub-goal. Each section is *jointly* oriented to – indeed *co-constructed* – by both participants as involving a task to be achieved. (1997: 167; 2004: 228)

Looking at the section boundaries, one can observe whether the parties seem to agree on the task and its parts, or whether this is less apparent. Identifying these sections helps to grasp the 'task-orientations which the *participants* routinely co-construct in routine ways'. He stresses that such an organization should not be used as a fixed 'framework to fit data into', but as an evolving structure 'that the parties orient to it in organizing their talk' (1997: 168; 2004: 229–30).

With *sequence organization*, we come, of course, to the heart of the CA enterprise:

> In analysing sequences, we essentially look at how particular courses of action are initiated and progressed and, as part of this, how particular action opportunities are opened up and activated, or withheld from and occluded. (1997: 169; 2004: 230)

Heritage elaborates this point mostly by a detailed analysis of an example, which I will not try to reproduce here. In essence, sequencing involves the ways in which participants arrange for each to talk about specific issues in specific ways, for instance as 'questions' and 'answers'.

Analysing *turn-design* involves two different aspects, because:

> When we talk about a turn being 'designed,' we are pointing to two distinct selections that a person's speech embodies: (1) the action that the talk is designed to perform and (2) the means that are selected to perform the action [...]. (1997: 170; 2004: 231)[5]

Heritage suggests that in agent–client interaction, agents tend to develop routines which seem to minimize the chance for a client's 'resistance', for instance by 'presupposing' the client's goodwill and legitimate reasons for his or her actions. Heritage calls this a 'wind tunnel' effect: because agents endlessly repeat similar actions, these actions and the turn-designs that bring them about become 'smooth'.

Under the heading *lexical choice*, Heritage discusses issues like the choice of descriptive terms (rather 'official' ones), self-reference (the organizational 'we'), and what he calls 'institutional euphemisms', ways of talking that seem designed to minimize the expressed reproachability or painfulness of the situation or the actions under discussion.

Finally, Heritage suggests four different kinds of *asymmetry* as the last topic in his list: (1) 'asymmetries of participation'; (2) 'asymmetries of interactional and institutional "knowhow"'; (3) epistemological caution and asymmetries of knowledge; and (4) rights of access to knowledge. The first refers to the observation that institutional agents often act in a task-based, directive manner, for instance when a doctor questions a patient. The second has to do with the unequal involvement in the case, which for the professional is generally routine, but for the client unique. Furthermore, clients quite often do not know what the agent is up to, according to what kind of 'protocol' or 'agenda' he or she is working. The third point has to do with a tendency of professionals to act cautiously, that is to avoid taking a firm position on the issues under discussion. On the other hand, both professional agents and clients quite often seem to co-produce their relation as 'expert' versus 'layperson', sometimes to the point of ignoring important aspects of lay experience. The final point seems to underlie the others: while professionals are given a large share of 'right to know', at least within their mandate, clients quite often 'hide' some relevant knowledge they have, because they do not have the 'right to know'; and when they do they often point out the source of their knowledge, which is often the, or another, professional.

In effect, then, John Heritage has provided an interesting 'shopping list' for students of institutional interaction, especially those interactions that bring professionals and clients together. He stresses that these aspects are intimately related, with turn-taking systems and the asymmetries being complex overall phenomena, while the other points concern elements that are 'nested' into one another. This approach may be helpful in inspiring a detailed, data-based study of institutional practices. Although it is focused on agent–client interactions, it could also be helpful, I think, in studying other kinds of institution-bound interactional formats, such as various kinds of meetings (cf. Boden, 1994; Meier, 1997).

Demonstration: standardized survey interviewing[6]

For my 'demonstration' in this chapter, I have chosen a rather specific type of institutionalized interaction, namely questioning in standardized survey interviews. Surveys, by the way, are large-scale research projects in which data are gathered on a vast number of persons by way of standardized interviews. Today, these interviews are mostly done using the technology of computer-assisted telephone interviewing (CATI). This involves implementing a questionnaire in a computer program and having interviewers call (often randomly) selected telephone numbers to ask for cooperation. The CATI computer screen presents the interviewer with organized instructions for the interview: firstly, to *read* the displayed questionnaire sections to the respondent; and, secondly, to *record* the answers by choosing options from an available set of possibilities, by typing a corresponding code on the keyboard. The interviewers are instructed to follow the 'script' of the computer-implemented questionnaire very closely. They should read the questions as worded, probe in a neutral fashion, and not show any evaluation of the answers given. Interactional research of actual survey interviewing shows that interviewers do not follow these instructions literally (cf. Houtkoop-Steenstra, 1995; 1996; 1997; 2000; Maynard et al., 2002; Maynard & Schaeffer, 1997; Schaeffer & Maynard, 1996; Suchman & Jordan, 1990; Stax, 2004). These interviews, then, provide an interesting 'test case' for 'applied CA'.

While many types of institutional interviews are to a certain extent based on 'instructions' available as broadly formulated 'rules', in standardized survey interviews the professional participant has, like an actor, to vocalize a text written by someone else. But at the same time, the lay respondent has to be guided by the professional to choose from the proposed answer options as if these represent the respondents' actual opinions, experiences, or whatever. So the interaction is to a large extent 'scripted', but apart from bringing this script to life,[7] the interviewer also frequently has to *negotiate* with the respondent to produce a codable answer.

I will quote and discuss a few excerpts from actual survey interviews in order to explore some interactional characteristics of this special format. This discussion will not be systematically ordered using a 'shopping' list like the one provided by Heritage, but the elements he has noted will be taken up in my explorations. Here is a first excerpt:

EXCERPT 9.1, TRANSCR. RJM (WISCONSIN SURVEY 01)[8]

```
80   [IV:   ·hhhh okay(gh): a::[::nd? now we have some questions=
81                              [##
82   IV:    =about government agencies.·hhh as you know:? every
            ten year
83          there is a census of the population of the united states.
            ·hhh
84          how confident are you: (.) that the census bureau
            protects the
85          privacy of personal information about individuals and
            does not
```

```
86          share it with other government agencies. ·hhh very
            confident
87          (0.4) somewhat ↑confident (0.5) not ↑too confident?
            (0.2) or
88          not at all ↑confident. {q5}
89          (1.0)
90   FR:    share it with what other governments
91   IV:    (tch) ·hh well the question doesn't specify: but (0.3) it just
92          says other government agen[cie]s
93   FR:                              [oh ]
94   FR:    probably very confident
95          (0.5)
96   IV:    °oh kay° people have different ideas about what
            the
```

We enter the interaction at the moment the interviewer accepts a previous answer to a preliminary question with 'okay' (80) and enters it in the computer (81). She immediately continues with announcing the first set of substantive questions 'about government agencies' (80, 82), and proceeds to ask the first of these (82–8). The respondent initiates a repair on one part of the question (90), which is dealt with by the interviewer (91–2) and accepted (93), followed by an answer to the question (94). After an accepting 'okay' the interviewer starts the next question in the series. So we have a 'set announcement' and a question, both largely conforming to the script, then an inserted repair sequence, followed by a hedged scripted answer to the question, and an unscripted acceptance, which closes the sequence.

The 'question' actually is constructed using three different components:

1 an introductory statement, which 'actualizes' a piece of supposedly common knowledge (82–3);
2 a question-formatted question (84–6);
3 four answer options, from which the respondent can make a choice (86–8).

In his unpublished paper 'Some design specifications for turns at talk in a job interview', Graham Button (1989) has coined concepts that are very useful to discuss *multi-unit questioning turns* like these. As he notes, the fact that many turns in a setting like the job interview are 'built out of multiple turn constructional units [...] contrasts with ordinary conversation where there is a pressure for the *mini-mization* of turn size'. He suggests that the general possibility for such complex, multi-TCU turns depends on a suspension of the pressure for the minimization of turn size that is operative in ordinary conversation. That pressure stems from the strictly local, turn-by-turn organization of turn-taking in conversation (Sacks et al., 1978). The suspension of this pressure depends on the participants' practical acceptance that it is the interviewer who does the questioning. This means that when the interviewer, after an acceptance of the previously given answer, takes a turn which starts with objects like announcements, assertions, etc., anything other than a question, the expectation is that the turn is still incomplete. In examining his materials, Button has distinguished three different *question components*: a *Question Delivery Component* (QDC), the unit which actually asks the question, and two others that may precede it, a *Question Target Component* (QTC) and a *Personal Relevance Component*. The QTC is that part of the turn which 'is used to develop a target for the eventually delivered question', while the Personal Relevance Component 'displays that the relevance of the question resides in the candidate's expressed experiences'. It is only after the QDC has been produced that the questioned can take the floor to work towards giving an answer.[9]

Returning to the three question components in our example (excerpt 9.1), we can say that item 1, the assertion that precedes the actual question, can be characterized as the QTC. Item 2 is the QDC, which in general tends to be the last in the turn, but is here followed by item 3, a list of options, which is not evident in Button's materials. There is no Personal Relevance Component in these survey interviews, as they are 'audience designed' rather than 'recipient designed' (Houtkoop-Steenstra, 1995; 2000: 67), as are job interview questions as well as conversational questions. So, the multi-component question format used here is *essentially* connected with the turn-taking system that is operative in these interviews, as it is in job interviews and news interviews. Because interviewers are expected to ask questions, especially as this activity has been announced as it is here, any component that is *not* recognizable as 'doing questioning', such as an assertion of supposedly common knowledge, is therefore taken as preliminary to an upcoming real question and therefore as a part of an as-yet-unfinished multi-component turn. In other settings where multi-component questions are regularly used, like news interviews as well as job interviews, they tend to be *last* in their turn. The fact that this is not the case here, as item 3, the answer option list, still follows, is a special feature of survey interviews to which I will return.

When the question in excerpt 9.1 is delivered, and the options list is brought to conclusion, there is a 1-second pause before the respondent initiates a repair in the following terms: 'share it with what other governments' (90); that is, she repeats the target phrase, changing 'government agencies' into 'governments', with an inserted 'what'. The interviewer explains: 'well the question doesn't specify: but (0.3) it just says other government agencies' (91–2). After an oh-receipt (93), the respondent answers the question in (94), which, although preceded by the qualifying 'probably', is accepted by the interviewer. By using a phrase like 'the question doesn't specify: but (0.3) it just says …', the interviewer maintains a distance from the questionnaire and refuses to take the task of providing for such a specification on her own account.[10]

Since this is a partially scripted kind of interaction, which is enacted again and again with different participants, it is interesting to compare the instance cited and discussed above with another one from the same set of interviews:

EXCERPT 9.2, TRANSCR. RJM (WISCONSIN SURVEY 02)

```
61  [IV:  ·hh two a:nd now we have some questions about
             government agencies
62         ·hhh ↑as you know every ten years (.) there's a census of
63         the population of the united states ·hhh how confident
             are you
```

```
64        that the census bureau protects the privacy of
          personal information
65        about individuals? ·hhh and doesn't share it with other
66        government ↑agencies? ·hh are you very confident (.)
          somewhat
67        ↑confident (.) not too confident (.) or not at all
          ↑confident?
68        {q5}
69        (2.1)
70   MR:  oh kay yer- you're talkin' (rapidly here you-)
71   IV:  ·hh o[kay
72   MR:       [protect information from
73        (1.8)
74   MR:  keep (things) confidential?
75        (0.7)
76   IV:  (tch) well um ·hhh the:: question actually asks how
          confident
77        are you that the census bureau ·hh protects the privacy of
78        personal information about individuals and doesn't
          share it
79        with other government agencies {q5}
80        (2.0)
81   IV:  so:: do you think the census bureau keeps the
          information that
82        people give them? do you think they keep that private?
          and they
83        don't share it?
84        (2.0)
85   MR:  eh:: i think they'd- they'd have to share it if
86        (0.6)
87   MR:  gatherin' information
88   IV:  ·hhh okay:? so:: how confident are you that (.) they::
          don't
89        share it(h) huh·hh
90        (0.8)
91   MR:  uh::m not very con[fident]
92   IV:                    [·hhh ] o[kay (.) A:ND people have=
93                                   [#
94   IV:  =different ideas about what the census is
```

In excerpt 9.2, a repair initiation by the respondent is introduced by a complaint about fast speech (70). The indicated trouble source is, again, the question. The respondent repeats some key terms (72, 74), after which the interviewer repeats the question (76–9), then paraphrases it (81–3), at which the respondent answers (85, 87). The interviewer, however, repeats the original question in truncated form (88–9), which the respondent answers in the required format (91), which is accepted (92) and entered into the computer (93).

Observe that, like the previous case, the repetition of the question is introduced with a 'distancing' move: 'well um ·hhh the:: question actually asks' (76). When this strategy of repeating the question does not produce an immediate answer (a 2.0

silence in line 80), the interviewer uses a paraphrasing tactic (81–3), which leads, after another (2.0) silence (in 84), to a hesitant start of the answering (85, 87). We can observe here a typical order of repairing an understanding problem in these materials, first by a repeat, and when this does solve the problem, by a paraphrase.

When we consider the interviewer's uptake of the respondent's tentative answers (85, 87), we might say that in initiating a repair on these answers, she demonstrates that these are possible 'trouble sources' for her. Her truncated repeat of the question (88–9) serves as a reminder of the *required format* for an answer that in itself has already been accepted ('·hhh okay:?', 88). The 'so::' suggests that the respondent can produce the required formatted answer on the basis of her earlier spontaneous one. This episode, then, has a structure that can be modelled as: Respondent: tentative answer; Interviewer: provisional acceptance, plus format instruction; Respondent: formal answer; Interviewer: formal acceptance.

The fact that we see some trouble on this item in several interviews may be related to the fact that it is the first 'real' question. Respondents need some experience to adapt to the actual interview routine, such as: the rather unspecific ways in which questions are worded; the way in which they are produced vocally; and the format requirements for answers that are contained in them. But I must also concede that I have purposely selected relatively 'troubled' examples, because these seem more instructive for present purposes.

In the collection from which these excerpts were taken, it can be observed that interviewers routinely produce an 'unscripted' vocal *acceptance* of the answer, mostly something like 'okay' or 'mhm'. Furthermore, we may note that the audible keyboard clicks (marked as # in the transcripts) provide additional indications that the answer has been sufficient to have the interviewer enter a code.[11] By closing the previous question–answer sequence in this way, they also serve to open the floor for the next question–answer sequence, expected to be started by the interviewer. This expectation is routinely reinforced by the interviewer making vocal indications of starting a (longer) turn, by audible inbreath and 'u:m:'-like sounds. Furthermore, some of the questions start with a scripted 'And', while such an object can also be produced on the interviewer's own initiative (cf. Heritage & Sorjonen, 1994). So there seem to be a cluster of indications and devices to mark the end of one sequence and the start of a next one, all serving to pass the turn to the interviewer for a unit of speech that will have a question as its ultimate component.

The next fragment can be fruitfully analysed against this background.

EXCERPT 9.3, TRANSCR. RJM (WISCONSIN SURVEY 01)

```
147   IV:  ↑a:n' sharing information between different agencies of
           government
148        when both want the same information (0.4) saves time [( )
149   FR:                                                        [but
150        see now who's the different agencies of government.
151   IV:  ·hhhh we:ll (0.4) the- you know the government (0.2) is made
           up
```

```
152        of different asiancies: one of which: is the census bureau
153        (0.9)
154    IV: so (0.2) they're just talking abou:t
155        (0.5)
156    IV: whatever: (0.4) the other government agencies are:
157    FR: within the united states
158    IV: >right<
159    FR: oh okay=
160    IV: =so w- y'know
161    FR: now i'm more clear
162    IV: ok(h)ay(h) huh huh ·hhh AH: sharing information between
           defferent
163        agencies of government [when both-]
164    FR:                       [i forgot    ] what was your question?
165        (0.3)
166    IV: Oh i'm- this is just the lead in
167        (0.3)
168    FR: oh o[kay
169    IV:      [we're just starting.·hhh ah:: sharing information between
170        different agencies of government when both want the same
           information
171        (.) saves time and money? but it also mean some loss in
172        privacy for the individual.·hhh do you think the benefits? of
173        saving time and money (0.4) outweigh the costs in privacy, ·hh
174        or: do you think the loss of privacy outweighs the benefits of
175        saving time and money {q7d}
176        (1.0)
177    FR: the first one
178    IV: okay benefits of saving time and money: outweigh:
179        (0.5)
180    IV: costs in privacy.
181    FR: °mm hmm°
182    IV: okay ·hhh you've given me your general views
```

The respondent here initiates a repair on an introductory statement (147–8), with a request for clarification (150). After a collaboratively produced explanation, the respondent produces a statement of satisfaction, closing this inserted repair sequence (159, 161). With a laughing 'okay' and an inbreath, the interviewer starts reading the multi-unit question again, repeating the statement that has just been discussed (162). The respondent then interrupts this reading, saying 'I forgot what was your question?' (164). Whereupon the interviewer explains: 'Oh i'm- this is just the lead in' (166), which the respondent accepts (168), followed by another explanation: 'we're just starting.' (169). It is only then that the multi-unit question can be produced in full. In other words, the interruptive request for clarification has disrupted both the scheduled reading of the complex question and its hearability as such. It is only when the interactional table has been cleared that the questioning interaction can return to normal flow.

As noted above, Button has observed that the QDC tends to be *the last one* in the multi-unit questioning turn in his job interview materials, while similar observations have been made on news interviews (cf. for instance Clayman & Heritage, 2002a). In the data on survey interviews used here, this is also the case generally, except when a larger number of answer options are given after the QDC, as in excerpts 9.1 and 9.2. That may be a problem, since respondents may start answering the question as soon as a QDC has been heard (Houtkoop-Steenstra, 1995: 105, n. 6; 2000: 88–106). In the previously cited data, this does not happen, but in excerpt 9.2 we have seen some disturbances that can be related to this issue. The respondent apparently was at first unable to answer the question (69), after which he complained about the interviewer talking too rapidly (70). She then repeated *just* the QDC (76–9), omitting the two introductory statements and the answer options. After a further paraphrase, a tentative answer, and a truncated repeat of the QDC, a final answer was produced that resembled the options enough to be accepted. In this episode, then, the QDC was treated as the *core* element in the turn, while the other units seemed to have a less essential, supportive function.

In the larger data set, however, there are a number of instances of respondents answering before all options have been enumerated. Here is one example:

EXCERPT 9.4, TRANSCR. RJM (WISCONSIN SURVEY 01)

```
[first part of multi-unit question skipped]
206   IV:  ·hh in order to reduce the cost of the census and make
207        the census simpler, ·hhh how would ↑you feel: about a
208        national health system. providing information about
209        you to the census bureau for use in the population
210        census.
211        ·h[hh
212   FR:  [good idea
213   IV:  (h)ok(h)ay(h) would you (.) favor it strongly (.)
214        favor it somewhat (.) oppose [it somewhat] or oppose=
215   FR:                               [ stro:ngly     ]
216   IV:  =it stro:ngly
217   FR:  strong[ly
218          [#
219   IV:  °okay.° favor it strongly.
220   FR:  mm hmm
221   IV:  ·hhh would you be willing to give your social security
```

In line 211, we see that after the QDC, the interviewer takes an inbreath, which seems to demonstrate that she is not finished yet. The respondent, however, already answers the question in her own words, 'good idea' (212). The interviewer laughingly accepts this, but continues with providing the options list *as scripted* (213, 214, 216). The respondent gives her response just after the relevant option is given, but before the option list is completed, and she gives it in truncated form: 'stro:ngly' (215). When the list is completed, she repeats it in the same format, 'strongly' (217), although in the meantime the oppose alternative has been mentioned using that same word (216). The interviewer enters the response into the computer (218), and subsequently verbally accepts it with a soft "°okay.°", followed by the fully formatted 'favor it strongly' (219), which is acknowledged by the respondent. It is clear, then, that respondents do expect the QDC to be the last one, and that producing an options list after it leads to a disturbance of the interactional flow, requiring extra interactional work from both parties.

Another aspect of sequence organization regards the elaboration of answers. Suchman and Jordan observe that in survey interviews,

> the interview schedule imposes external constraints on what form answers should take. These constraints result in somewhat contradictory problems: In some cases, responses that require elaboration are disallowed; in other cases, responses that in ordinary conversation are good enough in survey interviews require unreasonable elaboration. (1990: 235)

The point is, of course, that the answer has to be given in a form identical with, or closely resembling, one of the answer options. Quite often, respondents produce material from which answers can be inferred rather than complete answers, or answers in another form, which for purposes of understanding seems quite adequate. In short, many answers confront the interviewers with an inferential *coding* task.[12] Apparently, however, the interviewers are instructed to probe for formally adequate, rather than inferentially adequate, answers. This is what we see them doing in excerpts 9.2, 9.3, and 9.4. Such option-focused probes seem to instruct the respondents to limit themselves to formal answers, and abstain from any elaboration, demonstration, or explanation of their choices. At times, however, respondents do produce some indications of their personal reasons, but these tend to be disregarded, or acknowledged in a 'personal' fashion, with the interviewer stepping out of her professional role for a moment (Houtkoop-Steenstra, 1996).[13]

I now turn to another item on Heritage's list, the *overall structural organization* of these interviews, which can be characterized in the following way. After the opening, a number of preparatory tasks of confirmation, sampling, permission to tape-record the interview, and assurances of confidentiality have to be fulfilled before the actual interview can start. Then there are a series of questioning chunks or 'modules', as one of the interviewers explains in a fragment not quoted here. The series contains both general attitudinal questions, relating to general issues, as quoted, and a series of personal questions on respondents' characteristics, feelings, etc. The schedule ends with some factual questions for sampling purposes, and then the interview is closed off with further assurances and thanks. In this way, the interview is presented and enacted as the vocal filling of a form, consisting of a series of questions with fixed answer options. The order of the elements seems to be bureaucratically, rather than topically, motivated.

This overall format can be compared with that in other types of interviews, including medical interviews and semi-structured research interviews. In terms of its overall format, a *medical interview* has, as noted before, the 'naturally logical' form of a number of consecutive phases (Ten Have, 1989; 2006). The anchor point of this format is the complaint voiced by the patient on this or earlier occasions, which serves as a request for a service. It is this request which makes the ordinarily ensuing questioning by the physician relevant. The professional needs a clear conception of the expressed need, and additional information (in the medical case often involving physical examinations, tests, etc.), before the service (in the medical case: diagnosis and/or treatment) can be offered. Physicians tend to keep the agenda that presumably guides their questioning hidden from patients and they similarly tend to refrain from reacting to the information provided by patients, at least until they announce their overall assessment regarding the diagnosis and/or treatment. In short, physicians tend to maintain, and patients generally accept (at least openly, cf. Ten Have, 1995a; Heath, 1992) an asymmetrical *distribution of knowledge*, lay, experiential, and personal on the patient side, professional and general for the physician. The overall structural organization, then, is related to the last item in Heritage's 'list',[14] *epistemological and other forms of asymmetry*. Various institutional arrangements reflect presuppositions regarding the distribution of knowledge, as well as cognitive abilities and interests.

In his research on *semi-structured research interviews*, Harrie Mazeland (1992, summarized in Mazeland & Ten Have, 1996) has developed an interesting distinction that can be related to these issues. In his materials he encountered rather marked differences in the overall structural organization of such interviews, or at least the organization of extended episodes. Some of these consisted of a fast turnover of small question–answer sequences, starting with relatively simply shaped, one-unit question turns. These he has called *Turn-by-Turn (or TbT) Interviews*. The contrastive type is distinguished by the fact that here the two speakers each take rather extended turns-at-talk, at least as 'primary speaker'. These he has called *Discourse Unit (or DU) Interviews* (cf. also Houtkoop & Mazeland, 1985). Such interviews (or episodes within interviews) started with a complex turn in which the interviewer gave some explanation of the sorts of information requested, often inviting a story-like format. Rather than specifying a relatively closed set of answer options, as in survey interviews, these were invitations to speak in the informant's own terms.

These two forms, Mazeland suggests, presuppose different *distributions of knowledge*. In the DU format, the informant is constituted as a kind of *expert* on the knowledge sought by the interviewer, necessitating a kind of self-structured telling. Such formats are used with professionals like public prosecutors interviewed about their work organization, or interviews about extended personal experiences or exotic life styles. TbT interviews, on the other hand, are used with topics which are quite general and non-specialized, including 'face-sheet' data, household organization, and schooling careers. In such areas, the cognitive structure of the topical field is apparently supposed to be so general that 'any member', including the researcher, has access to its structure, while each respondent can quite easily fill in the slots in the structure from his or her private stock of knowledge.

In general, researchers who use semi-structured interviews take great care to structure the interviews in such a way that each topic seems to follow 'logically' from the preceding one and 'naturally' leads to the next. One of the dilemmas of this format is that such a kind of topical organization implies a sharing of control, which may lead to rather irrelevant episodes or markedly forced shifts in topic. In DU interviews, the interviewer initiates the topic, and then hands control over to the informant, restricting him- or herself to indirect control through selective reactions and probing questions. In TbT interviews, such dilemmas surface in negotiations about the extendibility of the answers (Mazeland, 1992). Tensions between the cognitive interests of researchers and informant seem unavoidable (cf. Mazeland & Ten Have, 1996; also Ten Have, 2004a: 56–87).

Returning now to *standardized survey interviews*, we can appreciate that the relatively arbitrary but strict topical organization of such interviews is related to different presuppositions regarding knowledge distributions and cognitive interests that are implicated in that 'form of life'. The respondents have no specific interest in some outcome of the interview, but seem to be motivated by a sense of civil duty. They sometimes acknowledge that they should have an interest in and opinion about the public issues about which they are questioned. The generality of the issues is quite often stressed in the introductory statements of the question or question series, such as 'As you know, every ten years there is a census of the population of the United States' (excerpts 9.1, 9.2). In comparison with less structured forms of interviewing, a standardized survey interview generally has little to offer in terms of the pleasure of being able to express oneself on topics of one's own interest. Interview schedules, interviewers, and respondents seem to differ in the extent to which such expressive behaviour is allowed or restricted. The 'audience design' of the survey interview, then, is reflected on all the levels of organization we have considered.

In this rather elaborate consideration of one particular genre of institutional interaction, I have tried to demonstrate how one can use CA to get a deeper understanding of its procedural infrastructure. This may be useful in a number of ways, for instance in questionnaire design, in training interviewers, and in the methodological evaluation of survey results (cf. Houtkoop-Steenstra, 2000; Maynard et al., 2002). The general sense of such usabilities will be discussed in the next chapter, where I will also discuss some less usual types of 'applied CA', including interaction among or with participants who are communicatively 'impaired', 'human–computer interaction', and 'workplace studies'.

EXERCISES

Since the conditions concerning the availability of data can be different as far as 'institutional' issues are concerned, I offer three different suggestions:

1   If the data you have been working with are 'institutional' in character, try to reanalyse them in terms of the perspectives on institutional interaction discussed in this chapter.
2   If your previously analysed data are *not* 'institutional', you might seek to obtain some institutional data and compare the two in terms of the contrasts between institutional and non-institutional as discussed above.

(Continued)

(Continued)

3   Alternatively, you might do a *reading* exercise, taking, on the one hand, the introductory chapter by Drew and Heritage (1992a: 3–65) and, on the other, one of the empirical case studies in that book in Chapters 4–14, or in Boden and Zimmerman (1991: Chaps 5, 6, or 7). Explore the applicability of the general statements in Drew and Heritage's introduction to your chosen case study, and how the stated or demonstrated perspectives, approaches, and/or conceptualizations can be related to each other.

Now that you have developed a routine, further specifications regarding the four options seem superfluous.

RECOMMENDED READING

As a first recommendation, I mention John Heritage's chapter discussed above: Heritage (1997 or 2004). You might also want to read one or more of the general discussions of CA applied to 'institutional interaction' or 'social problems' that have been published previously, such as: Atkinson (1982); Drew and Heritage (1992b); Drew and Sorjonen (1997); Heritage (1984a: 280–90); Marlaire and Maynard (1993).

A challenging critique of the general CA approach of institutional interaction from an ethnomethodological perspective is offered in: Hester and Francis (2001).

Furthermore, you might want to read one or more papers in which CA is 'applied' to various kinds of institutional situations, such as the empirical contributions to the following two volumes: Boden and Zimmerman (1991); Drew and Heritage (1992a). Excellent examples of studies of institutional interaction in the medical field are available in: Heritage and Maynard (2006). Or select one of the following examples: Drew (1985); Gill et al. (2001); Komter (1994); Maynard (2004); Maynard and Marlaire (1992); Mazeland (2004); Peräkylä and Silverman (1991); Whalen and Zimmerman (1987); Zimmerman (1992).

Here are two books that discuss the issues raised in this and the next chapter in a more extensive fashion, the first concentrating on CA, the second also including other approaches to discourse: Arminen (2005); McHoul and Rapley (2001).

Notes

1. Originally published in 1974, but here used in the 1978 version; cf. my discussion in Chapter 7, section on turn-taking organization.
2. Cf. Duranti and Goodwin (1992) for an elaborate discussion of the issue of 'context' in analysing talk, and a collection of papers displaying a variety of positions on these issues.
3. My treatment of Drew and Heritage's introduction is, of course, rather incomplete; some points skipped here will be encountered later. The interested reader should consult the full text, as well as the collected studies in that volume and in Boden and Zimmerman (1991).

4. We have already encountered this expression in the discussion of Schegloff and Sacks' classic paper 'Opening up closings' (1973) in Chapter 2.

5. Cf. Pomerantz and Fehr's proposals discussed in Chapter 7, steps 2 and 3.

6. This section is in part based on earlier explorations presented in the workshop on 'Interaction in the Standardized Survey Interview', Free University Amsterdam, 18–21 November 1995, and at Essex '96, the Fourth International Social Science Methodology Conference, University of Essex, 1–5 July 1996. I would like to thank the participants on those occasions for their helpful remarks, and especially the late Hanneke Houtkoop, whose enthusiasm for the topic, as well as her published and unpublished writings, has been a real source of inspiration. The data, transcribed by Robert J. Moore, were provided through Nora Cate Schaeffer, University of Wisconsin–Madison. A collection of papers, partly first presented at the Amsterdam workshop, has been published in Maynard et al. (2002).

7. In the workshop, mentioned before, Michael Lynch used the expression 'the living questionnaire', which Hanneke Houtkoop-Steenstra also used for her book (2000).

8. In the transcripts in this section some special conventions are used. 'IV' stands for 'interviewer', while 'FR' indicates a female respondent and 'MR' a male respondent. The ## signs, like those in line 81, indicate 'typing', the interviewer entering codes to represent a just-given answer. Brackets as in '{q5}' refer to questions in the questionnaire. Furthermore, I have printed those parts of the spoken text that conformed to the 'script' implemented in the CATI computer in **bold**.

9. Although I use Button's unpublished paper here, similar arguments have been put forward elsewhere, for instance in: Button (1992); Greatbatch (1988); Heritage and Greatbatch (1991). It should be clear that three elements in Heritage's 'list', namely 'turn-taking organization', 'sequence organization', and 'turn-design', are intimately related in these encounters.

10. At the workshop mentioned before, Harrie Mazeland presented a number of instances of such 'distancing'. In terms of Erving Goffman's *Frame analysis* (1974: 517), the interviewer at such moments seems to excuse herself that she is not the *originator* of the words she speaks when she reads the script – that is, asks the question; she is only an *emitter*, and therefore not accountable for its wording and meaning. This aspect of survey interviewing is dealt with extensively by Hanneke Houtkoop-Steenstra (2000: 42-61).

11. Cf. Greatbatch et al. (1995) on the turn-taking relevance of keyboard work in a setting where interactional partners have visual access to the keyboard work of one of them, the physician in a consultation.

12. The idea that interviewers have a coding task has been elaborated by Tony Hak (2002).

13. It seems probable that such elaborative accounts will be more frequent and extensive in face-to-face interviews in the visual bodily presence of the interviewer, which Suchman and Jordan studied, compared with telephone interviews such as the ones studied here.

14. The one element that I will not use in these explorations is 'lexical choice'. For a fuller investigation, this could certainly be usefully explored as an aspect of the 'audience design' of survey questions.

10

Applied CA: Local Rationalities, Formal Knowledge, and Critical Concerns

Contents

In this chapter, the exploration of 'applied CA', started in the previous one, is continued with a general discussion of the possibilities of using CA to elucidate practical situations. The central idea is that CA can be used to explore the sense of 'local' practices, which tends to be ignored or seen as faulty in 'formal' plans, tests, and accounts. This is firstly discussed in general terms, and then by an overview of the 'application' of CA in three different areas. These are: interaction of or with people with 'impaired' communicative abilities, humans acting on or with computer systems, and situations relevant to feminist concerns. The issue in all these areas is how the knowledge that CA can produce relates to knowledge that is established or expected in some way. The chapter concludes with a reconsideration of the application of CA in relation to 'pure' or 'basic' CA.

On the usability of CA findings

In the introduction to the previous chapter, I noted a number of 'wider concerns' that might be a motive for using CA, or CA-like approaches, for studying talk-in-interaction in detail. In that chapter, I discussed the possibilities of using CA within a framework of a sociological study of institutional practices as one example of a 'neighbouring discipline'. In the present section, I will discuss the usability of CA for the concerns of 'people who have a practical, moral, and/or political interest in the practices studied, in terms of the situations, organizations, and/or institutions that are co-constituted by those practices'.

I will start with some ideas proposed by James Heap (1990) in an essay on applied ethnomethodology.[1] His starting point is the question of why one should undertake some activity, like doing ethnomethodological enquiries. This fits into the more general question of how one should live. This is not a 'scientific' question, of course, but a moral one. 'However, [scientific] inquiry can deliver some of what we need to know in order to make reasoned judgements in particular situations about how to act to achieve some end' (Heap, 1990: 39). So a research enterprise like ethnomethodology (EM) or CA might be useful in producing bits of knowledge that may help one to make choices among courses of action. Reflection on why someone should engage in such enterprises, then, requires reflection on the kind of knowledge that it might produce, what kind of 'news' it might deliver:

> Grossly, in EM the two types of warrants for speaking/writing, i.e. the two types of news, have been 'things are not as they appear' and 'X is organized this way.' An often used variant of the former type of warrant is 'others got it wrong as to how things are.' So, one writes a paper snaring the readers' attention by the explicit or implicit claim that others got it wrong, or things are not as they appear. Or one invokes the second type of warrant and boldly says 'X is organized this way (and that is why I am writing and you should be reading this).' (42)

In other words, there are two approaches to warranting EM (or CA) studies: Heap calls one the 'critical news approach' and the other the 'positive news approach'. The first offers a sustained critique of conventional and established conceptions of the organization of social life and of the practical application of knowledge based on such conceptions. What are criticized are especially the individualistic, rationalistic, and mentalistic modes or thinking that still dominate most of the human sciences and its practical applications (cf., for instance, Button, 1991; Button et al., 1995; Coulter, 1989; Suchman, 1987; 2007):

> Both the critical news and the positive news approaches presuppose not only that an audience is interested in the news which is delivered, but the approaches also presuppose that the news is worth knowing, worth writing and reading about. And here we are back to the big question of how one should live. Presumably, others have got it wrong about something important, or, alternatively, the organization of this X is important to know. These things are important because, at some point, they look like they can make a difference to how one can live. For example [...] if some activity is important in our lives, then knowing how it is organized may make a difference to how we act. (Heap, 1990: 43)

Whether it is worthwhile to do EM (or CA) depends on the value of the news it produces for an audience, and here Heap differentiates between a professional EM audience and a lay EM audience. What he calls 'straight-ahead EM' is done for a professional EM audience and studies things chosen for their contribution to the development of ethnomethodological knowledge. This parallels what I have called 'pure CA':

'Applied EM' is done for, and reported to, persons perhaps having only a nodding acquaintance with EM. The affairs studied are those whose formal structures may have consequences important to this audience of 'lay ethnomethodologists.' The affairs chosen for study have value for, and to, them.

Hence [. . .] [i]t is worth writing or reading about applied EM because such effort may deliver news about the structures of phenomena, and especially about the consequences of those structures for realizing ends and objectives regarded as important outside of ethnomethodology's analytic interests. The state of affairs may be other than they appear, other than they have been reported to be by others, or may be of interest independently of what others have said, rightly or wrongly. (44)

In other words, 'pure' EM (or CA) is analytically motivated and can study *any* activity for what it can add to 'our knowledge of how social order is made possible'. 'Applied EM' (or CA), on the other hand, is done in the hope that it can deliver some news about the organization of valued activities, which may help to generate ideas as to how things may be done differently. The contrast between 'pure' and 'applied' should not be overdrawn, however:

There is no reason why straight-ahead EM cannot be done in domains and on topics of importance to non-ethnomethodologists. To render such an EM effort applied, one simply has to draw out the implications, the values of the discovered formal structures of activities or reasoning for those persons having a professional interest in the affairs studied. (44)

What applied EM is all about, ultimately, is the study of the *local rationality* of members' practices, why it makes sense, for participants, locally, in their practical context, to do things as they are done, even if this is at odds with how these practices are planned, evaluated, or accounted for 'elsewhere', 'in theory', or at higher hierarchical levels in an organization. In this way, I think, Heap's sketch is a useful basis for a reflection on 'applying' CA (as, in a certain sense, included in the EM enterprise, cf. Chapter 4) to various topics that may have a practical interest for lay members. What I would oppose, however, is a possible implication of his arguments that studying topics of obvious lay/practical interest should *in principle* be preferred. Heap himself suggests that 'straight-ahead EM' studies could 'add up' or 'be collected in some way which renders transparent how social order is made possible in general and in particular ways', in such a manner that 'ultimately any straight-ahead piece of work could be seen as making a difference to how we live' (45).

Furthermore, I do not think one can *know beforehand* whether a piece of work, or multiple pieces of similar work, will ultimately be seen to have added to a corpus which has made a difference to how we live our lives. Therefore, no piece of work should be excluded, let alone banned or made suspicious, because its *future* usability is not obvious, or even hard to imagine. And, as regards the researcher's attitude or 'study policy', it seems wise, in 'pure' as well as in 'applied' research, to 'bracket' conventional ideas during the actual analysis of the data, as is suggested by the earlier discussed notion of 'unmotivated looking'. This is especially urgent in EM and CA, since, as Heap argues, an important part of the news to be delivered might be that things are *different* from what established ideas suggest. This 'difference', however, should also not be presupposed or hunted for in itself, but rather should be allowed to emerge from the analysis. All this seems to be implied in the notion of 'ethnomethodological indifference' (see page 57).

A particularly strong example of the sensibility of 'unmotivated looking' in relation to 'applied CA' is provided by a book by Wayne Beach, entitled *Conversations about illness: family preoccupations with bulimia* (1996). As the author explains, this case study of a 17-minute conversation of a grandmother and her granddaughter about the latter's possible 'eating disorder' started off from an 'unmotivated' examination of a tape that happened to be available in a collection. As Beach writes:

> It is both the allure and defining characteristic of *unmotivated* data-driven observations that eventual recognition of the broader significance of materials examined are more retrospective than prospective in nature. [. . .]
>
> By not bringing social problems such as bulimia to the [. . .] interaction a priori, but instead working first toward explicating how and just what it is that these participants are contingently orienting to in meaningful ways [. . .], it has hopefully become possible to avoid the inherent seduction of prespecifying patterns of interaction by reference to what is known, and thus far too often taken for granted, about ways in which large-scale 'macro/societal' problems are evidenced in ordinary conversation. (1996: xii–xiv)

On the other hand, we shall see that in many cases the sensible application of CA will motivate researchers to acquire especially relevant kinds of data, given their particular interests.

Plans, practices, and accounts

It may be useful, in this context, to reflect a bit more on this 'difference' between the findings of EM and CA, on the one hand, and established conceptions, on the other. For this purpose, I will make use of a proposal by Harold Garfinkel, in a text written with Lawrence Wieder (1992: 187–9), for some conventions to 'render' the findings of ethnomethodological studies, extracting this element from a more complex argument. They write (Garfinkel & Wieder, 1992: 187): 'the locally produced, naturally accountable lived phenomenon of order⋆ is referred to with ticked brackets − [ ]'. Furthermore, 'An arrow, →, is used to refer to professional social analysts' skilled use of *methodic procedures*. Accounts, ( ), are specified by analysts with →.' So we get something like: '[order⋆] → (account)', where → is: 'the skilled use of methodic procedures'.

I would like to combine these notions with some ideas developed by Lucy Suchman in her *Plans and situated action* (1987). She discusses 'The planning model [which] treats a plan as a sequence of actions designed to accomplish some preconceived end' (Suchman, 1987: 28), and elaborates a contrasting view which stresses 'situated action'. 'The coherence of situated action is tied in essential ways not to individual predispositions or conventional rules but to local interactions contingent on the actor's particular circumstances' (27–8). In this view, plans never suffice as prescriptions for action. They have to be locally realized by changing the prescriptions in various ways. She suggests, however, that plans continue to be used to frame the actions, and that as such they are the basis for reports on and accounts for the actions, even if these have departed significantly from the plans.

Coming back to some of the 'findings' about survey interviewing discussed in the previous chapter, we can use these notions and ideas to construct a kind of overall *work-sequence* for standardized interviews as a production site for survey data. The questionnaire, which I often called the script, can be linked to the notion of a *plan*. As I have demonstrated, in its realization as an actual interview, the plan is used as a framework, but it is also changed by being worked on in various ways – through vocalization, reception work, and repair, for instance. In other words, the actual interview is a matter of *situated (inter)action*. The plan re-emerges, however, as the framework through which the respondent's reactions are (re)constituted as choices among the alternatives provided by the question-naire. The answers are *accounted* for in the plan's terms. This suggests a double task of the interviewers: asking questions, that is going *down* from the level of the plan to the level of the interaction; and noting answers, which amounts to bringing *up* the spoken reactions to the level of the plan again.

When we adapt Garfinkel's conventions to these findings, we get something like the following:

(questionnaire) → [interview] → (recorded answers)

---

or in more detail:

(questionnaire)   (recorded answers)

↓

['reading' questions, understanding questions, giving answers, understanding answers, record-ing answers; and possibly 'repairing' questions and/or answers]

What this amounts to is that there is an essential *gap* between 'plans' (including instructions) and actions, and between actions and 'accounts' (including reports). Ethnomethodological studies analyse and describe the local, 'situated' 'work' of participants to 'bridge' these 'gaps', for all practical purposes. There is a difference, however, in the analytic style of ethnomethodology in general and CA, in the sense that, while EM is focused on that work in itself, in its *local* particularities, CA tends to reason in terms of *repeatable* devices resulting in a *repeatable* order. In other words, and returning to some of James Heap's ideas discussed above, the 'news' that CA has to report 'that others got it wrong, or things are not as they appear', or that 'X is organized this way', may be more 'general' than that which ethnomethodology would produce. Such generality engenders both an opportu-nity and a danger. The opportunity is that one can summarize analytic findings in terms that seem communicable, apart from the instances used to produce them, but this also presents a danger of seeming to present *law-like* rules and allow for simplified *recipes* for action. I will return to these issues in the final section of this chapter, but before that I will touch on a number of examples that present a range of possibilities that is much larger than those discussed so far.

Examples of 'applied CA' 1: studies of 'impaired' communication[2]

In 'pure CA', the focus is on the local practices of turn-taking, sequential organization, etc., in and for themselves, while in 'applied CA' attention shifts to the tensions between those local practices and any 'larger structures' in which these are embedded, such as conventional membership categories, institutional rules, instructions, accounting obligations, etc. In 'applied' studies of 'institutional interaction', as discussed in the previous chapter, the focus of the analysis is still, as in 'pure CA', on *talk-in-interaction*. Part of the 'spirit', the approach, and the findings of CA can also be used, however, to explore interactional situations which *differ* in one or another respect from those studied in CA, for instance in the material conditions of communication. In other words, such studies focus on *action-in-interaction*, even if it does not only involve *talk*, as conceived of usually. I will sketch a few examples.

In 'classical' CA, material conditions of communication were not in focus, although they were not ignored either. The major issue was the difference between interaction in telephone calls and face-to-face interaction, where the latter provides a wider range of communicative facilities, including sight, smell, and touch. Therefore, analysing face-to-face interaction based on audio recordings could be seen to be essentially incomplete, in contrast to analysing telephone calls in the same manner. That was an important impetus for turning to video recording, as discussed in Chapter 5. There are, however, also people who are not able to use 'the audio channel' on which most of CA is based, namely deaf people. Does that mean that their communications cannot be analysed? Of course not. In his 'Seeing conversations: analysing sign language talk', Paul McIllvenny (1995) has applied CA's problems and methods to the interaction of deaf people who use *sign language* to communicate. As deaf people talk to each other, using their hands, face, and body to express themselves and their eyes to listen to what others have to say, they too have to solve organizational problems like turn-taking, including interruptions, simultaneous starts, etc. And in larger settings, they need special visual attention-getting devices and ways of showing appreciation in applause. In order to be able to analyse such interactions, one needs video recordings and access to the local sign language used. That is the way McIllvenny worked.

The applause example illustrates the overall point rather well. An auditory applause can be started by anyone in a room and all hearing people can monitor whether enough others are joining in. But in the gatherings of deaf people, where applauding is done by waving both hands above one's head, only those who can be seen by enough others can start an applause. So, an applause starting in the front row can be successful, while one from the back row is much less likely to succeed. If an applause-starter on the first row wants to know whether he or she has had any success with the others, he or she has to turn around to see whether this is the case (McIllvenny, 1995: 134–5). In short, such 'collective behaviour' depends, for deaf people, on *visual access*. The same applies to face-to-face conversation.

As McIllvenny stresses:

> The visual-spatial modality shapes the social organization of interaction and of talk-in-interaction specifically in that it must be accomplished in situ with hands, eyes, faces and bodies, but not with ears. (132)

As is clear from the sketch of the organization of applause among deaf people, the major problem is that sight is 'focused', that is the range of one's visual attention is essentially limited. Participants only have 'local access' through gaze, which leads to a 'mutual exclusivity of focal regions': when they look in one direction, they do not see what happens in others. Therefore, there is a lot of visual scanning in deaf gatherings, and quite often many people assist when someone tries to get the audience's attention (132–5). McIllvenny focuses his analytic attention on turn-taking in small encounters (135–45). The main concepts developed in the analysis of turn-taking in spoken interaction (cf. Sacks et al., 1978), such as turns and transitional relevance places, are still relevant. The major difference is that getting the floor, the next turn, requires not only that no other self-selects, but also that one gets the directed attention, the gaze, of the others. That is, the collaboration that is required between speakers and recipients in order to have a well-organized conversation is much more marked in this condition than in the one in which most people live their lives. McIllvenny's analysis (to which I cannot do justice here) suggests that the organizational *problems* deaf people face in interacting with others are essentially similar to those facing everyone, but that they have to use different *means* to solve them. Although 'impaired', deaf people may have to work harder to achieve a sociality hearing people tend to take for granted, but it does not mean they live an essentially defective life.

Sarah Collins and co-workers (1997) report on an aspect of an even more complicated situation: conversations between what they call 'natural speakers' and cerebral palsy patients using *alternative and augmentative communication* (AAC) *systems.* They focus specifically on conversational closings, starting from Schegloff and Sacks' (1973) study (discussed in Chapter 2), while also taking some of Graham Button's work into account, as well as Christian Heath's (1986) study of doctor–patient interaction, as most of the 'natural speakers' studied were professionals. From these studies, they note that closings ordinarily tend to be achieved in several *steps* in which both parties (in two-party conversations) participate, such as closing down a topic, pre-closings, and a closing exchange. In doctor–patient interactions, the closing tends to be initiated by the doctor, but mostly each step will involve the patient's cooperation (cf. West, 2006). However, in their study, using video recordings of 'invited' conversations between 'natural speakers' and cerebral palsy patients, with additional information from field observations and interviews, Sarah Collins and her co-workers found that closings here tend to be rather different. In the great majority of cases, closings were initiated by the 'natural speaker', mostly seeking some sort of acceptance from the patient, but sometimes also 'rushing through' the closing steps without waiting for cooperation from the patient:

> In these cases the actions of the 'natural' speaker display the difficulty of initiating a closing when he/she does not know whether the AAC user is ready to close the interaction at this point. The 'natural' speaker must either explicitly seek the AAC user's collaboration [...] or skirt around the issue by rushing through the closing components [...]. (Collins et al., 1997: 487)

In relatively few cases, the closing was initiated by the patient either through gesture or through the AAC, after which the 'natural speaker' produced an understanding check followed by an acceptance. These closings tend to be complicated because of the insertion of confirmation sequences. The closing initiatives are either hard to notice in the case of gestures or rather 'hard' by pointing to 'bye', for instance. In other words, the AAC-dependent patients seem to lack the facilities required to play the more subtle phases of a multi-step closing game adequately:

> They display an understanding of what is an appropriate sequential environment for closings, producing closing implicative moves at possible topic closure points, and thus recognizing this as a relevant juncture for the introduction of a closing implicative move. However, they do not appear to close down topics themselves, nor to use pre-closings of the kind found in conversations between 'natural' speakers. (485–6)

Interestingly, a single case of a conversation of two AAC-using patients is collaboratively brought to a close in a subtle step-like and implicit fashion, collaboratively, but without explicit topic closures or elicitations of acceptance:

> This case illustrates that it *is* possible for AAC users with cerebral palsy to accomplish closings implicitly. It suggests that there may be much to be learned from a more in-depth study of interactions between AAC users. (487)

The researchers conclude their paper by discussing various practical implications, relating to both the design of AAC systems, such as adding 'pragmatic markers', and training of both AAC users and their 'natural' speaking partners in using the subtleties of collaborative closing.

From the mid-1990s onwards, there has been quite a number of CA-based studies of interaction in which at least one of the participants is communicatively 'impaired' in one way or another. Charles Goodwin has edited a book, *Conversation and brain damage* (2003), which collects in 10 chapters work by the major contributors to this area, focusing on aphasia. The core message that is stressed in all of these contributions is that whatever communicative success is achieved in the encounters under study has to be seen as a *collaborative* achievement. This depends on the use of quite ordinary conversational methods, adapted to the particularities of the impairment in the case at hand, in which both the aphasics and their interlocutors have to be 'creative'. In this way, the book's essays have a polemical sub-theme vis-à-vis conventional psycho-linguistic and neurological approaches, which are oriented to individual rather than collective communicative productions.

A number of contributions deal explicitly with the contrast between, on the one hand, ordinary, real-life interactions with an aphasic, and formal test situations, on the other. In the latter type of situations, an aphasic may be asked, for instance, to tell a story based on a set of cartoon drawings, or to answer standardized questions, at the request of a tester who has only a professional interest in the performance displayed in those tellings or answers. This situation is contrasted with 'naturally occurring' situations in which an aphasic wants to tell the story of a personal experience to a close relative, for instance, or participate in the arrangement of eating-out with a family group. In such situations it is the achievement of shared understanding that matters, not the 'objective' assessment of the linguistic quality of an individual performance.

The chapter by Claus Heeschen, a psycho-linguist, and Emanuel Schegloff, entitled 'Aphasic agrammatism as interactional artifact and achievement', (Goodwin, 2003), offers an extensive substantiation of this theme. When an aphasic speaker is asked to tell a story on the basis of a set of cartoons, she produces a story which is marred by a range of production problems: long pauses, limitation to simple syntactic structures, misconstructions of various sorts, etc. In situations which allow for more interaction, a number of such features persist, but the pauses are less frequent and less long, and the speaker uses a special form of 'telegraphic' speech. Such syntactically simplified forms save her the time and effort to work at more complex structures, but requires more active co-productive work from the recipient. This work is mostly done by various form of 'repair': guesses, tentative completions, etc. In fact, a number of the other chapters also deal with various aspects of such repair work. It turns out that it can be done in various ways, which may have different relational implications in terms of the aphasic speaker's participation status.

A specially acute case is discussed in the chapter by the editor, Charles Goodwin, called 'Conversational frameworks for the accomplishment of meaning in aphasia'. Here the aphasic speaker can only produce three words, while he can only gesture with one arm. In the data examined, a family gathering of five people is discussing a dinner arrangement. By using just the words 'yes', 'no', and an intonated set of syllables and gestures with his one hand, the aphasic member is providing the others with the materials needed to infer his preferences, but this requires quite extensive collaborative work involving the choice between different 'competitive' frameworks (Goodwin, 1995).

The concept of 'aphasia' covers a range of impairments and the patients whose speech is exemplified and analysed in the various chapters suffer from a variety of types of linguistic insufficiencies, including quite prominently the inability to find the 'right' word in time. In such cases the speakers often use very general terms instead of a more specific one, requiring a more specific interpretation or (implicit or explicit) guess based on shared knowledge or situational cues. This also accounts for the fact that mutual understanding is best achieved in active collaboration with intimates.

These studies show that, while CA was developed as a study of audio-recorded talk-in-interaction, 'talk' that by necessity uses other means can be studied in a similar fashion, but using video recordings, while the researchers often had to acquire additional information and/or rely on locally competent 'interpreters' to get a basic understanding of what was going on in order to be able to analyse the interactions.

Examples of 'applied CA' 2: 'human–computer interaction' and 'workplace studies'

For quite some time now, there have been efforts to conceive of the possibilities of human beings 'communicating with' machines, and especially computer systems. Would it make sense, then, to 'apply' CA's methods and findings to this field of *human–computer interaction* or *HCI*? The first, and probably still most influential, study that needs to be discussed when considering this issue is *Plans and situated action: the problem of human–machine communication*, by Lucy Suchman (1987). As I explained earlier, she has contrasted two conceptions of practical action: one seeing it as following a systematic sequence of pre-planned steps leading to a goal; and another as a series of consecutive 'situated actions' which, while broadly oriented to a goal, are basically improvised on the spot, taking into account what seems to be the locally relevant knowledge available. Starting off from some anthropological studies of navigation at sea, Suchman presents an in-depth study of people working at an experimental copying machine, which had an 'instruction component' attached to it. She invited couples of novice users to carry out certain complicated copying tasks, on the basis of the 'instructions' provided by the machine. These trials were video taped and analysed using special kinds of transcripts. These were organized in four columns, two for the users and two for the machine. The first user column contained the talk between the users, under the heading 'Not available to the machine', while the second recorded their actions on the machine as 'Available to the machine'. The machine columns were similarly divided: the first, 'Available to the user', mentioning the displays provided for the users' information; and the second, 'Design rationale', explicating the 'reasoning' that was implemented in the design of the machine. The crux of the matter was that the machine had been designed on the basis of a rationalistic, systematic, step-like *plan* which was not available to the users, while these operated in terms of *situated action*, locally improvised guesses at what might have to be done next and what the machine displays and activities could 'mean'.

Suchman has used CA's general perspective and empirical findings in order to explore the *repertoire* of communicational resources that might be available in a communicative situation. She notes that face-to-face interaction can be considered to be 'the richest form of human communication', 'with other forms of interaction being characterizable in terms of particular resource limitations or additional constraints' (Suchman, 1987: 69). She discusses some basic properties of face-to-face interaction, such as local control, sequence-based coherence, and especially the possibilities for 'locating and remedying communicative trouble'. Then she turns to 'specialized forms of interaction', referring to interaction in institutional settings and specifically to issues of 'pre-allocation of turn-types' and 'the prescription of the substantive content and direction of the interaction, or the *agenda*' (88).

It is from this background that she analyses a number of cases of 'trouble' in the interaction between the users and the machine. These troubles can be seen as produced by particular 'misunderstandings' between the users and the machine, which are hard to detect for either party, and therefore hard to repair. The machine is designed in terms of a collection of stepwise plans, and checks its various parts in order to 'know' which is the current plan and at which phase it is currently. The users' actions on the machine are 'interpreted' accordingly. The users, however, may be mistaken as to either the current plan or the current action state. As she writes:

> The new user of a system [. . .] is engaged in ongoing, situated inquiries regarding the appropriate next action. While the instructions of the expert help system are designed in anticipation of the user's inquiries, problems arise from the user's ability to move easily between a

simple request for a next action, 'meta' inquiries about the appropriateness of the procedure itself, and embedded requests for clarification of the actions described within a procedure. (169)

In other words, the new user has a wider range of informational needs than has been, or maybe can be, anticipated by a pre-programmed system. Therefore, while Suchman's user may 'read' the machine's (non-)response as a reaction to her own enquiries, the machine does react in terms of what her actions suggest when seen in terms of the current procedure as planned:

> In reading the machine's response to her situated inquiries and taking the actions prescribed, the user imports certain expectations from human communication: specifically, that a new instruction in response to an action effectively confirms the adequacy of that action, while a non-response is evidence that the action is incomplete. (169)

This can lead to various kinds of ambiguities and impasses, which in themselves may be hard to detect.

The overall message of Suchman's book, then, is that in order to understand what can go wrong when users work with pre-planned action systems, one should study their *actual situated activity* in detail that is the local rationality of users' activities, rather than see it as faulty operation based on misconceptions regarding a rational system. In their interactional practices, people use 'a rich array of linguistic, nonverbal and inferential resources' (180):

> Today's machines, in contrast, rely on a fixed array of sensory inputs, mapped to a predetermined set of internal states and responses. The result is an asymmetry that substantially limits the scope of interaction between people and machines. Taken seriously, this asymmetry poses three outstanding problems for the design of interactive machines. First, the problem of how to lessen the asymmetry by extending the access of the machine to the actions and circumstances of the user. Secondly, the problem of how to make clear to the user the limits on the machine's access to those basic interactional resources. And finally, the problem of how to find ways of compensating for the machine's lack of access to the user's situation with computationally available alternatives. (180–1)

While this book was based on 'experimental' data on novice users' problems with this particular machine, Lucy Suchman later turned to field studies of real-life work situations, involving routine operations by experienced workers using a variety of technical devices. Best known is the large so-called 'Workplace Project' in which she worked with Françoise Brun-Cottan, Charles Goodwin, Marjorie Harness Goodwin, Brigitte Jordan, Randall Trigg, and others (see Brun-Cottan, 1990/1; Goodwin, 1996; Goodwin & Goodwin, 1996; M.H. Goodwin, 1995; Suchman, 1992; 1996; Suchman & Trigg, 1991). Most of this project was focused on work in an airline operations room at a local airport, considered as a 'coordination centre'. In the papers in which this project's studies are reported, one can see a combination of various methods and approaches being used to elucidate the endogenous logic of setting-based work practices, especially video analysis, based largely on CA, and ethnography, including various documents. Such an approach has, in the meantime, become known as that of *workplace studies*.

A major example from the UK is a series of studies by Christian Heath, with Paul Luff, on work in the line control rooms of the London Underground (Heath

& Luff, 1996; 2000: 88–124). Here too, a combination of CA-inspired video analysis and ethnography is used to study especially the implicit coordination of the various people who work in these rooms, based on aural and visual monitoring of each other's activities, in combination with the various electronic displays available. As they write, in the summary of a paper:

> The accomplishment of specialized tasks, and the conventional use of complex technologies to support those activities, are dependent upon a realm of tacit interactional competencies that inform the very production and intelligibility of organizational conduct. Tasks are accomplished in and through interaction, and it is only by detailing the socially sanctioned and 'publicly' available competencies used by individuals within real-world situations that we will begin to uncover the systematics that undoubtedly underlie human–computer interaction and computer-supported cooperative work. (Heath & Luff, 1996: 127)

They contrast their work with earlier studies of work and occupations, in the tradition of Chicago sociologist E.C. Hughes:

> [...] while recognizing the importance of the mundane and routine in work, such studies, often by virtue of the conceptual framework they employ, ignore the ways in which tasks and work-based activities are accomplished in actual circumstances within organizational settings. In particular, despite Hughes's recognition of the importance of social interaction to the accomplishment of work and organizational life, the ways in which specialized tasks [...] are produced in and through interaction remains unexplicated, glossed in terms of 'organizational culture', 'operational philosophies', 'negotiation', or 'taking the role of the other', etc. (97)

In other words, what workplace studies try to do is substitute detailed knowledge of the local rationalities implied in situated work practices for the conceptual summaries of overall tendencies that were produced by earlier generations of ethnographies of work, namely 'informal organization', 'subculture', and the like. Heath and Luff also hint at the contributions 'workplace studies' might make to recently emerging fields like 'human–computer interaction' (HCI) and 'computer-supported cooperative work' (CSCW),

> in which it has been recognized that many innovative and advanced applications fail not so much as a result of technological inadequacy, but as a consequence of the systems' 'insensitivity' to the ways in which individuals ordinarily interact and collaborate in the workplace [...]. Indeed, it is being increasingly argued that the requirements for complex systems need to be derived from a deeper understanding of real world, technologically supported cooperative work, which in turn might lead to a distinctive, more social scientific, approach to user-centered design. (98)

By explicating locally used practices, then, workplace studies might provide a unique contribution to an empirically based requirements analysis that does not seem to be available by other means, such as experiments, interviews, or user surveys. The recognition of this possibility seems to have gained more strength in this recently emerging field of human enterprise than in more traditional fields of CA-based study, such as medical work or psychiatric practice. This may be related to the fact that 'troubles' in computer-based work are more obviously dependent on in-work details, while those in the 'social' professions can more easily be 'explained away' or 'glossed over' in global, social psychological terms.

Examples of 'applied CA' 3: feminist CA studies

In Chapter 4, when discussing 'CA and feminist concerns', I came to the conclusion that 'feminist CA' could be seen as a type of 'applied CA'. It seems fit, therefore, to continue my discussion started there in the present chapter, shifting from programmatic themes to actual research efforts. The earliest example mentioned there was the report by Don Zimmerman and Candace West, 'Sex roles, interruptions and silences in conversation' (1975). It was taken as an example of an approach that has fallen into disrepute, as it seemed to objectify both gender categories and conversational phenomena. I also suggested, in Chapter 4, that more current proposals for a 'feminist CA' tended to stress either sequential aspects of talk-in-interaction or membership categorization.

A very early example of the latter is a short paper by Maria Wowk, 'Blame allocation, sex and gender in a murder interrogation' (1984). She examines a suspect's story about an encounter with a 'girl' that ended in her death, with a focus on how he depicts her and her actions as 'provoking' him in various ways, and especially how these depictions rely on membership categorizations. '[T]hese descriptions of the victim do not select one definitive categorization for her so much as they select a sub-set of categories from the M.C.D. "moral types of female"' (77). In these ways, she shows, the suspect makes an effort to shift the blame of her death to a certain extent to the victim. The case is used as a demonstration of the importance of (gender) categories and associated predicates as a 'machinery' for producing 'social facts', in this case facts that function in 'sexual politics'. Wowk ends her essay by referring to Sacks' (1979) remarks to the effect that changing categories can be a 'revolutionary' activity, which she then links to feminist activities at 'conscience raising': 'With this in mind, I hope to have provided, at least at the analytical level, some part of a formal basis for such social change' (79).

Wowk's paper seems to be mostly ignored by later feminists. An exception is Elisabeth Stokoe, who, as I mentioned in Chapter 4, has strongly argued for the applicability of MCA for feminist purposes. In a paper with the challenging title 'Mothers, single women and sluts: gender, morality and membership categorization in neighbour disputes' (2003), she has put these ideas into practice, often referring to the paper by Wowk. She uses two kinds of data concerning neighbour disputes, from mediation sessions and TV shows, to study 'participants' situated descriptions of themselves and their neighbours in order to track the emergence of cultural knowledge about such relationships and also to pursue the discursive production and maintenance of normative gender identities' (Stokoe, 2003: 319). Her analysis reveals that 'talk between and about neighbours is saturated with moral work as people's actions, as either appropriate to or as breaches of the social and moral order, are formulated' (319). In her data, speakers evoke categories relating to women (rather than men). The categories of 'mother' and 'single women' were used in both an offensive and a defensive manner, that is either to boost or to ward off complaints. Activity descriptions were often linked, positively or negatively, to gendered categories in order to support or suggest moral evaluations. Especially, failure to live up to category-related standards was used in this way. For instance, 'the juxtaposition of certain predicates and activities with the category "woman" constituted breaches of the moral order and (…) such categorizations were treated as acceptable warrants for complaints among disputing neighbours' (332). The author stresses both the force of the conventions related to (gendered) categorizations and the flexible ways in which they can be used, adapted to local rhetorical needs. This also implies that category-related conventions can change, again referring to Wowk. She also quotes Carolyn Baker to the effect that MCA 'provides a "critical edge" to ethnomethodological work. 'MCA is therefore a useful method for feminist researchers because it allows analysts to see how participants both construct, and manage their conduct in relation to, conventional expectations for women and men's behaviour and character' (339).

Referring back to the critical remarks rendered earlier in Chapter 4 about MCA, it can be said that Stokoe seems to have taken at heart the warnings given by Hester and Eglin not to take membership categories and their associated predicates as fixed. She does indeed stress both the flexibility and the cultural availability of categories and predicates. Her analysis fits into the style of *discursive psychology* in its rhetorical interest. As is often the case, her data involve talk (absent) people addressed to third parties, such as mediators, interviewers, or a studio audience. Their reactions to the categorizing descriptions are hardly taken up as an explicit resource for the analysis. In fact, the reactions available in the data quotes are mostly minimal acknowledgements. There are two fragments that are exceptions to this: one concerns an opponent who just denies some of the charges against him; and another is from a 'chat show' which has stimulating questions and remarks from the interviewer and laughter from the audience. This is taken to demonstrate the shared character of the activity/category pairs being discussed there. What we could call 'Schegloff's complaint' about the unanalyzed 'obviousness' of MCA results (cf. page 47) does seem to have some relevance here.

In a chapter presenting an overview of feminists' research interests, Celia Kitzinger (2004) has noted that researchers inspired by the 'second feminist wave' wanted to represent in their work the 'voice' of women's experience in general and of their research subjects in particular. They therefore relied heavily on qualitative interviews and later focus groups, that is self-reports, 'talk about experience as evidence for what that experience is actually like' (126). After discussing some uses and problems of this approach in feminist qualitative research in general, she presents CA as a possible alternative approach to the relationship between 'voice' and 'experience'. Her move into CA began as she 'started to take seriously the local interactional context in which women's voices were being elicited' (133). After some work on interview/focus group interactions, she moved on to analyse more 'natural' data. I will, in a summarizing fashion, discuss some of these more recent analyses.

I have selected three papers (Kitzinger, 2005a; 2005b; Land & Kitzinger, 2005) that deal with what she calls 'heteronormativity', 'the myriad ways in which heterosexuality is produced as a natural, unproblematic, taken-for-granted, ordinary phenomenon' (Kitzinger, 2005a: 478). In this paper she uses a corpus of after-hours calls to family doctors, in which she looks for the non-recognitional terms of person reference (i.e. not names) that are used by the callers to refer to the patient for whom they are making the call. In most cases these terms indicated a family relationship (33 out of 50 in which the caller is not the patient). Using a term from the categorization device 'family' can be seen as a choice, as terms from other devices might also have been taken. In many more or less subtle ways the doctors answering the calls show that they take it as obvious that the caller and the patient are members of a conventional family, a married couple with their pre-adult biological children living together, in which the wife is the main care-provider, which involves intimate knowledge of the patient's medical history. Similar presumptions are visible in what the callers mention, or do not mention. These and other invocations and inferences based on conventional images of family compositions and responsibilities are used as *resources* to transact the business of the call, to negotiate an after-hours home visit. In an analysis such as Kitzinger provides in this paper, as well as a parallel one, based on more general data (2005b), the ordinary resources are topicalized for the work they also do, if unintended, of reproducing 'heteronormativity'.

In the many ways in which such a normative obviousness is reproduced, a range of deviations from conventional formats of family life, such as parents living with children from a previous relationship or adopted children, as well as same-sex relationships, are in a way excluded. The practical upshot for those who are deviant in these respects is that it creates dilemmas of whether to contradict these assumptions or not, and if so in which ways.

The two other papers are called 'Speaking as a heterosexual' (Kitzinger, 2005b) and 'Speaking as a lesbian' (Land & Kitzinger, 2005). In the first, Kitzinger uses data from what she calls the foundational data sets of CA, the data used in the papers of 'the first generation', to explore how speakers represented in those data presented themselves and others as 'naturally heterosexual'. 'These practices include heterosexual topic talk and person reference terms: husband and wife; in-law terminology; identification of the other with reference to their spouse; the production of heterosexual "couples"; and the use of locally initial proterms.' The paper with Land is based on recordings of 150 telephone conversations to and from 'lesbian households'. There was an important difference, in these calls, between those with friends and acquaintances who were aware of the lesbian identity of a speaker, and those with institutional parties who did not know about it. In the first type, lesbian identities were indicated in an 'of course' manner similar to the ways in which heterosexuality is presupposed in calls of heterosexual people. In the second type, of lesbian callers with unaware others, mostly institutional agents, their sexual identity can lead to quite delicate episodes, as the lesbian speaker is confronted with expressions based on the 'heterosexist presumption'.

There are basically three alternatives: choosing not to 'come out' as a lesbian, by passing up the opportunity to correct; coming out explicitly; or coming out discreetly. Not correcting the heterosexist presumption, the first alternative, can be chosen because a correction would interrupt the interactional flow, for instance when it occurs as the other party asked a question about the 'husband', while the caller previously used 'partner' or 'spouse', and the exact gender of the partner does not seem to be important for the matter at hand. In technical terms, in these cases the 'preference for progressivity' (Stivers & Robinson, 2006) prevails. The authors label the two coming-out alternatives, following Jefferson (1987), 'exposed correction' and 'embedded correction'. An exposed correction occurs only once in their corpus and it gets quite an explicit excuse, as well as an extensive effort to deal with an administrative difficulty caused by the same-sex marriage. Overwhelmingly, however, the lesbian callers in the corpus try to do their corrections discreetly, 'embedded'. In such cases, the correction does not take a full turn, but is built into the design of a sequentially relevant next turn, such as an answer to a previous question. The paper also provides a subtle example of an embedded correction by a call-taker, who apparently became aware of the female gender of the caller's 'spouse' by an overheard off-line conversation. So embedded formats seem to be preferred because of their delicacy:

> The cointeractants' capacity to bring off the job of identifying and correcting error without disrupting the smooth progressivity of the talk – without the business of error correction ever rising to the surface of the conversation – means that no account, explanation, or apology is made relevant from (nor is one offered by) either party. (Land & Kitzinger, 2005: 403)

Keeping a denial of a heterosexist presumption 'below the interactional surface' may on occasion require quite a lot of work, however, and although the corrector may use an embedded format, this work may lead the corrected to bring the issue to the surface anyhow (see 403–8).

What this research documents is, in a way, a historical moment in between an earlier generalized 'homophobia' and secrecy surrounding any deviation from heteronormativity and a still-to-be-achieved openness and general acceptance of what Kitzinger calls LGBT people (referring to lesbian, gay, bisexual, and transgendered folk). The political point, of course, is that CA studies like the ones discussed only superficially here can show *how* such a change can come about in and through everyday practices, and possibly can be helpful in promoting it. In the instances analysed here, 'coming out' was not a purposeful (and dramatic) event, but a by-product, so to speak, of speakers going about their lives as ordinary people. The point of CA in general is how 'doing being ordinary' (Sacks, 1984b) gets done and these applied studies do provide sensible contributions to that task. One can enlarge Sacks' (1979) remarks about 'revolutionary' categories, as referred to by Wowk (1984), to suggest that formerly deviant categories can gradually become ordinary ones.

Doing CA: 'pure' and 'applied'

The distinction between 'pure' and 'applied' CA, as I have used it throughout the book, should not be overdrawn. As long as the CA part in 'applied CA' is faithful to the core of the CA approach, the 'applied' aspect can be seen as a useful addition to 'good solid CA'. Quite often, the focus in applied CA on special types of data occasions the emergence of insights and results that are of value to CA generally, not just for some applied purpose or that special kind of data. I will mention just a few themes from the present chapter. Looking at the studies of 'impaired communication' can make one aware of the use of resources such as being able to hear or to speak that seem so obvious that they almost escape analysis. They can be seen as natural 'breaching' studies and therefore can be used in a similar way to Garfinkel's 'breaching' experiments (Garfinkel, 1967; see also Clayman & Maynard, 1995; Ten Have, 2004a: 38-41). Workplace studies do often demonstrate the importance of seeing the 'context sensitivity' of talk. This is clear, for instance in Marjorie Goodwin's (1996) analysis of special ways of making announcements in noisy settings, or Maurice Nevile's (2004) studies of pronoun use and the precise coordination of talk and non-talk activity in the work of airline pilots. In recent feminist studies, such as Land & Kitzinger (2005) that I discussed above, we become aware of the mostly unnoticed implications of gendered pronouns and ordinary family terms. Such work can also be seen as an excellent example of combining sequential CA and MCA, which have often been presented as separate endeavours (cf. Chapter 4).

Comparing talk in institutional settings with informal talk among peers can be useful for more than just characterizing the first in terms of restrictions on systems for the latter. Studies in institutional settings can suggest topics that can then also be researched for informal situations. Douglas Maynard, for instance, did extensive studies of the delivery of 'bad news' in clinical settings, but in his book *Bad news, good news: conversational order in everyday talk and clinical settings* (2003) he spent most pages on ordinary conversations. Another example can be found in a paper by Tanya Stivers and Jeffrey Robinson (2006) on the confluence of two preferences, one for an addressed person to answer a question, and a more general one for having a question answered as such. This theme came to their attention through Stivers' observation in her earlier work on paediatric encounters involving parents, children, and physicians that physicians often selected children to respond to questions, but parents did most of the answering (368), which incidentally is similar to my own observations on Dutch consultations. In other words, it would be a mistake to see applied CA as just a 'second' to pure CA.

Returning to applied CA as such, let me add some remarks on using CA for practical purposes. As I suggested before, detailed studies of organizational practices will tend to find discrepancies between, on the one hand, those *actual* practices and, on the other, the overall *plans* for those practices and the ways in which they are *accounted* for. The small demonstrative exploration of survey interviewing given in the previous chapter provided some indications of the kinds of discrepancies one might encounter.

I have stressed that a CA study (or an ethnomethodological study generally) is committed to elucidate the *local logic*, the *emic rationality*, of situated practices. One way in which one could conceive of 'applied CA' in such fields would be to try to influence the *plans* for such practices, in the sense of making them more respectful of the local rationalities one has discovered. One could, for instance, invite the people who design survey interview schedules, or those who train interviewers, to take CA-like findings into account. One might suggest that interview questions could best be constructed in such a way that they end with a Question Delivery Component, or one could invite trainers to deal with the apparent situational 'need' of interviewers to vocalize the reception of an answer as recordable (with 'okay'). The idea would be, then, to make questionnaire design and interview training more 'realistic', to the benefit of all. In other words, the research would provide a platform for a dialogue between (representatives of) the parties with a diverse interest in the practice. Although this seems a sensible direction to take, one should, I think, not have too high hopes that all discrepancies can be dissolved. Designers are focused on generality and standardization, while practice requires flexibility and local sensitivity. Studies of local practices bring to light just how professional workers *achieve* standardization *in situ*, and these might be evaluated from a designer's point of view. Some discrepancy may be inevitable, however.

There seems to be a tendency in such situations to summarize the conclusions of a consideration of practical problems and general interests in terms of relatively simple *recipes* or 'rules of thumb'. In current practices, such recipes are often based on one or another theoretical 'model' based on ideas from social psychology, as in the interview training for physicians. Medical students may be encouraged, for instance, to provide frequent support to patients' reporting with hmm-like sounds, colloquially known as 'humming'. From CA research we know, however, that variations within this category of 'supportive' vocalizations can be quite important interactionally (cf. Jefferson, 1984b, on 'Yeah' and 'Mm hm'). The important point, then, would be not to 'hum' frequently, but to do so in a sensitive manner, which, of course, is much harder to train people in.

Similarly, it is often recommended that physicians (as well as qualitative interviewers) should frequently 'summarize' their understanding of what patients tell them, as a kind of understanding check. As the late Hanneke Houtkoop (1986) has demonstrated in a case study, this strategy may backfire due to the 'preference for agreement', as Sacks (1987) has formulated, which may lead the patient to confirm a summary given by the doctor, even if it is apparently leading in another direction than the patient was planning to take. As with 'humming', then, adequate 'summarizing' requires a sensitivity to the context and the specifics of utterance design that is not covered by general recommendations to 'hum' or to 'summarize'.

Rather than providing packaged easy-to-use solutions to felt problems, CA might only be helpful in terms of developing an overall sensitivity for the intricacies of talk-in-interaction. And that takes time, a basic openness, and long-term collaboration between conversation analysts, on the one hand, and designers, trainers, and practitioners, on the other.

Conclusion

The general idea of this book has been that you can only become a conversation analyst through practice. I have discussed various practical aspects of 'doing conversation analysis' in order to facilitate this process and I have provided summary indications of a number of theoretical and methodological issues. For all of these, more extensive readings are recommended: just follow the suggestions I have provided. My hope, then, is that this book will be a useful supporting device for aspiring 'new' conversation analysts. Feedback from users will be appreciated. Various kinds of information on CA and ethnomethodology, as well as on recent publications, conferences, etc., are available at the continuously updated Ethno/CA News website: www.paultenhave.nl/EMCA.htm.

EXERCISE

Go back one more time to the data you were analysing before, and try to explicate the 'local rationalities' on display there. Confront these data-based explications with what might be the global, common-sense, or 'social-scientific' characterization that might be given of the interactional situation from which the data are taken, as 'gossip', 'call-for-assistance', 'professional dominance', or whatever. Think about what CA might add to such a characterization as (re)specification, critique, support, grounds for suggestion for redesign, training, etc.

For options C and D, this seems a challenging topic for a group discussion, based on individual 'position papers'.

RECOMMENDED READING

The following three papers have been major resources for this chapter: Heap (1990); Schegloff (1991; 1997).

On 'impaired' communication the major source is Goodwin (2003); the first two chapters, by Goodwin and Schegloff, offer a very useful general perspective.

On 'human–computer interaction', Lucy Suchman's book has appeared in a second edition, with five additional chapters on developments in the field since the first: Suchman (2007).

On workplace studies see the following books: Heath and Luff (2000); Luff et al. (2000); Nevile (2004).

Examples of challenging feminist CA studies are: Kitzinger (2005a); Land and Kitzinger (2005); Stokoe (2003); Wowk (1984).

Notes

1. While Heap talks about 'ethnomethodology', and not about conversation analysis, I take it that what I make of his arguments can be applied to CA as well. My treatment is not designed to do justice to his arguments, only to use these for my purposes at this juncture.

2. See also some remarkable ethnomethodological studies situation of 'impaired' communication, such as David Goode's (1994) book on studying the life of children born deaf and blind, and Albert Robillard's (1999) book on his own situation of communicative impairment.

APPENDICES

Appendix A: Transcription Conventions

The glossary of transcript symbols given below is meant to explain the major conventions for rendering details of the vocal production of utterances in talk-in-interaction as these are used in most current CA publications. Most if not all of these have been developed by Gail Jefferson, but are now commonly used with minor individual variations. The glosses given below are mostly based on, and simplified from, the descriptions provided in Jefferson (1989: 193–6; see also 2004a), at times using those in Heritage and Atkinson (1984), Psathas and Anderson (1990); see also Psathas (1995) and Ten Have and Psathas (1995). I have restricted the set given below to the ones most commonly used, omitting some of the subtleties provided by Jefferson.

Sequencing

[A *single left bracket* indicates the point of overlap onset.
]   A *single right bracket* indicates the point at which an utterance or utterance-part terminates vis-à-vis another.
=   *Equal signs*, one at the end of one line and one at the beginning of a next, indicate no 'gap' between the two lines. This is often called *latching*.

Timed intervals

(0.0)   *Numbers in parentheses* indicate elapsed time in silence by tenth of seconds, so (7.1) is a pause of 7 seconds and one-tenth of a second.
(.)   *A dot in parentheses* indicates a tiny 'gap' within or between utterances.

Characteristics of speech production

word   *Underscoring* indicates some form of stress, via pitch and/or amplitude; an alternative method is to print the stressed part in *italics*.
::   *Colons* indicate prolongation of the immediately prior sound. Multiple colons indicate a more prolonged sound.
–   A *dash* indicates a cut-off.

.,??,   *Punctuation marks* are used to indicate characteristics of speech production, especially intonation; they are not referring to grammatical units; an alternative is an italicized question mark:*?*
.   A *period* indicates a stopping fall in tone.
,   A *comma* indicates a continuing intonation, like when you are reading items from a list.

?	A *question mark* indicates a rising intonation.
,?	The *combined question mark/comma* indicates a stronger rise than a comma but weaker than a question mark.
	The absence of an utterance-final marker indicates some sort of 'indeterminate' contour.
↑↓	*Arrows* indicate marked shifts into higher or lower pitch in the utterance-part immediately following the arrow.
WORD	*Upper case* indicates especially loud sounds relative to the surrounding talk.
º	Utterances or utterance-parts bracketed by *degree signs* are relatively quieter than the surrounding talk.
< >	*Right/left carets* bracketing an utterance or utterance-part indicate speeding up.
·hhh	A *dot-prefixed row of* hs indicates an inbreath. Without the dot, the *hs* indicates an outbreath.
w(h)ord	A parenthesized *h*, or a *row of* hs *within a word*, indicates breathiness, as in laughter, crying, etc.

Transcriber's doubts and comments

( )	*Empty parentheses* indicate the transcriber's inability to hear what was said. The length of the parenthesized space indicates the length of the untranscribed talk. In the speaker designation column, the empty parentheses indicate inability to identify a speaker.
(word)	*Parenthesized words* are especially dubious hearings or speaker identifications.
(( ))	*Double parentheses* contain transcriber's descriptions rather than, or in addition to, transcriptions.

Appendix B: Glossary

accountability   as used in ethnomethodology: a general feature of action that the one responsible for it can always be taken to account, having to explain, justify, etc., the action

adjacency pair   a two-part sequence in which the first part makes relevant the production of a second pair-part of the type suggested by the first part to follow immediately after the first one, as in question–answer, greeting–greeting, invitation–acceptance/declination

analytic induction   a strategy to produce general statements about a collection of instances, by a case-by-case inspection; when a 'deviant case' is encountered previous conclusions have to be reconsidered

assessment   a turn which expresses an evaluative reaction to an aspect of (what is reported in) the preceding turn

collection studies   (CA) studies based on a substantial amount of comparable instances

conditional relevance   in adjacency pairs, the expectability of a particular type of next action on the basis of the occurrence of an earlier one

continuer   a short contribution like 'uhuh' that invites continuation of the other speaker

conversation analysis (CA) – applied   CA as applied to particular kinds of data, analysed in terms of their context or specific (practical) interests

conversation analysis (CA) – pure   CA used to analyse talk-in-interaction relatively independent of contextual considerations or particular interests

deviant case analysis (*see* analytic induction)   the detailed analysis of any case that seems to depart from a previously formulated rule or pattern, in order to explicate the sense and/or to revise the characterization of that rule or pattern

discourse unit   a larger episode of talk-in-interaction in which one participant is the 'primary speaker', while others limit their contributions to shows of attention, requests for elaboration, etc.

emic/etic distinction   etic refers to a viewpoint to study behaviour as from outside a particular (cultural) system, while an emic approach tries to study it from inside the system

ethnography   the study of a way of life by using a range of data gathering methods, including most prominently participant observation and qualitative interviewing

ethnomethodology   an 'alternate sociology' developed by Harold Garfinkel, studying the folk methods used to constitute social states of affairs

ethnomethodological indifference   the research policy to study members' accounts 'wherever and by whomever they are done, while abstaining from judgments of their adequacy, value, importance, necessity, practicality, success, or consequentiality' (Garfinkel & Sacks, 1970: 845)

expansion, sequence expansion   the enlargement of a sequence beyond a two-item core sequence (adjacency pair) by a pre-sequence, an insertion sequence, or a post-sequence/third-turn item

formulation   an utterance which 'formulates' what is going on, or is implied, in the conversation, often the preceding interaction

indexicality, indexical expressions   the general property of expressions and other actions that their meaning depends on the occasion of use

insertion sequence   a sequence (adjacency pair) positioned between the first and second parts of a base adjacency pair

institutional interaction   a generalized category of interactions that typically take place in various institutional settings

membership categorization analysis (MCA)   analysis of the ways in which person-categories are used in talk and text

naturalness   'natural' data are data about interactions not 'provoked' by the researcher, in contrast to 'experimental' ones

other-initiation of repair   an initiation of repair by a speaker other than the one who produced the trouble source

other-repair   a repair done by a different speaker than the one who produced the 'trouble source'

post-sequence   a sequence dealing with aspects of a base sequence, positioned after that sequence

pre-sequence   a sequence which in some way is designed to prepare for or explore the fitness of a base sequence

preference, preference organization   the structural property of responses and other actions that alternatives are not equally valued; 'positives' and 'negatives' tend to be constructed differently, with the 'preferred' (positive) ones coming quick and short, while the 'dispreferred' (negative) ones come slow, hesitantly, and with explanatory comments

recipient design   refers to 'a multitude of respects in which talk by a party in a conversation is constructed or designed in ways which display an orientation and sensitivity to the particular other(s) who are the co-participants' (Sacks et al., 1978: 42–3)

repair   ways of dealing with various kinds of trouble in the interaction's progress, such as problems of (mis)hearing or understanding; it occurs in various phases: a (possible) trouble source, a repair initiator, by the same or a different speaker, and a repair, which may be a case of self-repair or other-repair

self-repair   a repair done by the speaker who produced the 'trouble source'

sequence, sequence organization   refers to the ordered progression of turns, often based on an adjacency pair

summons–answer sequence   a two-part (pre-)sequence, in which the first part works as an appeal, such as a telephone ring, and the second an answer to it, such as picking up the phone and saying 'hello'

topic/resource distinction   the ethnomethodological idea that what ordinarily is used as a taken-for-granted resource should be taken as a topic for analysis

transcription, transcript   rendering the information available from a recording by noting not just what is said, but also how the talk is produced

transition relevance place (TRP)   the moment in the production of a turn-at-talking in which that turn might be possibly complete and another speaker might take over

turn, turn-taking   turns are parts of spoken discourse by one speaker, after the speech of another and before others take over again; turn-taking refers to the organization of speaker change

turn constructional unit (TCU)   the part of an utterance that might be a complete turn, after which another speaker might take over

unique adequacy requirement   coined by Harold Garfinkel: states that the analyst must be 'vulgarly competent' in the activity studied

unmotivated looking   a strategy in which the analyst tries to be 'open to discovering phenomena rather than searching for instances of already identified and described phenomena or for some theoretically pre-formulated conceptualization of what the phenomena should look like' (Psathas, 1990a: 24–5, n. 3)

workplace studies   a style of research of work in technologically complex environments, including various ICT components; it uses ethnography for background information and video recordings as focal data

Appendix C: Tips for Presentations and Publications

Because of the rather special character of the CA enterprise, it may be useful to give some suggestions for the presentation of CA research, both oral and written.

Oral presentations

Oral presentations, whether of preliminary findings, work-in-progress, or finished products, are standard practice in all sciences, especially in the context of conferences. Most problems of presentation design and performance are quite general, but some are rather specific for CA research, especially those having to do with providing access to data. A common experience is that the *time slots* allotted for presentations are rather small: 20 minutes, with 10 minutes for 'questions'. Many speakers tend to take too much time to introduce their project, then have to rush through their findings, and in the end have no time left for conclusions or a discussion. If you want to give your audience a sense of the data and some argumentative reasoning as well, you are bound to run into trouble. In the following paragraphs, I will discuss some dilemmas and provide a few suggestions.

When preparing a presentation, try to restrict your talk to *one* major argument, which you should keep as simple as possible. You may start with some data, formulate an analytic problem, and offer a solution based on a careful consideration of at least part of the data. You will have to cut out all digressions and be short on background explanations, interesting exceptions, and scholarly references.

A very important dilemma is whether to *read* a pre-written text or to *speak* freely from notes. The tone of many speakers tends to degenerate to a drone when they read. This will make it very hard for an audience to keep its attention focused on the argument, especially when the presenter speaks fast in order to finish on time. Speaking from notes tends to be more lively, and, because the speaker has to search for the right formulations, the audience gets more time to digest the message. When speaking from notes, it may also be easier to coordinate the talk with the data presentation. Even if less attractive, many presenters do choose to read, however, because they want to be sure they present the right argument, in the required detail. So if your reading style is clear and lively, and if you insist on getting your message across in finely worked-out detail, you can choose to read your paper. But if you want to raise the audience's interest and if you are content with offering an overall impression of your work, you might do better to speak from notes.

As presentation programs, like MS-PowerPoint or Corel Presentations, are now in general use, I will treat them as the default technique, with printed handouts with major points, transcripts, and references as a major support. You can use a program to play recorded data while the audience can also read the transcript, preceded by an overview and interspersed with major concepts and ending with a summary. Be sure *not* just to read the slides as they are projected, but talk a bit around them.

Be sure to test the local system *before* the audience comes in. The best solution is to bring your own laptop computer with the required cables to connect to the system.

It is my experience that it is very hard for an audience to focus on an *audio* tape, so I would, in general, advise against it. It takes more repetitions to *hear* a phenomenon from an audio record only, than to *see* it on a video, or even to *hear* it while trying to *see* what is happening. In any case, whether you play a video or an audiotape, you should provide a transcript in order to assist the audience to see/hear what you want to focus on. There is no time, really, to allow the audience to discover phenomena on its own, so what you want to achieve is an *instructed* viewing or hearing.

Ask someone else to distribute your handouts *before* you start your presentation. Add clear number codes to the fragments, so you can just cite the numbers in your presentation. Use arrows or other marks to highlight the utterances you are specifically analysing. It is probably best to see the oral presentation as an occasion to raise an interest in your work and suggest what you are after, and where you are going. If at all possible, have a number of copies of a full paper with you to distribute to people who want to know more about it, or whom you want to interest in your work. Always give your (email) address on the handout. Take care to design a nice layout and use clear headings, mentioning the occasion, your name, and a title.

In all kinds of publication, you should consider the kind of *audience* you can expect to have, and adapt your presentation to the audience's interests and capabilities. When you present to an audience of professional CA practitioners, for instance, do not spend time explaining what CA is, or what the transcription conventions are. But if you are addressing a general or mixed audience, comprising a substantial number of lay persons or people with a different disciplinary background, you may be required to do so. For such an audience you might also check your text for hard-to-understand jargon, and you might choose to use simplified transcripts in standard orthography. In any case, concentrate on putting across what you want *this* audience to take home regarding you and your work.

Written papers, collections, and books

When you read CA papers, like the ones recommended in Chapters 2, 7, and 8, take a look at the way they are constructed: how they introduce the project, formulate the problem, use the data, propose a solution, and discuss its implications – to name a few obvious elements. You will see that there is not one fixed framework, like those required in some other fields (for instance, theory, method, results, discussion). In any paper, there should be an introduction and a conclusion, but for CA there is not one ideal ordered way to use the data or refer to the literature. Choose a design that best fits your particular argument.

It is essential that a CA paper contains a representation of the relevant *data*, most often in the form of transcribed fragments. You should select these fragments carefully, in terms of their contribution to the argument. Some will be used to exemplify the standard form of the phenomenon, others can function to differentiate sub-types, while still others will be the object of a 'deviant case analysis'. Whatever the function of the excerpt, it should be clearly indicated in the text.

In the context of a written paper, your argument is also accountable in terms of the *literature*. As I suggested, the usual CA format does not include a required 'review of the literature' section. Some papers do have such a section, however, sometimes at the request of a more conventionally oriented editor. A more usual way to refer to various published sources is to do so at the moment it is needed to support the argument that is being developed. Such references may support a concept being used, suggest a pattern that has been proposed by another researcher, or even provide a piece of data quoted from the source referred to. Whatever kind of referencing is being done, you should be alert to its 'fit' in the local argument and with the data under consideration. When a particular turn-shape, for instance, has been analysed as having a specific function in the literature, and you think that is also the case in your data, you are still under the obligation to demonstrate, or at least to make plausible, that it is so for the participants. CA, after all, is not oriented to find or formulate permanent and absolute 'structures', and to apply these 'mechanically', but rather to explicate locally used resources. The function of the literature is, therefore, different from the one in other types of social science research (cf. the discussions in Chapter 3).

In CA, papers, rather than book-length monographs, are the most often used form of publication. Papers may be distributed at conferences or through networks, often in draft form, or they may be published in journals, or as collections in a special journal issue or a book. As will become clear from scanning any CA bibliography, there are a wide range of journals that publish CA papers: some do so regularly, others rarely. There are no journals specialized in only presenting CA work.

The fact that papers are the most common format for CA reporting does not mean that there are no *monographs* at all. But as this option will be rarely open to beginning researchers, I will not treat it here. PhD dissertations are a special case, of course. Their overall format is strongly dependent on national and local regulations and traditions regarding the length, literature review, etc. If your supervisor and/or dissertation committee is not very knowledgeable about CA's approach, you may have to negotiate in order to save as many of CA's characteristics as is possible to have your thesis accepted. The most important point, I think, is the inclusion of the data you need to support your arguments. One solution is to include most of these in an appendix, possibly even in a separate volume. You may have to include more or less extensive accounts for your specific design decisions regarding issues like 'sampling' and (not) working with prede-fined hypotheses (cf. Chapters 3, 4, and 7). I hope my text, and the references, will supply you with the necessary arguments. Be sure to explore the local requirements and sensitivities at an early stage in order to prevent last-minute difficulties.

So, whatever the format, the distinguishing characteristic of written CA reports is that they include data in the shape of transcripts. Only rarely are tapes offered, as is the case in a book by Wayne Beach (1996: 113). Supplementing transcripts with more lively, detailed, and realistic data information has become much easier in recent years, as 'electronic publishing' becomes much usual. Some CA researchers have made data extracts available on their home page, with of course the consent of the recorded persons (see Chapter 5)

Bibliography

Alasuutari, P. (1995) *Researching culture: qualitative method and cultural studies*. London: Sage

Arminen, I. (2005) *Institutional interaction: studies of talk at work*. Aldershot: Ashgate

Atkinson, J.M. (1982) 'Understanding formality: the categorization and production of "formal" interaction', *British Journal of Sociology* 33: 86–117

Atkinson, J.M. (1984a) *Our masters' voices: the language and body language of politics*. London: Methuen

Atkinson, J.M. (1984b) 'Public speaking and audience responses: some techniques for inviting audience applause'. In: J.M. Atkinson, J. Heritage, eds, *Structures of social action: studies in conversation analysis*. Cambridge: Cambridge University Press: 370–407

Atkinson, J.M. (1985) 'Refusing invited applause: preliminary observations from a case study of charismatic oratory'. In: T.A. van Dijk, ed., *Handbook of discourse analysis*, vol. III. London: Academic Press: 161–81

Atkinson, J.M., P. Drew (1979) *Order in court: the organisation of verbal interaction in judicial settings*. London: Macmillan

Atkinson, J.M., J. Heritage, eds (1984) *Structures of social action: studies in conversation analysis*. Cambridge: Cambridge University Press

Beach, W.A. (1996) *Conversations about illness: family preoccupations with bulimia*. Mahwah, NJ: Lawrence Erlbaum

Benson, D., J. Hughes (1991) 'Method: evidence and inference for ethnomethodology'. In: G. Button, ed., *Ethnomethodology and the human sciences*. Cambridge: Cambridge University Press: 109–36

Bergmann, J.R. (1987) *Klatsch: zur Sozialform der diskreten Indiskretion*. Berlin/New York: Walter de Gruyter [translated as Bergmann, 1993]

Bergmann, J.R. (1992) 'Veiled morality: notes on discretion in psychiatry'. In: P. Drew, J. Heritage, eds, *Talk at work: interaction in institutional settings*. Cambridge: Cambridge University Press: 137–62

Bergmann, J.R. (1993) *Discreet indiscretions: the social organization of gossip*. New York: Aldine de Gruyter [translation of Bergmann, 1987]

Billig, M. (1999a) 'Whose terms? Whose ordinariness? Rhetoric and ideology in conversation analysis', *Discourse & Society* 10: 543–58

Billig, M. (1999b) 'Conversation analysis and the claims of naivety', *Discourse & Society* 10: 572–6

Bjelic, D., M. Lynch (1992) 'The work of a (scientific) demonstration: respecifying Newton's and Goethe's theories of prismatic color'. In: G. Watson, R.M. Seiler, eds, *Text in context: contributions to ethnomethodology*. London: Sage: 52–78

Boden, D. (1990) 'The world as it happens: ethnomethodology and conversation analysis'. In: G. Ritzer, ed., *Frontiers of social theory: the new synthesis*. New York: Columbia University Press: 185–213

Boden, D. (1994) *The business of talk: organizations in action*. Cambridge: Polity Press

Boden, D., D.H. Zimmerman, eds (1991) *Talk and social structure: studies in ethnomethodology and conversation analysis*. Cambridge: Polity Press

Bogdan, R., S.J. Taylor (1975) *Introduction to qualitative research methods: a phenomenological approach to the social sciences*. New York: Wiley

Bogen, D. (1992) 'The organization of talk', *Qualitative Sociology* 15: 273–96

Bogen, D. (1999) *Order without rules: critical theory and the logic of conversation*. New York: SUNY Press

Boyd, E. (1998) 'Bureaucratic authority in the "company of equals": the interactional management of medical peer review', *American Sociological Review* 63: 200–24

Brun-Cottan, F. (1990/1) 'Talk in the workplace: occupational relevance', *Research on Language and Social Interaction* 24: 277–95

Burns, T. (1992) *Erving Goffman*. London: Routledge

Button, G. (1987a) 'Answers as interactional products: two sequential practices used in interviews', *Social Psychology Quarterly* 50: 160–71

Button, G. (1987b) 'Moving out of closings'. In: G. Button, J.R.E. Lee, eds, *Talk and social organisation*. Clevedon: Multilingual Matters: 101–51

Button, G. (1989) 'Some design specifications for turns at talk in a job interview', Unpublished paper

Button, G. (1990) 'On varieties of closings'. In: G. Psathas, ed., *Interactional competence*. Washington, DC: University Press of America: 93–147

Button, G., ed. (1991) *Ethnomethodology and the human sciences*. Cambridge: Cambridge University Press

Button, G. (1992) 'Answers as interactional products: two sequential practices used in job interviews'. In: P. Drew, J. Heritage, eds, *Talk at work: interaction in institutional settings*. Cambridge: Cambridge University Press: 212–31

Button, G., N.J. Casey (1984) 'Generating the topic: the use of topic initial elicitors'. In: J.M. Atkinson, J. Heritage, eds, *Structures of social action: studies in conversation analysis*. Cambridge: Cambridge University Press: 167–90

Button, G., N. Casey (1985) 'Topic nomination and pursuit', *Human Studies* 9: 355

Button, G., N. Casey (1989) 'Topic initiation: business-at-hand', *Research on Language and Social Interaction* 22: 61–92

Button, G., J.R.E. Lee, eds (1987) *Talk and social organisation*. Clevedon: Multilingual Matters

Button, G., J. Coulter, J.R.E. Lee, W. Sharrock (1995) *Computers, minds and conduct*. Cambridge: Polity Press

Cicourel, A.V. (1981) 'Notes on the integration of micro- and macro-levels of analysis'. In: K. Knorr-Cetina, A.V. Cicourel, eds, *Advances in social theory and methodology: toward an integration of micro- and macro-sociologies*. London: Routledge & Kegan Paul: 51–80

Cicourel, A.V. (1992) 'The interpenetration of communicative contexts: examples from medical encounters'. In: A. Duranti, C. Goodwin, eds, *Rethinking context: language as an interactive phenomenon*. Cambridge: Cambridge University Press: 291–310

Clayman, S.E. (1988) 'Displaying neutrality in television news interviews', *Social Problems* 35: 474–92

Clayman, S.E. (1992) 'Footing in the achievement of neutrality: the case of news interview discourse'. In: P. Drew, J. Heritage, eds, *Talk at work: interaction in institutional settings*. Cambridge: Cambridge University Press: 163–98

Clayman, S.E. (1993) 'Booing: the anatomy of a disaffiliative response', *American Sociological Review* 58: 110–30

Clayman, S., V.T. Gill (2004) 'Conversation analysis'. In: A. Bryman, M. Hardy, eds, *Handbook of data analysis*. London: Sage: 589–606

Clayman, S., J. Heritage (2002a) *The news interview: journalists and public figures on the air*. Cambridge: Cambridge University Press

Clayman, S., J. Heritage (2002b) 'Questioning presidents: journalistic deference and adversarialness in the press conferences of Eisenhower and Reagan', *Journal of Communication* 52: 749–77

Clayman, S.E., D.W. Maynard (1995) 'Ethnomethodology and conversation analysis'. In: P. ten Have, G. Psathas, eds, *Situated order: studies in the social organization of talk and embodied activities*. Washington, DC: University Press of America: 1–30

Collins, S., I. Marková, J. Murphy (1997) 'Bringing conversations to a close: the management of closings in interactions between AAC users and "natural" speakers', *Journal of Clinical Linguistics and Phonetics* 11/6: 467–93

Coulter, J. (1983) 'Contingent and *a priori* structures in sequential analysis', *Human Studies* 6: 361–74

Coulter, J. (1989) *Mind in action*. Cambridge: Polity Press

Coulter, J. (1991) 'Logic: ethnomethodology and the logic of language'. In: G. Button, ed., *Ethnomethodology and the human sciences*. Cambridge: Cambridge University Press: 20–50

Couper-Kuhlen, E., M. Selting (1996) 'Towards an interactional perspective on prosody and a prosodic perspective on interaction'. In: E. Couper-Kuhlen, M. Selting, eds, *Prosody in conversation: interactional studies*. Cambridge: Cambridge University Press: 11–56

Davey, B., K. Gramkow Andersen (1996) 'Some practical and legal aspects concerning the collection of empirical data'. In: K.A. Jensen, J. Steensig, eds, *Datadag*. Aarhus: ADLA (Danish Association for Applied Linguistics)

Davidson, J.A. (1978) 'An instance of negotiation in a call closing', *Sociology* 12: 123–33

Davis, K. (1988) *Power under the microscope: toward a grounded theory of gender relations in medical encounters*. Dordrecht/Providence, RI: Foris Publications

Douglas, J.D. (1976) *Investigative social research: individual and team field research*. London: Sage

Drew, P. (1985) 'Analyzing the use of language in courtroom interaction'. In: T.A. van Dijk, ed., *Handbook of discourse analysis*, vol. III. London: Academic Press: 133–47

Drew, P. (2003) 'Conversation analysis'. In: Smith, J., ed., *Qualitative psychology: a practical guide to research methods*. London: Sage: 132–58

Drew, P. (2005) 'Conversation analysis'. In: K.L. Fitch, R.E. Sanders, eds. *Handbook of language and social interaction*. Mahwah, NJ: Lawrence Erlbaum: 71–102

Drew, P., J. Heritage, eds (1992a) *Talk at work: interaction in institutional settings*. Cambridge: Cambridge University Press

Drew, P., J. Heritage (1992b) 'Analyzing talk at work: an introduction'. In: P. Drew, J. Heritage, eds, *Talk at work: interaction in institutional settings*. Cambridge: Cambridge University Press: 3–65

Drew, P., M.-L. Sorjonen (1997) 'Institutional dialogue'. In: T.A. van Dijk, ed., *Discourse studies: a multidisciplinary introduction*. London: Sage: 92–118

Duranti, A. (1997) *Linguistic anthropology*. Cambridge: Cambridge University Press

Duranti, A., C. Goodwin, eds (1992) *Rethinking context: language as an interactive phenomenon*. Cambridge: Cambridge University Press

Edwards, D., J. Potter (2001) 'Discursive psychology'. In: A. McHoul, M. Rapley, eds, *How to analyse talk in institutional settings: a casebook of methods*. London: Continuum: 12–24

Edwards, D., J. Potter (2005) 'Discursive psychology, mental states and descriptions'. In: H. te Molder, J. Potter, eds, *Conversation and cognition*. Cambridge: Cambridge University Press: 241–59

Edwards, J.A., M.D. Lampert, eds (1993) *Talking data: transcription and coding in discourse research*. Hillsdale, NJ: Lawrence Erlbaum

Eglin, P. (2002) 'Members' gendering work: "women", "feminists" and membership categorization analysis', *Discourse & Society* 13: 819–25

Erickson, F., J. Shultz (1982) *The counselor as gatekeeper: social interaction in interviews*. New York: Academic Press

Fairclough, N. (2001) 'Critical discourse analysis'. In: A. McHoul, M. Rapley, eds, *How to analyse talk in institutional settings: a casebook of methods*. London: Continuum: 25–38

Fenstermaker, S., C. West (2002) *Doing gender, doing difference: inequality, power, and institutional change*. New York, London: Routledge

Fine, G.A., D.D. Martin (1995) 'Humor in ethnographic writing: sarcasm, satire, and irony as voices in Erving Goffman's *Asylums*'. In: J. Van Maanen, ed., *Representation in ethnography*. Thousand Oaks, CA: Sage: 165–97

Firth, A., ed. (1995a) *The discourse of negotiation: studies of language in the workplace*. Oxford: Pergamon

Firth, A. (1995b) 'Talking for a change: commodity negotiating by telephone'. In: A. Firth, ed., *The discourse of negotiation: studies of language in the workplace*. Oxford: Pergamon: 183–222

Firth, A. (1995c) 'Multiple mode, single activity: telenegotiating as a social accomplishment'. In: P. ten Have, G. Psathas, eds, *Situated order: studies in the social organization of talk and embodied activities*. Washington, DC: University Press of America: 151–72

Firth, A. (1995d) '"Accounts" in negotiation discourse: a single case analysis', *Journal of Pragmatics* 23: 199–226

Fisher, S. (1986) *In the patient's best interest: women and the politics of medical decisions*. New Brunswick, NJ: Rutgers University Press

Fishman, P. (1978) 'Interaction: the work women do', *Social Problems* 25: 397–406

Ford, C.E., B.A. Fox, S.A. Thompson, eds (2002) *The language of turn and sequence*. New York: Oxford University Press [Dedicated to Emanuel A. Schegloff]

Ford, C.E., B.A. Fox, S.A. Thompson (2003) 'Social interaction and grammar'. In: M. Tomasello, ed., *The new psychology of language: cognitive and functional approaches to language structure*, vol. 2. Mahwah, NJ: Lawrence Erlbaum: 119–43

Ford, C.E., S.A. Thompson (1996) 'Interactional units in conversation: syntactic, intonational, and pragmatic resources for the management of turns'. In: E. Ochs, E.A. Schegloff, S.A. Thompson, eds, *Interaction and grammar*. Cambridge: Cambridge University Press: 134–84

Francis, D., S. Hester (2004) *An invitation to ethnomethodology: language, society and interaction*. London: Sage

Frankel, R.M. (1984) 'From sentence to sequence: understanding the medical encounter through micro-interactional analysis', *Discourse Processes* 7: 135–70

Frankel, R.M. (1989) '"I wz wonderinguhm could *Raid* uhm *effect* the Brain permanently d'y know?": some observations on the intersection of speaking and writing in calls to a poison control center', *Western Journal of Speech Communication* 53: 195–226

Garcia, A. (1991) 'Dispute resolution without disputing: how the interactional organization of mediation hearings minimizes argument', *American Sociological Review* 56: 818–35

Garfinkel, H. (1967) *Studies in ethnomethodology*. Englewood Cliffs, NJ: Prentice Hall

Garfinkel, H. (1991) 'Respecification: evidence for locally produced, naturally accountable phenomena of order*, logic, reason, meaning, method, etc. in and as of the essential haecceity of immortal ordinary society (I) an announcement of studies'. In: G. Button, ed., *Ethnomethodology and the human sciences*. Cambridge: Cambridge University Press: 10–19

Garfinkel, H. (1996) 'An overview of ethnomethodology's program', *Social Psychology Quarterly* 59: 5–21

Garfinkel, H., H. Sacks (1970) 'On formal structures of practical action'. In: J.C. McKinney, E.A. Tiryakian, eds, *Theoretical sociology: perspectives and developments*. New York: Appleton-Century-Crofts: 338–66

Garfinkel, H., D.L. Wieder (1992) 'Two incommensurable, asymmetrically alternate technologies of social analysis'. In: G. Watson, R.M. Seiler, eds, *Text in context: studies in ethnomethodology*. Newbury Park, CA: Sage: 175–206

Gill, V.T., T. Halkowski, F. Roberts (2001) 'Accomplishing a request without making one: a single case analysis of a primary care visit', *Text* 21: 55–81

Glaser, B.G., A.L. Strauss (1967) *The discovery of grounded theory: strategies for qualitative research*. Chicago: Aldine

Glenn, Ph.J. (2003). *Laughter in interaction*. Cambridge: Cambridge University Press

Goffman, E. (1963) *Behavior in public places: notes on the social organization of gatherings*. New York: Free Press

Goffman, E. (1974) *Frame analysis: an essay on the organization of experience*. New York: Harper & Row

Goffman, E. (1981) *Forms of talk*. Oxford: Basil Blackwell

Goffman, E. (1983) 'The interaction order', *American Sociological Review* 48: 1–17

Goode, D. (1994) *A world without words: the social construction of children born deaf and blind*. Philadelphia, PA: Temple University Press

Goodwin, C. (1979) 'The interactive construction of a sentence in natural conversation'. In: G. Psathas, ed., *Everyday language: studies in ethnomethodology*. New York: Irvington: 97–121

Goodwin, C. (1980) 'Restarts, pauses and the achievement of a state of mutual gaze at turn beginning', *Sociological Inquiry* 50: 272–302

Goodwin, C. (1981) *Conversational organization: interaction between speakers and hearers*. New York: Academic Press

Goodwin, C. (1984) 'Notes on story structure and the organization of participation'. In: J.M. Atkinson, J. Heritage, eds, *Structures of social action: studies in conversation analysis*. Cambridge: Cambridge University Press: 225–46

Goodwin, C. (1986) 'Gesture as a resource for the organization of mutual orientation', *Semiotica* 62: 29–49

Goodwin, C. (1987) 'Unilateral departure'. In: G. Button, J.R.E. Lee, eds, *Talk and social organisation*. Clevedon: Multilingual Matters: 206–18

Goodwin, C. (1994a) 'Recording human interaction in natural settings', *Pragmatics* 3: 181–209

Goodwin, C. (1994b) 'Professional vision', *American Anthropologist* 96: 606–33

Goodwin, C. (1995) 'Co-constructing meaning in conversations with an aphasic man', *Research on Language and Social Interaction* 28: 233–60

Goodwin, C. (1996) 'Transparent vision'. In: E. Ochs, E.A. Schegloff, S.A. Thompson, eds, *Interaction and grammar*. Cambridge: Cambridge University Press: 370–404

Goodwin, C. (2000a) 'Action and embodiment within situated human interaction', *Journal of Pragmatics* 32: 1489–522

Goodwin, C. (2000b) 'Practices of seeing: visual analysis - an ethnomethodological approach'. In: T. v. Leeuwen and C. Jewitt, eds, *Handbook of visual analysis*. London: Sage: 157–82

Goodwin, C., ed. (2003) *Conversation and brain damage*. Oxford: Oxford University Press

Goodwin, C., M.H. Goodwin (1996) 'Seeing as situated activity: formulating planes'. In: Y. Engeström, D. Middleton, eds, *Cognition and communication at work*. Cambridge: Cambridge University Press: 61–95

Goodwin, C., J. Heritage (1990) 'Conversation analysis', *Annual Review of Anthropology* 19: 283–307

Goodwin, M.H. (1990) *He-said-she-said: talk as social organization among black children*. Bloomington: Indiana University Press

Goodwin, M.H. (1995) 'Assembling a response: setting and collaboratively constructed work talk'. In: P. ten Have, G. Psathas, eds, *Situated order: studies in the social organization of talk and embodied activities*. Washington, DC: University Press of America: 173–86

Goodwin, M.H. (1996) 'Informings and announcements in their environment: prosody within a multi-activity work setting'. In: E. Couper-Kuhlen, M. Selting, eds, *Prosody in conversation: interactional studies*. Cambridge: Cambridge University Press: 436–61

Greatbatch, D. (1988) 'A turn-taking system for British news interviews', *Language in Society* 17: 401–30

Greatbatch, D. (1992) 'On the management of disagreement between news interviewers'. In: P. Drew, J. Heritage, eds, *Talk at work: interaction in institutional settings*. Cambridge: Cambridge University Press: 268–301

Greatbatch, D., C. Heath, P. Luff, P. Campion (1995) 'Conversation analysis: human–computer interaction and the general practice consultation'. In: A. Monk, N. Gilbert, eds, *Perspectives on HCI: diverse approaches*. New York: Academic Press: 199–222

Gumperz, J.J., D. Hymes, eds (1972) *Directions in sociolinguistics: the ethnography of communication*. New York: Rinehart & Winston

Guthrie, A.M. (1997) 'On the systematic deployment of okay and mmhmm in academic advising sessions', *Pragmatics* 7: 397–415

Haakana, M. (2001) 'Laughter as a patient's resource: dealing with delicate aspects of medical interaction', *Text* 21: 187–219

Haegeman, P. (1996) 'Business English in Flanders: a study of lingua franca telephone interaction', PhD dissertation, University of Ghent

Hak, T. (2002) 'How interviewers make coding decisions'. In: D.W. Maynard, H. Houtkoop-Steenstra, N.C. Schaeffer J. van der Zouwen, eds, *Standardization and tacit knowledge: interaction and practice in the survey interview*. New York: Wiley: 449–69

Hammersley, M., P. Atkinson (1983) *Ethnography: principles in practice*. London: Tavistock

Have, P. ten (1989) 'The consultation as a genre'. In: B. Torode, ed., *Text and talk as social practice*. Dordrecht/Providence, RI: Foris Publications: 115–35

Have, P. ten (1990) 'Methodological issues in conversation analysis'. *Bulletin de Méthodologie Sociologique*, 27: 23–51 [also: http://www.paultenhave.nlmica.htm]

Have, P. ten (1991a) 'The doctor is silent: observations on episodes without vocal receipt during medical consultations'. In: B. Conein, M. de Fornel, L. Quéré, eds, *Les formes de la conversation*, vol. 2. Issy les Moulineaux: CNET: 55–76

Have, P. ten (1991b) 'Talk and institution: a reconsideration of the "asymmetry" of doctor–patient interaction'. In: D. Boden, D.H. Zimmerman, eds, *Talk and social structure: studies in ethnomethodology and conversation analysis*. Cambridge: Polity Press: 138–63

Have, P. ten (1995a) 'Disposal negotiations in general practice consultations'. In: A. Firth, ed., *The discourse of negotiation: studies of language in the workplace*. Oxford: Pergamon: 319–44

Have, P. ten (1995b) 'Medical ethnomethodology: an overview', *Human Studies* 18: 245–61

Have, P. ten (1999) 'Structuring writing for reading: hypertext and the reading body', *Human Studies* 22: 273–98

Have, P. ten (2002) 'Reflections on transcription', *Cahiers de Praxématique* 39: 21–43

Have, P. ten (2004a) *Understanding qualitative research and ethnomethodology*. London: Sage

Have, P. ten (2004b) 'Ethnomethodology'. In: C. Seale, D. Silverman, J. Gubrium, G. Gobo, eds, *Qualitative research practice*. London: Sage: 151–64 [reprinted in paperback in 2007 at pages 139–52]

Have, P. ten (2006) 'On the interactive constitution of medical encounters', *Revue Française de Linguistique Appliquée* 11/2: 85–98

Have, P. ten, G. Psathas, eds (1995) *Situated order: studies in the social organization of talk and embodied activities*. Washington, DC: University Press of America

Heap, J.L. (1990) 'Applied ethnomethodology: looking for the local rationality of reading activities', *Human Studies* 13: 39–72

Heath, C. (1982) 'Preserving the consultation: medical record cards and professional conduct', *Journal of the Sociology of Health and Illness* 4: 56–74

Heath, C. (1986) *Body movement and speech in medical interaction*. Cambridge: Cambridge University Press

Heath, C. (1988) 'Embarrassment and interactional organization'. In: P. Drew, A. Wootton, eds, *Erving Goffman: exploring the interaction order*. Cambridge: Polity Press: 136–60

Heath, C. (1989) 'Pain talk: the expression of suffering in the medical consultation', *Social Psychology Quarterly* 52: 113–25

Heath, C. (1992) 'The delivery and reception of diagnosis in the general practice consultation'. In: P. Drew, J. Heritage, eds, *Talk at work*. Cambridge: Cambridge University Press: 235–67

Heath, C. (1997) 'The analysis of activities in face to face interaction using video'. In: D. Silverman, ed., *Qualitative research: theory, method and practice*. London: Sage: 183–200

Heath, C. (2004) 'Analysing face to face interaction: video, the visual and material'. In: D. Silverman, ed., *Qualitative research: theory, method and practice,* Second edition. London: Sage: 266–82

Heath, C., P. Luff (1993) 'Explicating face-to-face interaction'. In: N. Gilbert, ed., *Researching social life.* London: Sage: 306–26

Heath, C., P. Luff (1996) 'Convergent activities: line control and passenger information on the London Underground'. In: Y. Engeström, D. Middleton, eds, *Cognition and communication at work.* Cambridge: Cambridge University Press: 96–129

Heath, C., P. Luff (2000) *Technology in action.* Cambridge: Cambridge University Press

Hepburn, A. (2004) 'Crying: notes on description, transcription, and interaction', *Research on Language & Social Interaction* 37: 251–91

Hepburn, A., J. Potter (2004) 'Discourse analytic practice'. In C. Seale, D. Silverman, J. Gubrium, G. Gobo, eds, *Qualitative research practice.* London: Sage: 180–96

Hepburn, A., S. Wiggins, eds (2005). 'Developments in discursive psychology', Special Issue. *Discourse & Society* 16/5: 595–747

Heritage, J. (1984a) *Garfinkel and ethnomethodology.* Cambridge: Polity Press

Heritage, J. (1984b) 'A change-of-state token and aspects of its sequential placement'. In: J.M. Atkinson, J. Heritage, eds, *Structures of social action: studies in conversation analysis.* Cambridge: Cambridge University Press: 299–345

Heritage, J. (1985) 'Analyzing news interviews: aspects of the production of talk for an overhearing audience'. In: T.A. van Dijk, ed., *Handbook of discourse analysis.* vol. III. London: Academic Press: 95–117

Heritage, J. (1988) 'Explanations as accounts: a conversation analytic perspective'. In: C. Antaki, ed., *Analyzing everyday explanation: a casebook of methods.* London: Sage: 127–44

Heritage, J. (1990/1) 'Intention, meaning and strategy: observations on constraints on interaction analysis', *Research on Language and Social Interaction* 24: 311–32

Heritage, J. (1995) 'Conversation analysis: methodological aspects'. In: U.M. Quasthoff, ed., *Aspects of oral communication.* Berlin/New York: Walter de Gruyter: 391–418

Heritage, J. (1997) 'Conversation analysis and institutional talk: analysing data'. In: D. Silverman, ed., *Qualitative research: theory, method and practice.* London: Sage: 161–82

Heritage, J. (1999) 'CA at century's end: practices of talk-in-interaction, their distributions and their outcomes', *Research on Language and Social Interaction* 32: 69–76

Heritage, J. (2004) 'Conversation analysis and institutional talk: analysing data'. In: D. Silverman, ed., *Qualitative research: theory, method and practice,* Second edition. London: Sage: 222–45

Heritage, J., J.M. Atkinson (1984) 'Introduction'. In: J.M. Atkinson, J. Heritage, eds, *Structures of social action: studies in conversation analysis.* Cambridge: Cambridge University Press: 1–15

Heritage, J., D. Greatbatch (1986) 'Generating applause: a study of rhetoric and response at party political conferences', *American Journal of Sociology* 92: 110–57

Heritage, J., D. Greatbatch (1991) 'On the institutional character of institutional talk: the case of news interviews'. In: D. Boden, D.H. Zimmerman, eds, *Talk and social structure: studies in ethnomethodology and conversation analysis.* Cambridge: Polity Press: 93–137

Heritage, J., D.W. Maynard, eds (2006) *Communication in medical care: interaction between primary care physicians and patients.* Cambridge: Cambridge University Press

Heritage, J., M.L. Sorjonen (1994) 'Constituting and maintaining activities across sequences: *And*-prefacing as a feature of questioning design', *Language in Society* 23: 1–29

Heritage, J.C., D.R. Watson (1979) 'Formulations as conversational objects'. In: G. Psathas, ed., *Everyday language: studies in ethnomethodology*. New York: Irvington: 123–62

Heritage, J.C., D.R. Watson (1980) 'Aspects of the properties of formulations in natural conversations: some instances analysed', *Semiotica* 30: 245–62

Hester, S., P. Eglin (1997) 'Membership categorization analysis: an introduction'. In: S. Hester, P. Eglin, eds, *Culture in action: studies in membership categorization analysis*. Washington, DC: University Press of America: 1–24

Hester, S., D. Francis (2001) 'Is institutional talk a phenomenon? Reflections on ethnomethodology and applied conversation analysis'. In: A. McHoul, M. Rapley, eds, *How to analyse talk in institutional settings: a casebook of methods*. London: Continuum: 206–17

Hopper, R., ed. (1990) 'Ethnography and conversation analysis after Talking Culture', *Research on Language and Social Interaction* 24: 161–387

Hopper, R. (1992) *Telephone conversation*. Bloomington: Indiana University Press

Hopper, R. (1995) 'Episode trajectory in conversational play'. In: P. ten Have, G. Psathas, eds, *Situated order: studies in the social organization of talk and embodied activities*. Washington, DC: University Press of America: 57–72

Houtkoop, H. (1986) 'Summarizing in doctor–patient interaction'. In: T. Ensink, A. van Essen, T. van der Geest, eds, *Discourse and public life*. Dordrecht/Providence, RI: Foris Publications: 201–21

Houtkoop, H., H. Mazeland (1985) 'Turns and discourse units in everyday conversation', *Journal of Pragmatics* 9: 595–619

Houtkoop-Steenstra, H. (1991) 'Opening sequences in Dutch telephone conversations'. In: D. Boden, D.H. Zimmerman, eds, *Talk and social structure: studies in ethnomethodology and conversation analysis*. Cambridge: Polity Press: 232–50

Houtkoop-Steenstra, H. (1995) 'Meeting both ends: standardization and recipient design in telephone survey interviews'. In: P. ten Have, G. Psathas, eds, *Situated order: studies in the social organization of talk and embodied activities*. Washington, DC: University Press of America: 91–106

Houtkoop-Steenstra, H. (1996) 'Probing behavior of interviewers in the standardized semi-open research interview', *Quality & Quantity* 30: 205–30

Houtkoop-Steenstra, H. (1997) 'Being friendly in survey interviews', *Journal of Pragmatics* 28: 591–623

Houtkoop-Steenstra, H. (2000) *Interaction and the standardized interview. The living questionnaire*. Cambridge: Cambridge University Press

Hutchby, I. (1996) *Confrontation talk: arguments, asymmetries, and power on talk radio*. Mahwah, NJ: Lawrence Erlbaum

Hutchby, I., R. Wooffitt (1998) *Conversation analysis: principles, practices and applications*. Oxford: Polity Press

Jayyusi, L. (1991) 'Values and moral judgement: communicative praxis as moral order'. In: G. Button, ed., *Ethnomethodology and the human sciences*. Cambridge: Cambridge University Press: 227–51

Jefferson, G. (1972) 'Side sequences'. In: D. Sudnow, ed., *Studies in social interaction*. New York: Free Press: 294–338

Jefferson, G. (1973) 'A case of precision timing in ordinary conversation: overlapped tag-positioned address terms in closing sequences', *Semiotica* 9: 47–96

Jefferson, G. (1974) 'Error correction as an international resource', *Language in Society* 2: 181–99

Jefferson, G. (1979) 'A technique for inviting laughter and its subsequent acceptance/declination'. In: G. Psathas, ed., *Everyday language: studies in ethnomethodology*. New York: Irvington: 79–96

Jefferson, G. (1980) 'On "trouble-premonitory" response to inquiry', *Sociological Inquiry* 50: 153–85

Jefferson, G. (1983) 'Issues in the transcription of naturally-occurring talk: caricature versus capturing pronunciational particulars', Tilburg: Tilburg University (Tilburg papers in language and literature 34)

Jefferson, G. (1984a) 'On the organization of laughter in talk about troubles'. In: J. M. Atkinson, J. Heritage, eds, *Structures of social action: studies in conversation analysis*. Cambridge: Cambridge University Press: 346–69

Jefferson, G. (1984b) 'Notes on a systematic deployment of the acknowledgement tokens "Yeah" and "Mm hm"', *Papers in Linguistics* 17: 197–206

Jefferson, G. (1985a) 'On the interactional unpacking of a "gloss"', *Language in Society* 14: 435–66

Jefferson, G. (1985b) 'An exercise in the transcription and analysis of laughter'. In: T.A. van Dijk, ed., *Handbook of discourse analysis*, vol. III: London: Academic Press: 25–34

Jefferson, G. (1986) 'Notes on "latency" in overlap onset', *Human Studies* 9: 153–84

Jefferson, G. (1987) 'On exposed and embedded correction in conversation'. In: G. Button, J.R.E. Lee, eds, *Talk and social organisation*. Clevedon: Multilingual Matters: 86–100

Jefferson, G. (1989) 'Preliminary notes on a possible metric which provides for a "standard maximum" silence of approximately one second in conversation'. In: D. Roger, P. Bull, eds, *Conversation: an interdisciplinary perspective*. Clevedon: Multilingual Matters: 166–96

Jefferson, G. (1990) 'List-construction as a task and a resource'. In: G. Psathas, ed., *Interaction competence*. Washington, DC: University Press of America: 63–92

Jefferson, G. (1996) 'A case of transcriptional stereotyping', *Journal of Pragmatics* 26: 159–70

Jefferson, G. (2004a) 'Glossary of transcript symbols with an introduction'. In: G.H. Lerner, ed., *Conversation analysis: studies from the first generation*. Amsterdam/Philadelphia: John Benjamins: 13–31

Jefferson, G. (2004b) A sketch of some orderly aspects of overlap in natural conversation'. In: G.H. Lerner, ed., *Conversation analysis: studies from the first generation*. Amsterdam/Philadelphia: John Benjamins: 43–59

Jefferson, G., J.R.E. Lee (1981) 'The rejection of advice: managing the problematic convergence of a "Troubles Telling" and a "Service Encounter"', *Journal of Pragmatics* 5: 399–422 [reprinted in P. Drew, J. Heritage, eds, *Talk at work: interaction in institutional settings*. Cambridge: Cambridge University Press: 521–48]

Jefferson, G., H. Sacks, E.A. Schegloff (1987) 'Notes on laughter in the pursuit of intimacy'. In: G. Button, J.R.E. Lee, eds, *Talk and social organisation*. Clevedon: Multilingual Matters: 152–205

Jefferson, G., J. Schenkein (1978) 'Some sequential negotiations in conversation: unexpanded and expanded versions of projected action sequences'. In: J.N. Schenkein, ed., *Studies in the organization of conversational interaction*. New York: Academic Press: 155–72 [reprinted from *Sociology* 11 (1977): 87–103]

Jordan, B., A. Henderson (1995) 'Interaction analysis: foundations and practice', *The Journal of the Learning Sciences* 4: 39–101

Kendon, A. (1990) *Conducting interaction: patterns of behaviour in focused interaction*. Cambridge: Cambridge University Press

Kirsner, R.S., J.Y. Deen (1990) '*Het mes snijdt aan twee kanten*: on the semantics and pragmatics of the Dutch sentence-final particle *hoor*'. In: M. Bruijn Lacy, ed., *The Low Countries: multidisciplinary studies*. Lanham, MD: University Press of America: 1–12

Kitzinger, C. (2000) 'Doing feminist conversation analysis', *Feminism and Psychology*, 10: 163–93

Kitzinger, C. (2004) 'Feminist approaches'. In: C. Seale, D. Silverman, J, Gubrium, G. Gobo, eds, *Qualitative research practice*. London etc: Sage: 125–40

Kitzinger, C. (2005a) 'Heteronormativity in action: reproducing normative heterosexuality in "after hours" calls to the doctor', *Social Problems* 52(4). *Special Section: Language Interaction and Social Problems*: 477–98

Kitzinger, C. (2005b) ' "Speaking as a heterosexual": (how) does sexuality matter for talk-in-interaction?', *Research on Language & Social Interaction* 38: 221–65

Komter, M.L. (1991) *Conflict and cooperation in job interviews: a study of talk, tasks and ideas*. Amsterdam: John Benjamins

Komter, M.L. (1994) 'Accusations and defences in courtroom interaction', *Discourse & Society* 5: 165–87

Kuhn, T.S. (1962) *The structure of scientific revolutions*. Chicago: University of Chicago Press

Labov, W. (1972) *Language in the inner city: studies in the Black English vernacular*. Philadelphia: University of Pennsylvania Press

Land, V., C. Kitzinger (2005) 'Speaking as a lesbian: correcting the heterosexist presumption', *Research on Language & Social Interaction* 4: 371–416

Lerner, G.H. (1996) ' "Finding face" in the preference structures of talk-in-interaction', *Social Psychology Quarterly* 59: 303–21

Lerner, G.H., ed. (2004) *Conversation analysis: studies from the first generation*. Amsterdam/Philadelphia: John Benjamins

Levinson, S.C. (1983) *Pragmatics*. Cambridge: Cambridge University Press

Locker, D. (1981) *Symptoms and illness: the cognitive organization of disorder*. London: Tavistock

Lofland, J. (1980) 'Early Goffman: style, structure, substance, soul'. In: J. Ditton, ed., *The view from Goffman*. London: Macmillan: 24–51

Lofland, J., L.H. Lofland (1984) *Analyzing social settings: a guide to qualitative observation and analysis*, second edition. Belmont, CA: Wadsworth

Luff, P., J. Hindmarsh, C. Heath, eds, (2000) *Workplace studies: recovering work practice and informing systems design*. Cambridge: Cambridge University Press

Luke, K.K., Th. Pavlidou, eds (2002) *Telephone calls: unity and diversity in conversational structure across languages and cultures*. Amsterdam: John Benjamins

Lynch, M. (1985) *Art and artifact in laboratory science: a study of shop work and shop talk*. London: Routledge & Kegan Paul

Lynch, M. (1993) *Scientific practice and ordinary action: ethnomethodology and social studies of science*. New York: Cambridge University Press

Lynch, M. (2000) 'The ethnomethodological foundations of conversation analysis', *Text* 24: 517–32

Lynch, M., D. Bogen (1994) 'Harvey Sacks' primitive natural science', *Theory, Culture & Society* 11: 65–104

Lynch, M., D. Bogen (1996) *The spectacle of history: speech, text, and memory at the Iran–Contra hearings.* Durham, NC: Duke University Press

Lynch, M., E. Livingston, H. Garfinkel (1983) 'Temporal order in laboratory life'. In: K.D. Knorr-Cetina, M. Mulkay, eds, *Science observed: perspectives on the social study of science.* London: Sage: 205–38

Macbeth, D. (2004) 'The relevance of repair for classroom correction', *Language in Society* 33: 703–36

McCall, G.J., J.L. Simmons (1969) *Issues in participant observation: a text and reader.* Reading, MA: Addison-Wesley

McHoul, A. (1978) 'The organization of turns at formal talk in the classroom', *Language in Society* 7: 183–213

McHoul, A., M. Rapley, eds (2001) *How to analyse talk in institutional settings: a casebook of methods.* London: Continuum

McIllvenny, P. (1995) 'Seeing conversations: analyzing sign language talk'. In: P. ten Have, G. Psathas, eds, *Situated order: studies in the social organization of talk and embodied activities.* Washington, DC: University Press of America: 129–50

Manning, P. (1992) *Erving Goffman and modern sociology.* Cambridge: Polity Press

Marlaire, C.L., D.W. Maynard (1993) 'Social problems and the organization of talk in interaction'. In: J.A. Holstein, G. Miller, eds, *Reconsidering social problems: debates in social problems theory.* New York: Aldine de Gruyter: 173–98

Maynard, D.W. (1984) *Inside plea bargaining: the language of negotiation.* New York: Plenum

Maynard, D.W. (1997) 'The News Delivery Sequence: bad news and good news in conversational interaction', *Research on Language and Social Interaction* 30: 93–130

Maynard, D.W. (2003) *Bad news, good news: conversational order in everyday talk and clinical settings.* Chicago, University of Chicago Press

Maynard, D.W. (2004) 'On predicating a diagnosis as an attribute of a person', *Discourse Studies* 6: 53–76

Maynard, D.W., S.E. Clayman (1991) 'The diversity of ethnomethodology', *Annual Review of Sociology* 17: 385–418

Maynard, D.W., C.L. Marlaire (1992) 'Good reasons for bad testing performance: the interactional substrate of educational exams', *Qualitative Sociology* 15: 177–202

Maynard, D.W., H. Houtkoop-Steenstra, N.C. Schaeffer J. van der Zouwen, eds (2002) *Standardization and tacit knowledge: interaction and practice in the survey interview.* New York: Wiley

Maynard, D.W., N.C. Schaeffer (1997) 'Keeping the gate: declinations of the request to participate in a telephone survey interview', *Sociological Methods & Research* 26: 34–79

Maynard, D.W., N.C. Schaeffer (2000) 'Toward a sociology of social scientific knowledge: survey research and ethnomethodology's asymmetric alternates', *Social Studies of Science* 30: 323–70

Mazeland, H. (1992) *Vraag antwoord-sequenties* [Question/answer sequences]. Amsterdam: Stichting Neerlandistiek VU [also: PhD dissertation, University of Groningen]

Mazeland, H. (2004) 'Responding to the double implication of telemarketers', opinion queries', *Discourse Studies* 6: 95–115

Mazeland, H., P. ten Have (1996) 'Essential tensions in (semi)open research interviews'. In: I. Maso, F. Wester, eds, *The deliberate dialogue: qualitative perspectives on the interview.* Brussels: VUB University Press: 87–113 [also: http://www.paultenhave/et.htm]

Mehan, H. (1979) *Learning lessons: social organization in the classroom.* Cambridge, MA: Harvard University Press

Meier, C. (1997) *Arbeitsbesprechungen: Interaktionstruktur, Interaktionadynamiek und Konsequenzen einer sozialen Form* [Work meetings: interactional structure, interaction dynamics, and consequences of a social form]. Opladen: Westdeutscher Verlag

Mishler, E.G. (1984) *The discourse of medicine: dialectics of interviews.* Norwood, NJ: Ablex

Moerman, M. (1988) *Talking culture: ethnography and conversation analysis.* Philadelphia: University of Pennsylvania Press

Moerman, M. (1990/1) 'Exploring talk and interaction', *Research on Language and Social Interaction* 24: 173–88

Moerman, M. (1992) 'Life after CA: an ethnographer's autobiography'. In: G. Watson, R.M. Seiler, eds, *Text in context: contributions to ethnomethodology.* London: Sage: 30–4

Nevile, M. (2004) *Beyond the black box: talk-in-interaction in the airline cockpit.* Aldershot: Ashgate

Ochs, E., E.A. Schegloff, S.A. Thompson, eds (1996) *Interaction and grammar.* Cambridge: Cambridge University Press

O'Connell, D.C., S. Kowal (1994) 'Some current transcription systems for spoken discourse: a critical analysis', *Pragmatics* 4: 81–107

Peräkylä, A. (1995) *AIDS counselling: institutional interaction and clinical practice.* Cambridge: Cambridge University Press

Peräkylä, A. (1997) 'Reliability and validity in research based on tapes and transcripts'. In: D. Silverman, ed., *Qualitative research: theory, method and practice.* London: Sage: 201–20

Peräkylä, A. (2004a) 'Reliability and validity in research based on naturally occurring social interaction'. In: D. Silverman, ed., *Qualitative research: theory, method and practice,* Second edition. London: Sage: 283–304

Peräkylä, A. (2004b) 'Conversation analysis'. In: C. Seale, D. Silverman, J. Gubrium, G. Gobo, eds, *Qualitative research practice.* London: Sage: 165–79

Peräkylä, A. (2006) 'Communicating and responding to diagnosis'. In: J. Heritage, D.W. Maynard, eds, *Communication in medical care: interaction between primary care physicians and patients.* Cambridge: Cambridge University Press: 214–47

Peräkylä, A., D. Silverman (1991) 'Reinterpreting speech-exchange systems: communication formats in AIDS counselling', *Sociology* 25: 627–51

Pike, K. (1967) *Language in relation to a unified theory of the structure of human behavior.* The Hague: Mouton

Pollner, M. (1974) 'Sociological and common sense models of the labelling process'. In: Turner, R., ed., *Ethnomethodology: selected readings.* Harmondsworth: Penguin: 27–40

Pomerantz, A. (1978) 'Compliment responses: notes on the cooperation of multiple constraints'. In: J.N. Schenkein, ed., *Studies in the organization of conversational interaction.* New York: Academic Press: 79–112

Pomerantz, A. (1980) 'Telling my side: "limited access" as a fishing device', *Sociological Inquiry* 50: 186–98

Pomerantz, A. (1984) 'Agreeing and disagreeing with assessments: some features of preferred/dispreferred turn shapes'. In: J.M. Atkinson, J. Heritage, eds, *Structures of social action: studies in conversation analysis*. Cambridge: Cambridge University Press: 57–101

Pomerantz, A. (1986) 'Extreme case formulations: a way of legitimizing claims', *Human Studies* 9: 219–30

Pomerantz, A. (2005) 'Using participants' video-stimulated comments to complement analyses of interactional practices'. In: H. te Molder, J. Potter, eds, *Conversation and cognition*. Cambridge: Cambridge University Press: 93–113

Pomerantz, A., B.J. Fehr (1997) 'Conversation analysis: an approach to the study of social action as sense making practices'. In: T.A. van Dijk, ed., *Discourse studies: a multidisciplinary introduction*. London: Sage: 64–91

Potter, J., A. Hepburn (2003) ' "I'm a bit concerned": early actions and psychological constructions in a child protection helpline', *Research on Language and Social Interaction*, 36, 197–240

Potter, J., M. Wetherell (1987) *Discourse and social psychology: beyond attitudes and behaviour*. London: Sage

Psathas, G., ed. (1979) *Everyday language: studies in ethnomethodology*. New York: Irvington

Psathas, G., ed. (1990a) *Interactional competence*. Washington, DC: University Press of America

Psathas, G. (1990b) 'Introduction: methodological issues and recent developments in the study of naturally occurring interaction'. In: G. Psathas, ed., *Interactional competence*. Washington, DC: University Press of America: 1–30

Psathas, G. (1991) 'The structure of direction-giving in interaction'. In: D. Boden, D.H. Zimmerman, eds, *Talk and social structure: studies in ethnomethodology and conversation analysis*. Cambridge: Polity Press: 195–216

Psathas, G. (1995) *Conversation analysis: the study of talk-in-interaction*. Thousand Oaks, CA: Sage (Qualitative Research Methods 35)

Psathas, G., T. Anderson (1990) 'The "practices" of transcription in conversation analysis', *Semiotica* 78: 75–99

Ragin, C.C. (1987) *The comparative method: moving beyond qualitative and quantitative strategies*. Berkeley: University of California Press

Ragin, C.C. (1994) *Constructing social research: the unity and diversity of method*. Thousand Oaks, CA: Pine Forge Press

Robillard, Albert B. (1999) *Meaning of a disability: the lived experience of paralysis*. Philadelphia: Temple University Press

Roger, D., P. Bull, eds (1989) *Conversation: an interdisciplinary perspective*. Clevedon: Multilingual Matters

Roulston, K. (2006) 'Close encounters of the "CA" kind: a review of literature analysing talk in research interviews', *Qualitative Research* 6: 515–34

Sacks, H. (1967) 'The search for help: no one to turn to'. In: E.S. Shneidman, ed., *Essays in selfdestruction*. New York: Science House: 203–23

Sacks, H. (1972a) 'An initial investigation of the usability of conversational data for doing sociology'. In: D. Sudnow, ed., *Studies in social interaction*. New York: Free Press: 31–74

Sacks, H. (1972b) 'On the analyzability of stories by children'. In: J.J. Gumperz, D. Hymes, eds, *Directions in sociolinguistics: the ethnography of communication*. New York: Rinehart & Winston: 325–45

Sacks, H. (1974) 'An analysis of the course of a joke's telling in conversation'. In: J. Sherzer, R. Bauman, eds, *Explorations in the ethnography of speaking*. London: Cambridge University Press: 337–53

Sacks, H. (1978) 'Some technical considerations of a dirty joke'. In: J.N. Schenkein, ed., *Studies in the organization of conversational interaction*. New York: Academic Press: 249–70

Sacks, H. (1979) 'Hotrodder: a revolutionary category'. In: G. Psathas, ed., *Everyday language: studies in ethnomethodology*. New York: Irvington: 7–14

Sacks, H. (1984a) 'Notes on methodology'. In: J.M. Atkinson, J. Heritage, eds, *Structures of social action: studies in conversation analysis*. Cambridge: Cambridge University Press: 2–17

Sacks, H. (1984b) 'On doing "being ordinary"'. In: J.M. Atkinson, J. Heritage, eds, *Structures of social action: studies in conversation analysis*. Cambridge: Cambridge University Press: 413–29

Sacks, H. (1987) 'On the preferences for agreement and contiguity in sequences in conversation'. In: G. Button, J.R.E. Lee, eds, *Talk and social organisation*. Clevedon: Multilingual Matters: 54–69

Sacks, H. (1992a) *Lectures on conversation*, vol. I. Edited by G. Jefferson with an introduction by E.A. Schegloff. Oxford: Basil Blackwell

Sacks, H. (1992b) *Lectures on conversation*, vol. II. Edited by G. Jefferson with an introduction by E.A. Schegloff. Oxford: Basil Blackwell

Sacks, H. (2004) 'An initial characterization of the organization of speaker turn-taking in conversation'. In: G.H. Lerner, ed., *Conversation Analysis: Studies from the first generation*. Amsterdam/Philadelphia: John Benjamins: 35–42

Sacks, H., E.A. Schegloff (1979) 'Two preferences in the organization of reference to persons in conversation and their interaction'. In: G. Psathas, ed., *Everyday language: studies in ethnomethodology*. New York: Irvington: 15–21

Sacks, H., E.A. Schegloff, G. Jefferson (1978) 'A simplest systematics for the organization of turn taking for conversation'. In: J.N. Schenkein, ed., *Studies in the organization of conversational interaction*. New York: Academic Press: 7–55 (originally 1974)

Schaeffer, N.C., D.W. Maynard (1996) 'From paradigm to prototype and back again: interactive aspects of "cognitive processing" in standardized survey interviews'. In: N. Schwarz, S. Sudman, eds, *Answering questions: methodology for determining cognitive and communicative processes in survey research*. San Francisco: Jossey-Bass: 65–88

Schatzman, L., A.L. Strauss (1973) *Field research: strategies for a natural sociology*. Englewood Cliffs, NJ: Prentice Hall

Schegloff, E.A. (1968) 'Sequencing in conversational openings', *American Anthropologist* 70: 1075–95 [reprinted in: J.J. Gumperz, D. Hymes, eds, *Directions in sociolinguistics: the ethnography of communication*. New York: Rinehart & Winston: 346–80]

Schegloff, E.A. (1972) 'Notes on a conversational practice: formulating place'. In: D. Sudnow, ed., *Studies in social interaction*. New York: Free Press: 75–119

Schegloff, E.A. (1978) 'On some questions and ambiguities in conversation'. In: W.U. Dressler, ed., *Current trends in text linguistics*. Berlin: De Gruyter: 81–102 [reprinted in: J.M. Atkinson, J. Heritage, eds, *Structures of social action: studies in conversation analysis*. Cambridge: Cambridge University Press: 28–52]

Schegloff, E.A. (1979a) 'Identification and recognition in telephone conversation openings'. In: G. Psathas, ed., *Everyday language: studies in ethnomethodology*. New York: Irvington: 23–78

Schegloff, E.A. (1979b) 'The relevance of repair to syntax-for-conversation'. In: T. Givon, ed., *Syntax and semantics 12: discourse and syntax*. New York: Academic Press: 261–88

Schegloff, E.A. (1980) 'Preliminaries to preliminaries: "Can I ask you a question?"', *Sociological Inquiry* 50: 104–52

Schegloff, E.A. (1982) 'Discourse as an interactional achievement: some uses of "uh huh" and other things that come between sentences'. In: D. Tannen, ed., *Analyzing discourse: text and talk* (Georgetown University Roundtable on Languages and Linguistics). Washington, DC: Georgetown University Press: 71–93

Schegloff, E.A. (1986) 'The routine as achievement', *Human Studies* 9: 111–52

Schegloff, E.A. (1987a) 'Analyzing single episodes of interaction: an exercise in conversation analysis', *Social Psychology Quarterly* 50: 101–14

Schegloff, E.A. (1987b) 'Recycled turn beginnings: a precise repair mechanism in conversation's turntaking organization'. In: G. Button, J.R.E. Lee, eds, *Talk and social organisation*. Clevedon: Multilingual Matters: 70–85

Schegloff, E.A. (1987c) 'Between macro and micro: contexts and other connections'. In: J. Alexander et al., eds, *The micro-macro link*. Berkeley and Los Angeles: University of California Press: 207–34

Schegloff, E.A. (1988a) 'Goffman and the analysis of conversation'. In: P. Drew, A. Wootton, eds, *Erving Goffman: exploring the interaction order*. Cambridge: Polity Press: 89–135

Schegloff, E.A. (1988b) 'On a virtual servo-mechanism for guessing bad news: a single-case conjecture', *Social Problems* 35: 442–57

Schegloff, E.A. (1991) 'Reflections on talk and social structure'. In: D. Boden, D.H. Zimmerman, eds, *Talk and social structure: studies in ethnomethodology and conversation analysis*. Cambridge: Polity Press: 44–71

Schegloff, E.A. (1992a) 'Repair after next turn: the last structurally provided defense of intersubjectivity in conversation', *American Journal of Sociology* 98: 1295–345

Schegloff, E.A. (1992b) 'On talk and its institutional occasions'. In: P. Drew, J. Heritage, eds, *Talk at work: interaction in institutional settings*. Cambridge: Cambridge University Press: 101–34

Schegloff, E.A. (1993) 'Reflections on quantification in the study of conversation', *Research on Language and Social Interaction* 26: 99–128

Schegloff, E.A. (1996a) 'Turn organization: one intersection of grammar and interaction'. In: E. Ochs, E.A. Schegloff, S.A. Thompson, eds, *Interaction and grammar*. Cambridge: Cambridge University Press: 52–133

Schegloff, E.A. (1996b) 'Confirming allusions: towards an empirical account of action', *American Journal of Sociology* 104: 161–216

Schegloff, E.A. (1997) 'Whose text? Whose context?', *Discourse & Society* 8: 165–87

Schegloff, E.A. (1998) 'Reply to Wetherell', *Discourse & Society*, 9: 413–16

Schegloff, E.A. (1999a) ' "Schegloff's Texts" as "Billig's Data": a critical reply', *Discourse & Society* 10: 558–72

Schegloff, E.A. (1999b) 'Naivety vs. sophistication or discipline vs. self-indulgence: a rejoinder to Billig', *Discourse & Society* 10: 577–82

Schegloff, E.A. (2000) 'Overlapping talk and the organization of turn-taking for conversation', *Language in Society* 29:1–63

Schegloff, E.A. (2004) 'Answering the phone'. In: G.H. Lerner, ed., *Conversation analysis: studies from the first generation*. Amsterdam/Philadelphia: John Benjamins: 63–107

Schegloff, E.A. (2005) 'When "others" initiate repair', *Applied Linguistics* 21: 205–43

Schegloff, E.A. (2007a) *Sequence organization in interaction: a primer in conversation analysis*, vol.1. Cambridge: Cambridge University Press

Schegloff, E.A. (2007b) 'A tutorial on membership categorization', *Journal of Pragmatics* 39: 462–82

Schegloff, E.A., I. Koshik, S. Jacoby, D. Olsher (2002) 'Conversation analysis and applied linguistics', *Annual Review of Applied Linguistics*, 22: 3–31

Schegloff, E.A., E. Ochs, S. Thompson (1996) 'Introduction'. In: E. Ochs, E.A. Schegloff, S.A. Thompson, eds, *Interaction and grammar*. Cambridge: Cambridge University Press: 1–51

Schegloff, E.A., H. Sacks (1973) 'Opening up closings', *Semiotica* 8: 289–327

Schegloff, E.A., G. Jefferson, H. Sacks (1977) 'The preference for self-correction in the organization of repair in conversation', *Language* 53: 361–82 [also in: G. Psathas, ed., *Interactional competence*. Washington, DC: University Press of America, 1990: 31–61]

Schenkein, J.N., ed. (1978) *Studies in the organization of conversational interaction*. New York: Academic Press

Schwartz, H., J. Jacobs (1979) *Qualitative sociology: a method to the madness*. New York: Free Press

Seale, C. (1999) *The quality of qualitative research*. London: Sage

Silverman, D. (1985) *Qualitative methodology and sociology: describing the social world*. Aldershot: Gower

Silverman, D. (1993) *Interpreting qualitative data: Methods for analysing talk, text and interaction*. London: Sage

Silverman, D. (1998) *Harvey Sacks and conversation analysis*. Key Contemporary Thinkers. Cambridge: Polity Press

Silverman, D. (2006) *Interpreting qualitative data: methods for analysing talk, text and interaction*, Third edition. London: Sage

Sorjonen, M.-J. (1996) 'On repeats and responses in Finnish conversation'. In: E. Ochs, E.A. Schegloff, S.A. Thompson, eds, *Interaction and grammar*. Cambridge: Cambridge University Press: 277–327

Speer, S. (1999) 'Feminism and conversation analysis: an oxymoron?', *Feminism and Psychology* 9: 471–8

Speer, S.A. (2005) *Gender talk: feminism, discourse and conversation analysis*. London & New York: Routledge

Stax, H.-P. (2004) 'Paths to precision: probing turn format and turn-taking problems in standardized interviews', *Discourse Studies* 6: 77–94

Stivers, T. (2002) ' "Symptoms only" and "Candidate diagnoses": presenting the problem in pediatric encounters', *Health Communication* 14: 299–338

Stivers, T. (2005) 'Non-antibiotic treatment recommendations: delivery formats and implications for parent resistance', *Social Science & Medicine* 60: 949–64

Stivers, T., J.D. Robinson (2006) 'A preference for progressivity in interaction', *Language in Society* 35: 367–92

Stokoe, E.H. (2003) 'Mothers, single women and sluts: gender, morality and member-ship categorisation in neighbour disputes', *Feminism and Psychology* 13: 317–44

Stokoe, E. (2006) 'On ethnomethodology, feminism, and the analysis of categorial ref-erence to gender in talk-in-interaction', *Sociological Review* 54: 467–94

Stokoe, E.H., J. Smithson (2001) 'Making gender relevant: conversation analysis and gender categories in interaction', *Discourse & Society* 12: 243–69

Stokoe, E.H., J. Smithson (2002) 'Gender and sexuality in talk-in-interaction: consid-ering a conversation analytic perspective'. In: P. McIlvenny, ed., *Talking gender and sexuality: conversation, performativity and discourse in interaction*. Amsterdam: John Benjamins: 79–110

Strauss, A.L. (1987) *Qualitative analysis for social scientists*. Cambridge: Cambridge University Press

Strauss, A.L., J. Corbin (1990) *Basics of qualitative research: grounded theory procedures and techniques*. London: Sage

Suchman, L. (1987) *Plans and situated action: the problem of human–machine communica-tion*. Cambridge: Cambridge University Press

Suchman, L. (1992) 'Technologies of accountability: of lizards and airplanes'. In: G. Button, ed., *Technology in working order: studies of work, interaction and technology*. London: Routledge: 113–26

Suchman, L. (1996) 'Constituting shared workspaces'. In: Y. Engeström, D. Middleton, eds, *Cognition and communication at work*. Cambridge: Cambridge University Press: 35–60

Suchman, L.A. (2007) *Human-machine reconfigurations: plans and situated actions*, second edition. Cambridge: Cambridge University Press

Suchman, L., B. Jordan (1990) 'Interactional troubles in face-to-face survey inter-views', *Journal of the American Statistical Association* 85: 232–41

Suchman, L., R.H. Trigg (1991) 'Understanding practice: video as a medium for reflection and design'. In: J. Greenbaum, M. Kyng, eds, *Design at work: cooperative design of computer systems*. Hillsdale, NJ: Lawrence Erlbaum: 65–89

Sudnow, D., ed. (1972) *Studies in social interaction*. New York: Free Press

Sudnow, D. (1978) *Ways of the hand: the organization of improvised conduct*. London: Routledge & Kegan Paul

Sudnow, D. (2001) *Ways of the hand: a rewritten account*. Cambridge, MA: MIT Press

Tanaka, H. (1999) Turn-taking in Japanese conversation: a study in grammar and inter-action. Amsterdam: John Benjamins

Tanaka, H. (2000) 'Turn projection in Japanese talk-in-interaction', *Research on Language and Social Interaction* 33: 1–38

Tanaka, H., M. Fukushima (2002) 'Gender orientations to outward appearance in Japanese conversation: a study in grammar and interaction', *Discourse & Society* 13: 749–65

(Ten Have, P. see Have, P. ten)

Todd, A.D. (1989) *Intimate adversaries: cultural conflict between doctors and women patients*. Philadelphia: University of Pennsylvania Press

Turner, R. (1971) 'Words, utterances, activities'. In: J.D. Douglas, ed., *Understanding everyday life: towards a reconstruction of sociological knowledge*. London: Routledge & Kegan Paul: 169–87

Wagner. J., ed. (1996) 'Conversation analysis of foreign language data'. Special Issue. *Journal of Pragmatics* 26/2: 147–259

Watson, R. (1992) 'The understanding of language use in everyday life: is there a common ground?'. In: G. Watson, R.M. Seiler, eds, *Text in context: contributions to ethnomethodology*. London: Sage: 1–19

Watson, R. (1997) 'Some general reflections on "categorization" and "sequence" in the analysis of conversation'. In: S. Hester, P. Eglin, eds, *Culture in action: studies in membership categorization analysis*. Washington, DC: University Press of America: 49–76

West, C. (1984) *Routine complications: trouble with talk between doctors and patients*. Bloomington: Indiana University Press

West, C. (2006) 'Co-ordinating closings in medical interviews: producing continuity of care'. In: J. Heritage, D.W. Maynard, eds, *Communication in medical care: interaction between primary care physicians and patients*. Cambridge: Cambridge University Press: 379–415

West, C., A. Garcia (1988) 'Conversational shift work: a study of topical transition between women and men', *Social Problems* 35: 551–75

West, C., D.H. Zimmerman (1985) 'Gender, language, and discourse'. In: T.A. van Dijk, ed., *Handbook of discourse analysis*, vol. IV. London: Academic Press: 103–24

Wetherell, M. (1998) 'Positioning and interpretative repertoires: conversation analysis and poststructuralism in dialogue', *Discourse & Society* 9: 387–412

Whalen, J. (1995) 'A technology of order production: computer-aided dispatch in public safety communication'. In: P. ten Have, G. Psathas, eds, *Situated order: studies in the social organization of talk and embodied activities*. Washington, DC: University Press of America: 187–230

Whalen, J., D.H. Zimmerman, M.R. Whalen (1988) 'When words fail: a single case analysis', *Social Problems* 35: 333–62

Whalen, M.R., D.H. Zimmerman (1987) 'Sequential and institutional contexts in calls for help', *Social Psychology Quarterly* 50: 172–85

Wilson, T.P. (1991) 'Social structure and the sequential organization of interaction'. In: D. Boden, D.H. Zimmerman, eds, *Talk and social structure: studies in ethnomethodology and conversation analysis*. Cambridge: Polity Press: 22–43

Wodak, R. (2004) 'Critical discourse analysis'. In: C. Seale, D. Silverman, J. Gubrium, G. Gobo, eds, *Qualitative research practice*. London: Sage: 197–213 [reprinted in paperback in 2007 at pages 185–201]

Wooffitt, R. (2005) *Conversation analysis and discourse analysis: a comparative and critical introduction*. London: Sage.

Wootton, A.J. (1989) 'Remarks on the methodology of conversation analysis'. In: D. Roger, P. Bull, eds, *Conversation: an interdisciplinary perspective*. Clevedon: Multilingual Matters: 238–58

Wootton, A.J. (1997) *Interaction and the development of mind*. Cambridge: Cambridge University Press [reprinted in paperback, 2005]

Wowk, M.T. (1984) 'Blame allocation, sex and gender in a murder interrogation', *Women's Studies International Forum* 7: 75–82

Wowk, M. (2007) 'Kitzinger's feminist conversation analysis critical observations', *Human Studies* 30: 131–55

Yin, R.K. (1994) *Case study research: design and methods*, second edition. Thousand Oaks, CA: Sage

Zimmerman, D.H. (1988) 'On conversation: the conversation analytic perspective'. In: J. Anderson, ed., *Communication Yearbook 11*. Beverly Hills, CA: Sage: 406–32

Zimmerman, D.H. (1992) 'Achieving context: openings in emergency calls'. In: G. Watson, R.M. Seiler, eds, *Text in context: contributions to ethnomethodology*. London: Sage: 35–51

Zimmerman, D.H., D. Boden (1991) 'Structure-in-action'. In: D. Boden, D.H. Zimmerman, eds, *Talk and social structure: studies in ethnomethodology and conversation analysis*. Cambridge: Polity Press: 3–21

Zimmerman, D.H., C. West (1975) 'Sex roles, interruptions and silences in conversation'. In: B. Thorne, N. Henley, eds, *Language and sex: difference and dominance*. Rowley, MA: Newbury House: 105–29

Index